A Magical Classic for

"Many of Israel Regardie's book̶s̶ ̶s̶e̶e̶m̶ ̶t̶o̶ ̶b̶e̶ ̶m̶o̶r̶e̶ ̶o̶u̶t̶l̶i̶n̶e̶s̶ ̶o̶f̶ ̶t̶h̶e̶ intense ideas of his fertile mind. Here, the Cicero's have expanded Regardie's classic book to what it always should have been—a thorough, accessible examination and extension of the single ritual which has become the very embodiment of magic."

Donald Michael Kraig
author of *Modern Magic*

"The Middle Pillar Ritual is the skeletal structure upon which hangs the fabric of future ritual performances. Based as it is upon the Tree of Life, it is the core of all solar-based ceremonial magic. Magic is self empowerment. Through becoming aware of the power zones of the Tree of Life we are provided with the tools for being more than we are. Cognizance of the Tree of Life within ourselves, through using the Middle Pillar technique, awakens its energies so that our practices have a direct impact upon our everyday lives. This avoids the danger of ritual exercises becoming entertainment only. It empowers us to be vehicles of life, channels of change. Well annotated, illustrated, and greatly expanded by the Ciceros, The Middle Pillar offers a wider appeal to various viewpoints. We once again have this wonderful tool to offer seekers desiring practical material for entry into the world of ceremonial technique."

Roger Williamson
author of *The Sun at Night*, owner of Magus Books

"Regardie's classic work [*The Middle Pillar*] is now updated by the Ciceros with much new information. This revision is a must buy for any new student of the Qabalah, as well as all who have already read Regardie's original work. Now the Eastern tradition of the chakras has been integrated into the original text. In addition many cultural variations on the Middle Pillar ritual are offered here for the first time, as well as a musical key for vibrating the Hebrew God names during the ritual."

David Hulse
author of *The Eastern Mysteries* and *The Western Mysteries*

About the Author

Israel Regardie (1907-1985) was the author of a number of outstanding books on magic who was credited with removing the excessive secrecy surrounding modern occultism. Born in England, Regardie spent most of his life in the United States. In 1928 he took a job as Aleister Crowley's secretary and by 1932 he had become a esoteric teacher in his own right. In 1933 he joined the Stella Matutina, a offshoot of the Hermetic Order of the Golden Dawn. In 1937 he published the rituals of the Order in his classic book *The Golden Dawn*.

About the Editors

Chic Cicero was born in Buffalo, New York. A former musician and businessman, Chic has been a practicing ceremonial magician for the past thirty years. He was a close personal friend of Israel Regardie. Having established a Golden Dawn temple in 1977, Chic was one of the key people who helped Regardie resurrect a legitimate branch of the Hermetic Order of the Golden Dawn in the early 1980s.

Sandra Tabatha Cicero was born in Soldiers Grove, Wisconsin. She graduated from the University of Wisconsin-Milwaukee, with a Bachelor's degree in the Fine Arts. Both Chic and Tabatha are Senior Adepts of the Hermetic Order of the Golden Dawn. They are the authors of several books published by Llewellyn.

To Write to the Editors

If you wish to contact the editors or would like more information about this book, please write to the editors in care of Llewellyn Worldwide and we will forward your request. Please write to:

Chic Cicero and Sandra Tabatha Cicero
C/o Llewellyn Worldwide
P.O. Box 64383, Dept. K140-6
St. Paul, MN 55164-0383, U.S.A.

Please enclose a self-addressed, stamped envelope for reply, or $1.00 to cover costs.
If outside U.S.A., enclose international postal reply coupon.

THE

MIDDLE PILLAR

The Balance Between Mind and Magic

Israel Regardie

edited and annotated with new material by
Chic Cicero
Sandra Tabatha Cicero

2000
Llewellyn Publications
St. Paul, Minnesota 55164-0383, U.S.A.

THIRD EDITION, edited and annotated
Second Printing, 2000

Copyright © 1938 by Israel Regardie
Copyright © 1945 by Aries Press
Second Edition, revised and enlarged, Llewellyn Publications, 1970

Cover design: Tom Grewe
Illustrations: Sandra Tabatha Cicero

The diagram on page 126 from the book *Psychosynthesis* by Roberto Assagioli is reproduced by permission of Sterling Lord Literistic, Inc.

The diagram on page 112 from the book *The Psychology of C. G. Jung* by Jolande Jacobi is reproduced by permission of Yale University Press.

The Middle Pillar Ritual on pages 212–219 is from "The Middle Pillar, Revised Version by Israel Regardie." © 1996 by Darcy Küntz.

The musical notes in the Appendix are excerpts from *The Musical Qabalah,* © 1995 by Thom Parrott, used by permission.

Regardie, Israel.
      The middle pillar : the balance between mind and magic / Israel
Regardie ; edited and annotated with new material by Chic Cicero &
Sandra Tabatha Cicero. -- 3rd ed.
            p.   cm.
      Includes bibliographical references and index.
      ISBN 1-56718-140-6 (pbk.)
      1. Magic. 2. Occultism. 3. Jungian psychology.   I. Cicero,
Chic, 1936- . II. Cicero, Sandra Tabatha, 1959-   . III. Title.
BF1999.R42   1998
133--dc21   97-51493
                                                        CIP

Llewellyn Publications
A Division of Llewellyn Worldwide, Ltd.
P.O. Box 64383, Dept. K140-6
St. Paul, MN 55164-0383, U.S.A.

Printed in the U. S. A.

Other Books by Israel Regardie

The Golden Dawn
A Garden of Pomegranates
The Philosopher's Stone
The Tree of Life
The Art of True Healing
The Romance of Metaphysics
Twelve Steps to Spiritual Enlightenment
The Complete Golden Dawn System of Magic
Ceremonial Magic
Foundations of Practical Magic

Other Books by the Ciceros

The Golden Dawn Magical System
   including:
   The New Golden Dawn Ritual Tarot (deck)
   The New Golden Dawn Ritual Tarot (book)
Secrets of a Golden Dawn Temple
Self-Initiation into the Golden Dawn Tradition
The Golden Dawn Journal Series
   including:
   Book I: Divination
   Book II: Qabalah: Theory and Magic
   Book III: The Art of Hermes
   The Magical Pantheons: A Golden Dawn Journal
Experiencing the Kabbalah

DEDICATED
to the
revered memories
of
William Wynn Westcott
and
S. L. MacGregor Mathers

— *Israel Regardie*

To Francis,
whose light
shines as brightly now
as it ever did

— *Chic and Tabatha Cicero*

Contents

List of Illustrations ix

Introduction to the Third Edition
    by Chic Cicero and Sandra Tabatha Cicero xiii

Introduction to the Second Edition..xxv

Foreword xxxiii

Part One: The Middle Pillar

**A co-relation of the principles of analytical psychology
and the elementary techniques of magic.**

by Israel Regardie with annotation by Chic and Sandra Tabatha Cicero

Chapter One
    The Two Pillars of the Temple (*ed.*)..3

Chapter Two
    The Tree of Life (*ed.*)...25

Chapter Three
    The Qabalistic Cross and the Pentagram Ritual (*ed.*)...............47

Chapter Four
    The Middle Pillar Exercise (*ed.*)..69

Chapter Five
    Circulating the Light and the Formula of Vibration (*ed.*)....85

Part Two: The Balance Between Mind and Magic

**A further analysis of the relationship
between psychology and magic.**

by Chic Cicero and Sandra Tabatha Cicero

Chapter Six
    Psychology and Magic 103

Chapter Seven

    The Art of Relaxation..139

Chapter Eight

    Yoga, Chakras, and the Wisdom of the East........................159

Chapter Nine

    The Pentagram..175

Chapter Ten

    The Middle Pillar Exercise 209

Appendix

    The Musical Qabalah *by Thom Parrott* 243

Glossary...251

Bibliography 267

Index 273

Illustrations

Figure 1: Cover Art from the Second Edition xi

Figure 2: The Tree of Life 28

Figure 3: Lesser Banishing Pentagram.....................................59

Figure 4: The Middle Pillar 73

Figure 5: Jung's Model of the Psyche.....................................112

Figure 6: Assagioli's Model of the Psyche 126

Figure 7: The Divisions of the Soul.......................................132

Figure 8: The Tattva Symbols 164

Figure 9: The Chakras 168

Figure 10: Adam Kadmon, the "Reversed Tree" 182

Figure 11: Backing into the Tree...184

Figure 12: The Pentagram and Pentagon 189

Figure 13: Drawing a Pentagram...194

Figure 14: Ritual Signs and Symbols of Protection.............198

Figure 15: The Tree of Life in the Human Body 220

Figure 16: The Five Pillars 222

Figure 17: The Musical Qabalah: The Qabalistic Cross.............246

Figure 18: The Musical Qabalah: The LBRP 247

Figure 19: The Musical Qabalah: The Middle Pillar 248

Figure 20: The Musical Qabalah: Divine Names....................249

Acknowledgments

The editors would like to thank the following people for contributing material to this new edition of Israel Regardie's *The Middle Pillar*: Adam Forrest, Isidora Forrest, R. A. Gilbert, Darcy Küntz, Thom Parrott, Prof. Seàn O Mìadhachàin, and William Stoltz.

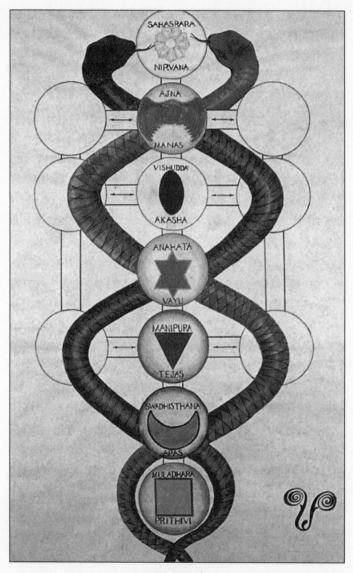

*Figure 1: Cover art from the Second Edition of The Middle Pillar.
(Painting by Marjory Paskaruk.)*

INTRODUCTION
TO THE THIRD EDITION

I n the early decades of this century, little was known about the techniques of western ceremonial magic due to the veil of secrecy which had shrouded these practices. Unless a person happened to be a member of a magical organization, there was little chance of learning the procedures and initiatory practices of high magic. This changed in 1937 when Israel Regardie published four volumes titled *The Golden Dawn*, a collection of ceremonies and teachings from the Hermetic Order of the Golden Dawn. Earlier, Regardie had published two books describing the magical principles of the Golden Dawn system. *The Middle Pillar*, published in 1938, gave step-by-step details on how to perform practical exercises of ceremonial magic, something which was quite revolutionary for its time. Perhaps even more radical was Regardie's daring attempt to correlate these magical techniques to the (then) new methods and hypotheses of psychoanalysis. Since the object of study in both magic and psychology was the human mind, it was Regardie's belief that magic could be regarded as a subdivision of the science of psychology. Such a thing was quite unheard of in 1938. In fact, Regardie postulated that psychotherapists could use the techniques of magic, such as the Lesser Banishing Ritual and the Middle Pillar exercise of the Golden Dawn, in a clinical setting for the benefit of patients.

In the mid-1930s Regardie's suggestion would have raised many eyebrows, but today several enlightened therapists are coming to the conclusion that the magicians of old were the psychotherapists of their day. Over the last few years there has been considerable reconciliation between occultism and analytical psychology. A large percentage of ancient magical knowledge is being rediscovered and renamed by modern psychologists for modern times. The "gods and angels" of magic are described by the science of mind as "archetypes," while "demons" have been converted into "neuroses." The goal of both magic and psychotherapy is the well-being of the individual—his or her growth and health on every level—physical, mental, and psychological. Magic, however, also includes *spiritual* well-being. Regardie sought to tear down the artificial walls that had been built up between the ancient art and the modern science.

Regardie's *The Middle Pillar* was a milestone which boldly stated these ideas long before they became popular. Today the exercise of the Middle Pillar, as a technique for self-development, has become standard fare—so much so that it is sometimes described in New Age self-help manuals, often without mentioning its source in the Golden Dawn tradition. *The Middle Pillar* shows the clarity of writing, expertise, and love for teaching that Regardie was famous for. To this day it remains a classic among magical texts.

Who was Israel Regardie and why did he write *The Middle Pillar*? The following brief biography should give readers an awareness of Regardie's prominent place in the history of modern magic and occultism, as well as his interest in psychology.

Before his death in 1985, Israel Regardie was considered by many to be the last living adept of a prestigious magical current known as the Golden Dawn. The tradition represented by the Golden Dawn and its sister spin-off groups, the Stella Matutina and the Alpha et Omega, attracted many influential occultists of the late nineteenth and early twentieth centuries. Among these were Dr. William W. Westcott, Samuel L. MacGregor Mathers, Arthur Edward Waite, William Butler Yeats, Dion Fortune, and Aleister Crowley. Yet among this extraordinary ensemble of knowledgeable magicians, Regardie ranks high as an authority of prominence.

Born on November 17, 1907, in London, Israel Regardie moved with his family to Washington, D.C. in 1921 when he was thirteen years old. At an early age he developed an interest in the theosophical works of Madame Blavatsky, Hindu philosophy, and yoga. At age sixteen Regardie frequented the Library of Congress, which he called his second home. It was through his contacts in the Library that he was able to find a Hebrew tutor. He learned to read Hebrew fluently, a skill that would aid him tremendously in his study of Qabalah. About this time, Regardie enrolled in an art school in Philadelphia. On March 18, 1926 Regardie discovered a newly published book which captivated his curiosity. The book was *Part One of Book Four* by Aleister Crowley. Regardie wrote to Crowley in Paris and eventually received a reply to his inquiry, suggesting that he contact Crowley's agent, Karl Germer, in New York. From Germer, Regardie bought a set of *The Equinox*, a series of magazines that Crowley published from 1909 to 1914. This was the beginning of Regardie's life-long interest in magic and mysticism which changed the course of his whole life, and he soon realized that art was not his calling. In March of 1926 the young Regardie became a member of the Washington College of the Societas Rosicruciana in America. A year or so later, Crowley offered Regardie a job as his secretary in Paris. Regardie took this as a great opportunity to learn magic from an authority.

In order to go to Paris, Regardie had to obtain a passport and a visa. He was still a minor, and was supposed to get permission from his father for the required documents. However, he never told his parents about Crowley or his own interest in mysticism. Crowley received a great deal of bad press in both the English and American tabloids, so Regardie was hesitant to tell his parents that he would be working with Crowley. Since Regardie had attended art school, he simply told them that he had been invited to study painting with an English artist in Paris. His parents gave him documents for the passport, but when it came time to obtain the French visa, Regardie typed up the papers himself and signed his father's name to it.

So in October of 1928 at the age of twenty, Regardie went to France to take the post that Crowley offered him. For the next three years Regardie lived a rather nomadic life as he tried to get his employer to teach him the magical arts.

However, Crowley did not offer to teach Regardie magic or yoga and Regardie, a shy and unobtrusive young man, did not press the issue. Instead he continued his own studies, reading every book or manuscript on these subjects that he could get his hands on.

Meanwhile, Regardie's sister, whom he scornfully referred to as "Nosey Parker," read some of Crowley's books and, since she understood nothing about magic, was appalled. She marched off to the French Consul in Washington and complained about her brother's "demise." The French Consul promised to look into the matter. This was the beginning of trouble. Four months after Regardie arrived in Paris, a French detective from the Surete Generale came to the apartment "to see what kind of wicked monster this man Crowley was." It just so happened that Crowley owned an unusual glass Silex coffee maker that the detective assumed was used for distilling drugs. The fact that Crowley was the British head of a German magical society (the Ordo Templi Orientis) led police to the false conclusion that Crowley was a German spy.

Crowley's problems came to a head when he had a falling out with his literary press agent who told French police that Crowley was a drug addict. As a result of all this, Crowley and his wife-to-be, Marie de Miramar, were given expulsion papers. The young Regardie, who had neglected to get a valid residence permit, was also told to leave the country. After spending six months in Brussels, Regardie went to England where he stayed with Crowley and his wife. By this time Crowley had discovered another publisher, Mandrake Press, but by now Crowley's notoriety in the tabloids as "the wickedest man in the world"[1] was enough to cause most booksellers to avoid him, and Mandrake Press soon went under. As a result, Crowley could no longer afford to keep his secretary. After attempting to repair Crowley's tarnished image by co-authoring a book called *The Legend of Aleister Crowley* (1930), Regardie and Crowley drifted apart though they remained friends. For a time Regardie, who had settled in London, served as a secretary for Thomas Burke, the novelist.

In 1932, Regardie published his first two important books, *A Garden of Pomegranates* and *The Tree of Life*. The former represented

Regardie's own Qabalistic studies, while the latter is usually considered Regardie's Magnum Opus and one of the most comprehensive
texts on practical magic ever written. The book was primarily a
restatement of the original teachings of the Golden Dawn and
contained very little "Crowleyanity." *The Tree of Life* was dedicated to Crowley under the name of Marsyas, a pseudonym that
Crowley used in his poem *Aha*. About five years later in 1937,
Regardie sent his old friend a copy of *The Tree of Life* with a warm
note. Unfortunately, Crowley's response to Regardie's kindness
was less than kind—chiding the sensitive young author with an
anti-Semitic slur about his recently adopted name of "Francis" (a
name given to Regardie by a lady friend who thought he had a lot
in common with St. Francis of Assisi). Regardie took offense and
wrote Crowley an inflammatory letter designed to "sting" him—
which apparently it did. Crowley retaliated by circulating an abu-
sive and slanderous letter about Regardie to all of his friends and
acquaintances. The result was a final and complete break between
the two men. Regardie was deeply wounded by the breakup of
the friendship and was only able to pardon Crowley in his later
years. (In 1970, when he wrote *The Eye in The Triangle: An Interpretation of Aleister Crowley*, Regardie's charitable nature and his
ability to be forgiving toward his old friend was evident.)

The publication of *The Tree of Life* caused quite a stir in magical
circles of the time. In the book Regardie outlined a few of the magical practices and teachings of the Hermetic Order of the Golden
Dawn. Although the original Order had ceased to exist in 1903, it
continued to live on in its successors, the Stella Matutina and the
Alpha et Omega. Many members of both Orders remembered
Crowley as a disruptive insurgent from years before, therefore
Regardie's previous connection to Crowley caused some members
to lash out at him. Other members, most notably Dion Fortune,
defended him. With her support, Regardie was invited to join the
Stella Matutina. In January of 1933, Regardie joined the Order and
made rapid progress through the grades, probably due to his
exceptional abilities. However, Regardie was terribly disappointed
with the chiefs of the Stella Matutina, who claimed extraordinarily
high degrees but seemed sorely lacking in magical knowledge. The

Order itself was in a state of demoralization and decay—the members and chiefs alike cared little for magic, other than as an irritating prerequisite for examinations in order to obtain exalted titles. Regardie concluded that the teachings of the Order would not survive unless they were published, so shortly after attaining to the grade of Theoricus Adeptus Minor in 1934,[2] Regardie left the Order in December of that year. In 1937 he published much of the Golden Dawn's ceremonies and teachings in four volumes titled *The Golden Dawn*. He clearly stated his reasons for doing this in his previous book *My Rosicrucian Adventure* (1936) which documented his own experiences with the Golden Dawn:

> ...(I)t is essential that the whole system should be publicly exhibited so that it may not be lost to mankind. For it is the heritage of every man and woman—their spiritual birthright. ... My motives have been to prove without a doubt that no longer is the Order the ideal medium for the transmission of Magic, and that since there have already been several partial and irresponsible disclosures of the Order teaching, a more adequate presentation of that system is urgently called for. Only thus may the widespread misconceptions as to Magic be removed.

Some members of the Order were incensed at this action, but others were quite happy—they no longer had to copy all the Order materials tediously by hand. In Regardie's words, "Some approved of the publication of these books; a very few disapproved. That's all there is to it." Nevertheless most temples of the Stella Matutina and the Alpha et Omega slowly stagnated and died, just as Regardie had predicted. But because of Regardie's actions, all students of magic today owe him an enormous debt of gratitude. According to Francis King and Isabel Sutherland: "That the rebirth of occult magic has taken place in the way it has can be very largely attributed to the writings of one man, Dr. Francis Israel Regardie."[3]

Regardie made a very difficult and courageous decision to break his oath of secrecy to a lethargic Golden Dawn in order to save the valuable teachings of the Order. Given the fact that many former chiefs had the appalling habit of destroying Order documents rather than passing them on to future generations of initiates, it was the right thing to do. As a result all true seekers, regardless of their education, background, location, or finances, could benefit from the

Order's teachings. Not only did Regardie's work on the Golden Dawn system ensure that its body of knowledge, sometimes called the Western Esoteric Tradition, would survive long after the original Order had ceased to exist, he is also credited with inspiring the Golden Dawn's modern revival. And of all the initiates who were associated with the original GD or its immediate offshoots (the SM and AO), Regardie, far more than any other person, demonstrated through his life, his work, and his writing, the essential wisdom and soundness of those teachings. He was the one initiate uniquely qualified for his appointed task—the task of successfully presenting magic as a therapeutic tool to the skeptical world of psychology, and ultimately, to bring psychotherapy and magic together.

In the winter of 1936-37, Regardie was bedridden in London for two weeks with a bad case of bronchitis. During this time he wrote most of what would be published as *The Philosopher's Stone*, a book about alchemy from a Jungian perspective. At the time Regardie was convinced that laboratory alchemy was fallacious, and that only theoretical, spiritual, or psychological alchemy was valid. (By 1970, however, interaction with practical alchemists such as Frater Albertus of the Paracelsus Research Society caused him to change his opinion on this. He began his own alchemical experiments in a small laboratory setting. Unfortunately, one of his experiments went awry and he seriously burned his lungs when fumes of antimony escaped in the lab. Regardie gave his alchemy equipment to a friend and for the rest of his life he suffered from the effects of the accident.)[4]

Seeing that war in Europe was imminent, Regardie returned to the U.S. in 1937, where he immersed himself for a number of years in the study of psychology and psychotherapy. He was grateful for his previous experience with the Golden Dawn and a lengthy Freudian analysis—"for both of which I can say in all humility and simplicity—Thank God!" These were the two influences which led him to write *The Middle Pillar* in 1938. *The Art of True Healing* would soon follow. In 1941 he graduated from the Chiropractic College of New York City with a degree in psychology, and took up practice as a lay analyst. He was particularly intrigued with the work of Wilheim Reich.

When America became involved in World War II, Regardie discontinued his practice and joined the army, something he later considered a huge mistake. When the war was over, he continued his studies and received a doctorate in psychology.

For a time he explored Christian mysticism with as much energy as he had previously pursued Hindu, Jewish, and Buddhist systems. He was especially drawn to Christian Science, New Thought, and the Unity School of Christianity, which taught that faith, belief, and the power of positive thinking could cure physical illnesses. He concluded that the healing techniques taught by these different schools had validity, and he explored these ideas in *The Romance of Metaphysics* (1946).[5]

In 1947, Regardie relocated to California and set up practice as a chiropractor and a Reichian therapist. He also taught psychiatry at the Los Angeles College of Chiropractic. During this time, he contributed articles to various psychology magazines, including *The American Journal of Psychotherapy* and *Psychiatric Quarterly*.

Throughout the 1950s Regardie distanced himself from occultists and concentrated on establishing his practice, which brought him a comfortable income. He had three marriages which all ended in divorce. He had no children.

His interest in magic never waned as can be seen by such books as *The Art and Meaning of Magic* (1964); *Twelve Steps to Spiritual Enlightenment* (1969); *A Practical Guide to Geomantic Divination* (1972); *How to Make and Use Talismans* (1972); and *Foundations of Practical Magic* (1979).

Regardie retired from his practice in 1981 and moved to Sedona, Arizona, where he continued to write. His later books included *Ceremonial Magic* (1980); *The Lazy Man's Guide to Relaxation* (1983); and *The Complete Golden Dawn System of Magic* (1984). He continued to give advice on health and magical matters until the end of his life.

We came to know Regardie through Grady McMurtry, former Caliph of the OTO. We had established our own independent Golden Dawn temple in Columbus, Georgia, in 1977 and were in the process of building the Vault of the Adepti.[6] At that time we were also involved with the OTO, because we were told that the Golden Dawn no longer existed in any form. Grady was well aware that our primary interest was the Golden Dawn,[7] and since he and Regardie were friends, eventually he was kind enough to give us Regardie's address. We were ecstatic—we had assumed that Regardie passed on years ago. We wrote to Regardie and initiated what was to become a rewarding magical adventure and a close friendship.[8]

Regardie, as we knew him, was small in stature but great in spirit. In his later years, the shyness and inhibition of his youth was gone. In its place was a vitality, a ready smile, a no-holds-barred honesty, and a mischievous Scorpio sense of humor. He enjoyed good food and drink, boxing, professional wrestling, Salvador Dali, and Mozart. He enjoyed the unique red rock outcroppings of Sedona as much as he enjoyed playfully teasing the local New Age inhabitants of that town.[9] Although Regardie believed that no magician should be poor or have to struggle to make a living, he was adamantly opposed to the idea of spiritual gurus or magical groups exploiting students for personal financial gain.[10]

On March 10, 1985, Regardie died of a massive heart attack while entertaining friends at a restaurant. We had visited him in his home just ten days prior. His death was a great blow to us. A few days later, we performed the Requiem ceremony from *The Golden Dawn* in his honor, in conjunction with the reading of one of his favorite pieces, "The Prayer of the Sylphs."[11] Although Regardie is gone, his written works continue to teach and inspire new generations of students.

Regardie's classic book, *The Middle Pillar*, introduces a psychological perspective on magic and occultism and presents an intelligent and viable rationale promoting the practice of certain magical techniques, the effects of which can be compared to the processes of analytical psychology. Regardie gave readers clear directions on how to perform the Qabalistic Cross, The Lesser Banishing Ritual of the Pentagram, and the Middle Pillar exercise, along with its accompanying methods of circulating the light, the Vibratory Formula, and the building up of the Tree of Life in the aura.

Regardie, more than any other individual, saw the vast potential of the Middle Pillar exercise, which was first published in a rather incomplete form in the manuscirpts of the Stella Matutina. Regardie realized that this simple ritual could be adapted into a variety of exercises with varying levels of complexity and spiritual development, or used for numerous purposes such as charging talismans and healing (healing oneself or healing others). He firmly advocated that the Middle Pillar exercise was an excellent and multifaceted tool that could be easily accessed and employed by any and all for the purpose of self-development and self-healing. Regardie must be credited for the popularity that the Middle Pillar exercise and its numerous variants have enjoyed among ceremonial magicians, mystics, and New Agers for the past several decades.

Regardie also brought the disciplines of analytical psychology and magic together as a holistic mechanism for human development. As an author, Regardie's style of writing was refreshing, inspiring, comprehensible, and non-elitist. Now, nearly sixty years since *The Middle Pillar* was first published, it remains a fine introduction to the psychological processes underlying all magical work.

It was with great pleasure, then, that we responded to Llewellyn publisher Carl Weschcke's suggestion that Regardie's classic *The Middle Pillar* be reprinted and its ideas expanded on so that new generations of seekers could benefit from it. We hope that the material we have contributed to this new annotated edition is a fitting tribute to Regardie's original work, which was so instrumental in our own spiritual growth.

Part One of the third edition of *The Middle Pillar* contains Regardie's masterpiece in its entirety. We have redrawn the illustrations and added titles for Regardie's chapters. We have also applied standard rules of capitalization to Regardie's text and changed the style of certain capitalized words to italic. All endnotes are ours.

In previous editions, differences in Regardie's spelling of Hebrew words (such as *Sephiros* in place of *Sephiroth*, *Keser* instead of *Kether*, *Tipharas* rather than *Tiphareth*, *Daas* for *Daath*, and *Malkus* in place of *Malkuth*) are due to a variation in dialect—Askenazic Hebrew versus Sephardic Hebrew. His early works, including *The Middle Pillar*, featured the Askenazic dialect which was a form of Hebrew pronunciation used in central Europe.[12] Later, he adopted the more common Sephardic (Mediterranean) dialect which was used by many Qabalistic authors, translators, and most Golden Dawn magicians. The Sephardic pronunciation is used almost exclusively by Western magicians today. With this in mind, we have changed the spelling of the words mentioned above in this edition of *The Middle Pillar* to reflect the modern usage that most readers are familiar with.

Part Two contains our own work titled *The Balance Between Mind and Magic*. This comprises a number of chapters which we have added to supplement and enhance many of the ideas introduced by Regardie in Part One. Chapter Six contains a further exploration of the principles of Jungian psychology and Qabalah. In the Foreword of *The Middle Pillar*, written in 1938, Regardie expressed a desire to add more information on the art of relaxation and its importance to the individual's well-being. Chapter Seven provides several exercises for this, and both solitary and group work is covered. Chapter Eight examines the Eastern system of the chakras including the similarities and differences between the Qabalistic and Yoga systems of self-growth. An exercise for activating the chakras is included. The use and symbolism of the Pentagram Ritual and the Middle Pillar Exercise are investigated in Chapters Nine and Ten, which also give Egyptian, Greek, Gaelic, and Shamanic versions of these rituals for the benefit of those readers who are not especially drawn to the language of Hebrew but nevertheless would like to experience the energies involved. Also included is a revised and expanded version of the Middle Pillar by Regardie himself, along with exercises for healing and charging talismans. The Appendix reflects a portion of a larger work called "The Musical Qabalah" by Thom Parrott, which builds upon the musical correspondences of Hebrew letters and words used in the Middle Pillar and Pentagram rituals. Also included is a glossary of psychological and magical terms.

Regardie's legacy lives on through each and every individual who values and finds meaning in his written works. We strongly suspect that readers of *The Middle Pillar* will discover that Regardie was an inspirational writer, an ethical magician, a skilled therapist, a caring healer, a great teacher, a consistent guide, and a companion on the path of the Magic of Light.

—Chic Cicero
Sandra Tabatha Cicero
Metatron House
Winter Solstice 1996

Endnotes

1. Although Crowley's reputation as "the wickedest man in the world" was undeserved, he nonetheless enjoyed the notoriety and had only himself to blame for it.

2. We have in our possession a copy of a ThAM-level Enochian Exam taken by Regardie and dated November 2, 1934. He was given a satisfactory grade by his temple chiefs.

3. From *The Rebirth of Magic* quoted in the Foreword of Regardie's *What You Should Know about the Golden Dawn*, ix.

4. In his later years, Regardie always needed a tank of oxygen nearby. Periodically, he would disappear to "take a puff."

5. Republished in 1983 as *The Teachers of Fulfillment*, (Falcon Press, 1983).

6. Not in Atlanta or Athens, Georgia, as some authors have mistakenly stated.

7. We had bought a house which was solely intended as a Golden Dawn temple. But it also became the site of our OTO temple. (Truly, a house divided!) At the time of Chic's Minerval initiation into the OTO in August of 1978, Grady had to walk through the framework of what would later become the walls of the Vault of the Adepti, a purely Golden Dawn creation. Grady's somewhat gruff response was "What the hell does this have to do with the OTO?" Both Grady and Regardie insisted time and time again that the two systems of magic "could not be mixed."

8. The events at the Isis-Urania temple at Columbus, Georgia, have been documented in the epilogue of our book *Secrets of a Golden Dawn Temple* (Llewellyn, 1992) so there is no need to repeat them here.

9. Sedona is a magnet for New Age groups. One time when we had stopped at a local Arby's for a quick lunch, Regardie could not resist engaging a group of people who were in line behind us. Regardie acted as if he was a complete novice and asked them what they were talking about. "Oh, it's very cerebral," one lady replied, and she continued to explain how they were interested in the mind's psychic abilities. "Oh," said Regardie, "you mean the mind has pish-ic abilities!" ("Pish-ic" was Regardie's favorite way of mispronouncing the word "psychic.") Regardie continued to play this good-natured game until our food arrived. I'm sure the group in question never had an inkling of who they were talking to. But the questioning look in their eyes as we walked away suggested that they were thinking to themselves, "Just who is that nice old guy?"

10. Regardie made this abundantly clear in a series of letters he wrote to us in the summer of 1984.

11. Since his death, we have maintained a respectful tradition of placing a personalized and hand-painted invitation to attend certain GD functions next to Regardie's headstone. We like to think that Regardie would have been pleased. (Or perhaps, like Edgar Allen Poe, he would have prefered a bottle half-filled with "spirits" to accompany him in the afterlife!)

12. This was probably the dialect he learned in his youth from his Hebrew tutor.

INTRODUCTION
TO THE SECOND EDITION

T he world is in crisis. Men of all ages look in despair on the chaos which is their inheritance from countless generations of forebears, and join in what has become a universal cry of disillusionment: "Stop the world—I want to get off."

Unfortunately, it isn't that easy to get off. Answers are not as simple as some might have supposed. And assuming they were, where would people go, once they got off the merry-go-round? Many centuries ago, certain sages approached the problem from another angle, and found what they considered a practical solution. If life is sorrow, then the only thing to do is to end this sorrowful existence by getting off the perpetually revolving wheel of existence.[1] Life follows life, incarnation follows incarnation—and all of them spell anxiety and sorrow. For these sages, it was apparent that it might be millions of years before the masses of humanity would develop enough insight to be able to terminate the sorrowful cycle of existence. But for the illuminated individual who will apply himself to a specific psycho-spiritual discipline, escape might come aeons sooner than for the average member of mankind.

This release, they learned, comes only through the achievement of a higher consciousness by the individual. Call it cosmic consciousness, the mystical experience, communion with God—all spell the same message—*release*. None may know it for another. Each man must himself attain *for himself* awareness of his own oneness with infinite life—the consciousness that a state of separateness exists only within his own mind.

Not until man does recognize that he is himself a microcosm of the macrocosm,[2] a reflection of the universe, a world within himself, ruled and governed by his own divinity, can he escape from the wheel. It is the achievement of this one realization which all schools of mysticism, magic, and various forms of occult teaching refer to as the Great Work.[3]

The Great Work is not accomplished overnight, or even in one lifetime. But the sooner the aspirant undertakes the task, the sooner will it be finished, and the quicker will he be released from the cycle of necessity, the wheel of evolution to which common humanity is bound. Millions of years may pass in the normal process of evolution before the mass of mankind will reach the state of freedom which those few individuals who apply themselves to this work can accomplish in a fraction of the time. And the paradox then dawns upon them that life, instead of being sorrowful, may just as well be the opposite. "Remember all ye that existence is pure joy; that all the sorrows are but as shadows; they pass and are done; but there is that which remains."[4] And as it has also been written: "I am divided for love's sake, for the chance of union. This is the creation of the world, that the pain of division is as nothing, and the joy of dissolution all."[5]

Herein lies the value of magic. Under ordinary conditions, months may be required for the flowering of a plant, but the use of a hot-house will produce identical results within a few weeks. An understanding and application of magic can telescope the time required for man to acquire the realization of his own divinity. Then, once he has become aware of the existence of his higher self, and works in cooperation rather than opposition to it, once he looks to it for guidance and direction, thenceforth regarding his ego as a tool, sharpened and polished to be employed now to fulfill the divine plan rather than in the indulgence of his own petty purposes—then will his way become easier. Long before obtaining his final release, then may he move forward on the upward path with joy and equanimity.

So it is that, at a time when the planet seems to be rocking beneath our feet, I derive great pleasure from writing an introduction to a new edition of *The Middle Pillar*. It is that pillar which stands dependable and relatively changeless as the sphinx, between the extremes of Mercy and Severity, the two outer pillars of the Qabalah's Tree of Life.[6] Equally important, it also provides basic principles of magic which can speed the student on his way to blessed release from the necessity of the accursed wheel. Once he has gained this new understanding, the student, it is to be hoped, will gradually but steadily progress until he has completed the Great Work. In so doing, not only will he help himself by stepping up his own evolutionary processes, but to that degree will he have raised the frequencies of his fellow man and even the planet itself, since all that is, is one.

Frances G. Wickes in *The Inner World of Choice* points out that we must "accept the experience that will bring to birth a latent potential," and be willing to dare the leap into the unknown, diving deep into the unconscious "in search of the other unborn or lost potentials of the self."[7]

The Middle Pillar should prove a trustworthy guide on this search. It involves several distinct methods, each of which has been designed for a specific purpose, yet all work together to accomplish the ultimate goal, to erase the barrier between the conscious self and the unconscious, and to enable the student to find within the self, the Great Self who is in reality the only saviour he will ever have.

The use of the Qabalistic Cross, as described in an early chapter, serves as an ideal means of aiding the ego to undergo an enormous expansion, to open up consciousness on a voluntary ordered level to the dictates of the unconscious. The so-called Banishing Ritual of the Pentagram[8] is a vital technique designed to eliminate undesirable elements from the psychic sphere, and thus to permit the process of consciousness expansion to proceed without harm or hindrance. The use of the archaic exercise referred to as the Middle Pillar will increase the field of attention, aid in the achievement of balance and equilibrium, and unfold to the aspirant a completely new and remarkable sphere of power and spiritual perception.

Every technique of magic is intended in various ways to widen the field of vision of the conscious ego to the deeper, more spiritual aspects of the divine nature—which, in reality, is his true or higher self. Of the numerous techniques available in the vast armamentarium of magic for this purpose, the most vital and essential ones are summed up in the simple exercises outlined in this book.

Ceremonial magic enables man to become an engine capable of harnessing and directing the enormous power that lies within. A multitude of basic principles are utilized to this end. Adoration, which is essential to attaining a sense of unity with godhead, concentration, development of will and the use of it to accomplish a given purpose, achievement of self-awareness, and the ability to breathe properly, these are but a few of the benefits to be derived from persistent application to the basic practices herein discussed.

Various symbolisms are employed in those phases which deal with adoration, but the choice of symbols is actually unimportant. Once it is realized that basically all religions are one and all prophets are true, it is quite logical to borrow any set of symbols from one religion for a certain purpose, and another set from a second religion for a different purpose. Nor will the practices be of passing value. On the contrary, the set of adorations the student will learn from this book are to be integrated for all time into the daily pattern of living. Next in importance is the achievement of a heightened sense of self-awareness. All other exercises and complex procedures actually begin from this heightening of self-awareness. To the degree that the horizon of one's self becomes expanded, to that extent does the self become enlarged.

The development of proper breathing habits will serve many purposes, including eradication of considerable neuromuscular tension, with a consequent increase of energy and vitality. The air by which we are surrounded, and in which we live and move and have our being, is the essence of life itself. Consequently we live, literally surrounded by a circumambient sea of energy and vitality—a divine force which can be assimilated by the simple process of learning to breathe in a proper rhythm, altogether apart from more abstruse occult theories.

Once he has gained control over his mental processes, the student can then learn to stimulate and direct his emotions. This becomes will. So complete and interlocking are the details of this system, that the emotions can then be utilized as a tool to be used in directing and holding the mind steady on a given objective. For fervor and conviction are essential to activating the productive and creative agency within man.

In the process, over a period of time, life becomes consecrated so that all one's energies become automatically concentrated in a continuous devotion to God or the one life that courses through all of us. In short, the student achieves a perfect and harmonious identification with divine power, life, and love. And then he will know that "existence is pure joy; that all the sorrows are but as shadows; they pass and are done...."[9]

The Middle Pillar was originally dedicated to S. L. MacGregor Mathers and Dr. William Wynn Westcott who were chiefs of the Hermetic Order of the Golden Dawn, to which I owe so very much. The book is merely the simplest possible representation of some of the elementary practices of that order. In actuality, it is an attempt to simplify and combine the practices both of the Golden Dawn with the insights and later developments of Aleister Crowley.[10]

The real virtue of the book lies in its correlation of the practice of magic to modern psychotherapy. For magic places the achievement of self-awareness second in importance only to the achievement of unity with God. And Jung's definition of psychotherapy was that which enabled one to become conscious of what hitherto was unconscious.

For untold thousands of years, man has lived in subjugation to the unconscious forces of nature—powerful instincts and drives which led him to act without deliberation or conscious volition, and in complete ignorance in fact of the forces at work which really motivated him. The Great Work recognizes that in these deep unconscious levels lies a great storehouse of power, awareness, and vitality which must not only be awakened but recognized and equilibrated for the human being to function at maximum capacity and efficiency. This in short is the major purpose and function of the teachings of this book.

I had first begun to read about psychoanalysis in the writings of Freud and Jung as early as 1926. I cannot say they meant very much to me, save as intellectual stimuli of a fascinating kind. When I first wrote *The Middle Pillar*, I had just entered psychoanalytical therapy, thanks to the influence of a very dear friend. The tremendous value and importance of psychotherapy as a prelude to any serious magical training was just beginning to dawn upon me.

My work with Dr. E. A. Clegg of Harley Street, and with Dr. J. L. Bendit,[11] a Jungian of Wimpole Street in London, led me to realize the importance of psychotherapy to the beginner in mysticism and magic. In fact, thirty-five years later, in 1968, I am more strongly of the opinion than I was then. So fervently do I feel about this that since that time I have acquired some of the qualifications necessary to practice various forms of psychotherapy, particularly that of Wilhelm Reich,[12] whose work I regard as a bridge between conventional psychotherapy and occultism. I doubt if Reich would be pleased to learn of this association of mine—but a fact it is nevertheless.

Today I will not so much as consider even discussion of the Great Work with a student until he has experienced some form of psychotherapy, I care not which. There is lacking, until then, a common frame of reference, and common medium of communication. In *The Middle Pillar* will be discovered the first glimmerings of insight I had in that particular direction. It still holds good today.

Endnotes

1. The "wheel of existence" or the "wheel of evolution" refers to the wheel of *karma* or destiny. *Karma* is a Sanskrit word that means "action." It is a destiny consciously chosen in life by each person, created by the total life experiences of all previous incarnations. Karma is the spiritual law of cause and effect—a law of consequence that plays itself out in psychic, moral, and physical ways in the life of human beings. One of the fundamentals of karma is that you get back what you give out. Thus evil that you do in one lifetime will come back to haunt you in the next. Likewise, the good that you do in one lifetime will come back to reward you in the next. In this manner, the individual human soul slowly evolves over the course of many lifetimes, gradually learning though its mistakes and growing a little wiser, a little closer to the divine each time. In Buddhism, the "Wheel of Life" or round of births is known as sasara. The mystic seeks to get off the wheel of incarnation as soon as possible, speeding up the process of spiritual

growth through various techniques of meditation and magic. Once freed from the wheel, the soul of the mystic can merge with the ultimate unity that is God. (The Hebrew term for this concept is *tikkun* or "redemption.")

2. The *macrocosm* is the "greater universe" or the totality of all that exists within the divine cosmos. Man is the *microcosm* or "lesser universe," a miniature version of the greater universe in every detail.

3. A term borrowed from the alchemical phrase "Magnum Opus." It refers to the path of spiritual evolution and growth. *Illumination*.

4. From the second chapter of *Liber Al vel Legis* or *The Book of the Law*, by Aleister Crowley (Samuel Weiser, Inc., 1976), 34.

5. Ibid., first chapter, 15.

6. The primary symbol of the ancient system of Hebrew mysticism known as Qabalah or "tradition." This system is the foundation of almost all western magic.

7. Frances G. Wickes, *The Inner World of Choice* (Sigo Press, 1988).

8. Sometimes referred to as the LBRP.

9. See Endnote 4.

10. The emphasis of the Golden Dawn was primarily Western, the study of the Hermetic occult sciences of Qabalah, astrology, spiritual alchemy, skrying, etc. Crowley's teachings, though based on Golden Dawn techniques, tended to be much more Eastern in focus.

11. John Laurence Bendit (1898–?) was a psychiatrist, author, and psychic researcher. Educated at Cambridge University, Dr. Bendit had a private practice as a psychiatrist from 1923 onwards. From 1958 to 1961 he was the General Secretary for the Theosophical Society in London, and from 1937 to 1946 he was a member of the Society for Psychical Research. Dr. Bendit's doctorate in medicine was granted for his work in parapsychology, the first of its kind granted by a university in Britain. His specialized field of study was the relationship between psychic ability and psychological problems. His published works included *Paranormal Cognition; The Psychic Sense; This World and That*; and *Man Incarnate*. In 1939 he married Phoebe Daphne Payne, a psychotherapist herself and a natural clairvoyant. Mrs. Bendit worked with her husband and co-authored some of his books.

12. See Part Two, Chapter Six for more on Wilhelm Reich.

The Wisdom of Enlightenment is inherent in every one of us. It is because of the delusion under which our mind works that we fail to realize it ourselves, and that we have to seek the advice and guidance of the highly enlightened one before we can know our essence of mind. You should know that so far as Buddha-nature is concerned, there is no difference between an enlightened man and an ignorant one. What makes the difference is that one realizes it, while the other is kept in ignorance of it.

—SUTRA OF WEI LANG

FOREWORD

This book was completed in February 1936, anterior to the writing of *The Art of True Healing*, whilst I was still resident in London. My point of view since that time has undergone considerable revision, mostly by way of extension. I could easily have altered the text to conform to my present thinking on such matters as the importance of the art of relaxation in relation to the welfare both of body and mind. But I have refrained from doing so since such alteration would interfere with the integrity and continuity of the book as an expression of myself at that time.

For me *The Middle Pillar* marks a certain stage of psychological development. I prefer not to tamper with temporal markings and inner milestones. Such a stage may correspond with that of other people who may thus find it of no little value, I hope, to themselves. Possibly in the near future I may dilate at greater length and freedom upon the important implications of relaxation and psychological analysis insofar as they have bearing upon spiritual development and unfoldment.

—Israel Regardie
(January 31, 1938, New York City)

Part One

The Middle Pillar

Israel Regardie

*A co-relation of the principles of analytical psychology
and the elementary techniques of magic.*

CHAPTER ONE

THE TWO PILLARS
OF THE TEMPLE

T o me one of the most significant and extraordinary characteristics of modern thought is the widespread circulation of books on psychology in its various branches. There is a general interest in matters dealing with the mind—especially with that aspect of the hinterland of the mind which has been named the unconscious for want of better words and also because its realm at the moment is so ambiguous to us. There could hardly be an educated individual who has not some slight degree of acquaintance with this analytical psychology. Even if this familiarity ran only to an acquaintance with several of the more commonly employed *cliches*—such as libido, the unconscious, conflicts and resistances, neuroses and complexes—that in itself would be indicative of a phenomenon which surely has occurred seldom before in the history of civilized thought.

To meet this widespread interest in matters psychological, a number of books have been written to give the general reader some notion of that peculiar world with which it is the province of the analyst to deal. Quite a number of these are extremely informative, providing a very sane and balanced view of the subject. On the other hand, as is inevitable, there is a large number which might just as well have remained unwritten. One of the

3

most curious misconceptions promulgated by some of these latter is the fact that analytical psychology—and here I use this term in its widest sense to cover the various schools inaugurated by Freud, Jung, Adler, etc.—is a thing quite apart, and that the one thing which stamped our ancestors as barbarians and savages was their utter lack of acquaintance with psychotherapy. It would be totally absurd for anyone to minimize all that has been achieved by modern psychology, due to the efforts of such astute investigators as Freud and Jung. But it is abundantly clear that their protagonists—psychological extremists—go entirely too far in disclaiming the intelligence and insight of our predecessors. For the facts are, as but little research indicates, that so far from being ignorant of analytical psychology, the ancients, and particularly those of the East and hither East, had evolved a highly complex and elaborate scheme not only of analysis, but also of spiritual development and synthesis.

Some orthodox diehards may question the relationship of modern psychology with discredited oriental and archaic techniques for the unfolding of man's higher or spiritual nature. In practice, however, such a relationship does indubitably exist. It is a fact of clinical and consulting-room experience. For, during the course of a protracted analysis, the cruder and more superficial unconscious levels having been uncovered and moral conflicts resolved, symbols and theme-motifs of a religious or spiritual nature do make their entry across the threshold of consciousness. This entry is by way of dream, intuition, and by direct apprehension. Not only is this so, but they exert a potent influence on the entire personality, producing integrity, a new and more equilibrated attitude towards life, and an unification of the various strata of consciousness which collectively we call man.

What modern psychology has quite possibly accomplished is an advance over the efforts of our predecessors in the way of a cathartic technique. Moreover, because of modern devices, the methods of analytical psychology have been brought nearer to the understanding and convenience of the ordinary man of the street. In the past, the techniques of attainment, mysticism, magic, and yoga, or by whatever name such systems were denoted, were always several removes from the ken of the average individual.

The psychologies of the past may be summarized by the use of the words yoga and magic. The subject of yoga has already been excellently dealt with by several able and competent writers, requiring therefore but little mention here. Such a book as *Yoga and Western Psychology* by Geraldine Coster must certainly take its place historically as a genuine and first-rate contribution to the progress of analytical psychology. There is also the compilation of the Buddhist Lodge *Concentration and Meditation,* a handbook on that subject of great merit.[1] A number of modern psychologists have also examined the subject of yoga and meditation as a whole, and have found much that is sympathetic to and explanatory of their own systems. And furthermore, the mystical systems posit a goal and a general schema which expand the rather hazy and indeterminate character of a very large part of our psycho-therapeutic systems.

Analytical psychology and magic comprise in my estimation two halves or aspects of a single technical system. Just as the body and mind are not two separate units, but are simply the dual manifestations of an interior dynamic "something," so psychology and magic comprise similarly a single system whose goal is the integration of the human personality. Its aim is to unify the different departments and functions of man's being, to bring into operation those which previously for various reasons were latent. Incidentally, its technique is such that neurotic symptoms which were too insistent upon expression either become eliminated or toned down by a process of equilibration.

It will be obvious, then, that by magic[2] we are not considering a theatrical craft or jugglery—and certainly not that mediaeval superstition which was the child of ignorance begotten by fear and terror. These definitions should be expunged from our thinking. For centuries magic has been quite erroneously associated with such pathologies as witchcraft[3] and demonolatry[4] due to the duplicity of charlatans and the reticence of its own so-called authorities. Even today, the custodians of this knowledge, harassed by personal problems and more especially by their own power complex are still adamant in their traditional refusal to circulate a more accurate description of the nature of magic. Possibly even they have lost all understanding of its principles. No wonder is it that misconception exists. With the exception of very few works which have attracted the attention of but a fractional part of the reading public, little has been written to act as a definitive exposition of what magic really is. Inasmuch as something of the nature of modern psychology is at least partially understood by a fair section of the educated world, were it said that magic is akin to and concerns itself with that same subjective realm of psychology, some notion of its character and objectives come within hailing distance.

So far as the average man or aspirant to magic is concerned, unquestionably the analytic technique should comprise the first stage of the routine employed in spiritual development. For until one understands himself according to that peculiarly penetrating light which psychology has thrown upon our motives, he cannot hope to bring effectively into operation the dormant side of his nature. And lest anyone casually dismiss this desirable self-knowledge as a goal easily attained to or, it may be, already obtained, one can only utter a solemn warning that this is not so simple as at first sight seems. That self-knowledge is necessary to the pursuit of magic is self-evident. At once we are faced at the portal by guardians armed to the teeth. Such queries confront us as: suppose the interest in spiritual culture were motivated by a desire to escape from the turbulence of physical life? What if one's stubbornly defended point of view were only an elaborate rationalization to conceal the sense of insecurity, the dull but insistent ache of inferiority? These are quite often the unrecognized factors which compel refuge in the religious avocation— even in various branches of science too. The search for, and quite often assumed discovery of some paternal-like God or a testy senior after the fashion of Jehovah, frequently has its origins in an adolescent rejection of the father. This, deliberately forgotten, has become so deep, that the inner psychic necessity for the authority and affection of the father is unconsciously projected outwards into a terrifying and awe-inspiring deity. Discernment of the true motives of conduct and attitude towards life is, therefore, an absolute essential. This accomplished, then may be examined that other side of the medallion which is man's own psyche.

As a practical system, magic is concerned not so much with analysis as with bringing into operation the creative and intuitive parts of man. A psychological technique can never be a wholly integrative one until it accepts this spiritual side of man and assists the analysand in the recognition of or acquaintance with its activity. At this moment, the treatment of these matters remains almost entirely within the domain of magic alone. Fully does it recognize the necessity for integration. Not only does it accept and recommend the results of analysis, but it proceeds still further. If analysis aims at the acceptance of the unconscious, and the validity of its co-existence with consciousness, then magic may be said to be a technique for realizing the deeper levels of the unconscious. These are levels of power and realization whose value we can but dimly grasp through contemplation of religious figures of the past. Buddha, Jesus, Krishna, St. Francis, and a host of others are instances of such illuminated men—of individuals who have striven, all in different ways, to know themselves and attain to a realization of their true divine nature. If so we wish, the techniques they employed we may call devotion, meditation, and contemplation. Fundamentally, however, they are identical in spirit with what we now propose to discuss as magic. In the latter, however, the entire process of attainment has been systematized and developed almost into an exact science, having as its foundation the discovery of godhead. While there may be very few in life who can attain to the full realization of their divine origin and nature, yet for all of us there is some value to magic, some degree of fulfillment or attainment available. There is none so small as cannot employ it to some good and noble end. None so great as cannot better himself morally and otherwise, thus rendering himself more efficient to cope with and understand life and the world both about and within him. These are objectives which, notwithstanding the magnitudes of their vision, are within the reach of every man.

It is not yet the moment to enter into a disquisition on the intricacies of magical ritual. But in order to expound fundamental psychological and spiritual principles it is necessary to refer to what are known technically as the *two pillars*.[5] Half-way between the east and west, and north and south, in a properly instituted temple are placed two upright pillars.[6] One of these is colored white, the other black. These pieces of lodge furniture are emblematical of the two opposites functioning in the diverse operations of nature. Just as the temple represents in miniature the whole of life by which we may ever be confronted, or, rather, the manifold parts of our own inner nature, so these two pillars symbolize some aspect of these phenomena. They represent light and darkness, heat and cold. In man, they stand for love and hate, joy and pain, mind and emotion, life and death, sleeping and waking. Every pair of opposites conceivable to the human mind find their representation in the implication of these two pillars.

Now one of the most important ideas communicated to the student of magic, in his ceremonial initiation when he is led from one station to another, is that an extreme leaning either to one or the other of the opposites is a very dangerous thing. It is unwise to swing to opposite poles of life's pendulum. "Unbalanced power is the ebbing away of life. Unbalanced mercy is but weakness and the fading out of the will. Unbalanced severity is cruelty and the barrenness of mind."[7]

Were we to change the terminology of the speech, instead of the word "mercy" we might substitute "emotion," or "generosity," or "love"; for "severity" we may substitute "power," "the rational side of us," or "justice," or "tyranny." Either of these qualities when carried to an extreme, unmodified by the other, is conducive to an unhealthy state of psyche. Thus it is, that in so religiously authoritative a book as the *Bhagavad-Gita*,[8] which some consider one of the finest pieces of devotional and philosophical literature yet penned, we find it stated "Be free from the pairs of opposites."

The whole of life—it is in fact the law of nature itself—seems to be dominated by these extremes or opposites. "Two contending forces and one which unites them eternally. Two basal angles of the triangle and one which forms the apex. Such is the origin of creation; it is the Triad of Life."[9] Only a little reflection will convince the reader of the truth of this theorem. Until we have acquired wisdom and understanding, we swing during the seventy year span of our lives between self-esteem and self-disgust, from an exaggerated estimation of our fellows to their utter and final condemnation. Age, it is true, does bring moderation and temperance with it. But were this more balanced attitude towards life cultivated, taught or adopted earlier or before middle age set in, how much more efficient could we not be, and what could we not achieve? The technique under consideration consists primarily in the conscious reconciliation of opposing forces. It is this which has been called the development of the Golden Flower.[10]

Before proceeding further, it is a very interesting piece of speculation to consider the trinities of various religions. Most of them resolve themselves when all theological argument and intellectual quibbling are eliminated, into some such relationship as Father, Mother, and Son. Osiris, Isis, and Horus are an excellent example. This is true also of the Christian system where, upon careful consideration we find the Holy Ghost defined as a feminine aspect of godhead.[11] And in the Hebrew Qabalah we have the Trinity on the Tree of Life of *Chesed* ("Mercy"), *Gevurah*[12] ("Might") and *Tiphareth* ("Equilibrium" or "Beauty"). Co-relating this latter triad with traditional symbolism, *Chesed* is masculine, referred to Jupiter, a paternal wisdom symbol. *Gevurah*, feminine, is attributed to Mars, indicative of great power. One alchemical aphorism expresses this duality in the words "Man is peace and woman is power." Bearing all these in mind, we conclude that as *Chesed* represents the Father and *Gevurah* the Mother,[13] so *Tiphareth* which is Beauty, is the reconciler between them. Interestingly enough, Tiphareth is referred to the Sun, and corresponds to the third member of the theological trinity, the Son.

Looking at these trinities as so many expressions of psychological fact—that is, as previously defined, as factors active within the psyche itself—we are struck by the similarity of the religious point of view with the idea of the Middle Way.[14] It is the pursuit of this middle path which leads to self-conquest and the steady growth of the Golden Flower, the wakening of the imprisoned soul within.

The Father and Mother may be said to correspond to the two pillars of the temple, to the two extremes or opposites. In this sense they are the tendencies exhibited by all the phenomena of nature. They are the extremes of spirit and matter, love and hate, life and death, ebb and flow, systole and diastole. Nature itself is the embodiment of the two extremes, the two opposites of the Trinity.

Man, unenlightened man, one in whom neither wisdom nor understanding has been brought to birth, likewise fashions his life in the way of these two extremes. Or rather, these extremes fashion his life for him. For he is, as though by compulsion, driven by some external force he knows not of, between the poles of extreme love and hate, swinging from kindness and maudlin generosity to bursts of uncontrolled anger, hate and meanness. His actions, almost without a single exception, are so many semi-hysterical flights from pole to pole of his emotions. He is, as it were, under the dominion of the Father and the Mother.

To the student of the psyche, to the one who seeks wisdom and the knowledge of his higher self, the counsel has always been given to avoid the opposites. His task is to refrain from the compulsion of extreme actions.

In certain schools of magic, where the rites of initiation were celebrated by adepts who at one time thoroughly understood the technique they employed, initiation ceremonies depicted the burial of the higher self and its rebirth by means of a technical system of magic and meditation. Therein, the higher self was always represented by some sacred figure of the major religions—a man who was nearly always shown as the Son of God. The essence of the ethical injunctions of these systems was to develop the Son within. "Unless Christ be born in you…." "Look within; thou are Buddha." I do not believe these images could possibly have reference to any historical individual we know of. But rather I surmise these refer to the gradual bringing into conscious operation of a spiritual point of view, of an equilibrated attitude towards life, an attitude not exclusively directed to any extreme. Recognizing the polarity of life, such a point of view sought to steer a middle way between the tortuous and extreme activity of nature. It is the way of the Reconciler, of keeping to the path between the two pillars, that balanced and harmonious position in which the candidates of the ancient initiation systems found themselves at the major crisis and climax of their initiation. This is the technique of bringing to birth the golden Sun of *Tiphareth*, the Sun of beauty and harmony who is the third person of the Trinity. Thus it is that one system nowadays[15] conceives of the Great Work as partaking of the recognition of the Crowned and Conquering Child

Horus—he who, while partaking necessarily of the nature of both the Father and the Mother, is simultaneously an entirely different and unique being. Through the result of the union of opposing forces, his nature tends to a new viewpoint in the conquest of life. For the Father and Mother are "those forces whose reconciliation is the key of life."[16]

To illustrate in another way the import of this concept, let us describe it from a practical and physical point of view. One of the major inconveniences which afflicts a large portion of mankind is constipation. In many instances of this disorder, no organic disturbance exists at all; the trouble being principally a functional one. (Though it must be here interpolated that even if it were organic, there is sufficient psychological evidence to indicate that this likewise may ensue from an identical series of causes.) Very often, this malady does not respond to any kind of medical treatment. It is not uncommon for patients to testify that they have been recommended massage, surgical operations, drugs, nature cure, and all the other types of cures. In spite of these the illness persists unchanged. Enquiry elicits that there is, frequently, a conscious conflict between two courses of conduct. More often than not, however, the real seat of the conflict is not in consciousness at all, but exists in a far deeper level of mind, in the unconscious. It was probably around puberty that an already existent conflict developed such acuteness and severity as to require for the psychic safety of the ego to be repressed completely out of sight.

From this, we might conclude—and there is some psychological evidence to this end—that the conflict is one between the instincts and social dictates. That is, because of parental training there is a blind refusal to recognize the necessity for the proper and legitimate expression of the instincts. It is a denial of one side of the personality, a denial without justification or reason. It is as though, while admiring the beauty and form of the lotus, we wished not to be reminded of the slimy source where grow the roots of the plant, and therefore cut the stalk right through, severing the flower from its necessary root. This cutting of the lotus stalk has its counterpart in human minds, many of us having been cut off from our roots. For this denial of the instinctual life, in which the conscious existence after all has its roots, and this persistent repression, cause some degree of dissociation. That is, a severance of the integrity and unity of the psyche. The psychosis,[17] if sufficiently intense and prolonged, produces symptoms of various sorts ranging from lack of vitality, irritability, constipation, and a host of other physical and nervous disorders.

With such a problem, there is but one logical method of attack. It is to recognize quite clearly that the physical symptoms are the results of an internal conflict, a conflict between the needs of the body and the self-sufficiency or cowardice of the mind. It is a conflict between the necessity to the expression of emotion and feeling, and the imperious urge of the ego to escape from a vulnerable constituent of its nature, that principle which at one time had been susceptible to hurt and injury. With the frank recognition of the conflict, one should endeavor to recollect the events of his early childhood, bringing up as many memories as possible of that period, experiencing neither shame nor remorse at his discoveries.[18] Confronting these memories with the knowledge that as an adult in whom is the light of reason, he understands that his mature mind can dissipate the infantile emotion connected with early experiences, in which shame or inferiority or insecurity was felt. In this way, he links and applies mind to emotion, thus avoiding within him the uncontrolled play of the opposites. Their existence is neither denied nor frustrated. This is a vital point to be understood. No denial or rejection should be countenanced of what manifestly is an actual fact, no stubborn refusal to admit and accept a part of his own nature. As we have seen, the denial of any function of the self leads to dissociation, and the latter results in nervous and physical disorders.

Face the fact that at one time there was a denial of one phase of life, and thus accept the conflict. Accept it, knowing that so long as we remain human, these conflicts are bound to be our lot. In our present stage of evolution, they are part and parcel of human nature, and so cannot be avoided. But what can be eliminated is the ignorant attitude so often adopted towards them. For these opposites, the two pillars of the temple, their magical images or prototypes, represent "those eternal forces betwixt which the equilibrium of the universe dependeth. Those forces whose reconciliation is the

Key of Life, whose separation is evil and death."[19] This, then, is the solution to conflict. They must be reconciled.

Let me recapitulate. There must be the clear recognition of the conflict. Its exact nature must be analyzed and faced, and its presence accepted in all its implications.

One must endeavor to bring up into consciousness, so far as the capabilities of the mind permit, all the memories of childhood. In a word, he should attempt to perform a species of what is called in the Buddhist system the *Sammasati* meditation. This consists in a cultivation and rigid examination of memory. The idea involved here is not that these recollections in themselves are worth anything, but that raising them up to the surface releases a great deal of tension associated with early experiences. There is often a tying up of nervous energy in childhood experiences, in trivial events which are allowed to be forgotten and to sink into unconsciousness. But this forgetfulness does not overcome the shock of nervous exhaustion connected with them. On the contrary, they set up what are called resistances—resistances to the flow of life and vitality from the primitive and vital layers of the unconscious level.

"What matters," remarks Georg Groddeck[20] the brilliant German physician-psychologist, "is not to make conscious anything at all of the unconscious, but to relieve what is imprisoned, and in so doing it is by no means rare for the repressed material to sink into the depths instead of coming into consciousness…. What is decisive in the success of treatment is the removal of resistance."

Beginning with the actual events of the day upon which the reader determines to commence this exercise, the meditation should gradually extend its field of vision until ultimately the events and occurrences of the earliest years are brought into the light of day. The technique is principally one of the training of the mind to think backwards. Difficult though at first it may seem, practice leads the student slowly and gradually to facility in the art of remembering. The facts of memory confronted fearlessly, without shame and discomfiture, the resistance to the flow of vitality between the various levels of consciousness is broken down, restoring physical, nervous, and spiritual health.

As the childhood memories are exposed, the student will see for himself in what way the conflict now bothering him came into manifestation. Since by definition a neurosis[21] is a maladaptation of the psyche to life itself, by this process of remembering he will see in what way he failed to respond properly to the phenomena of his existence.

Realizing this, and recognizing thoroughly the nature of his conflict, he must now endeavor to ignore it. More accurately a more positive attitude should be adopted. He must develop in an entirely new direction. It must be remembered, however, and this is important, that to ignore any symptom of conflict as manifested in mind or body, is dangerous until the conflict in question has been recognized and accepted. The unconditional acceptance almost invariably acts as its resolution. Any other attitude constitutes an escape.

The escape mechanism is that so frequently adopted by the neurotic and must be avoided. It is the way of the coward. To face the conflict is to rob it and its consequences of crippling fear. Honesty with oneself acts as a catharsis. One finds himself endued with a new courage and greater ability to face one's problem in an entirely new and more practicable way. Given the recognition of the conflict causing constipation, the symptom itself may be severely ignored, relying upon the bowel after the lapse of some days to recommence functioning of its own accord. The conflict and the warring between the two sides of the psyche, tied a knot as it were in consciousness preventing the perfect functioning of the whole. The immediate result of this is an impediment in the free movement of nervous energy in the body-mind system, causing stasis in that part of the system having a relationship or correspondence with the factors concerned in the conflict.

Occult theory as we have it from tradition may be extremely useful here. With some degree of practical experience, we could easily discover the precise nature of the original conflict by a consideration of that part of the organism to the symptoms of which our attention is attracted. For example, consider one troubled by nephritis.[22] One of the most significant aspects of the magical tradition is astrology. In this latter science the kidneys are referred to the operation of the planet Venus. As we know from mythology, Venus is the deity concerned with love, feeling, and emotion. We would surmise therefore that in the event that the love or emotional life of an individual has been frustrated or repressed to such a point where the psyche finally refused to continue living whilst hampered by such a neurosis, some expression of that frustration could be transferred to the neighborhood of the kidneys. Were the frustration complete and devastating to the psyche, it is not impossible that we should find a cancer—the symptom *par excellence* of the death-wish, the so-called suicide complex indicative of a division in the psyche's integrity.

Moreover, we could proceed a step further. We might enquire as to whether the affliction were on the right or left, remembering the Qabalistic definition of the Left Pillar as the side of Mercy, and that on the Right as the Pillar of Severity.[23] "Unbalanced mercy is weakness and the fading out of the will. Unbalanced severity is cruelty and the barrenness of mind."[24]

Enquiry might elicit the fact that an afflicted left kidney was symptomatic of one who had been afraid to taste life to the full. Or on the other hand, out of sheer compensation, had lived, so completely as to have over-indulged. The right kidney would indicate symptoms of severe and violent repression on principle—where the entire emotional life had been so subjected to continuous frustration because of an ethical standard that the outraged eros reacted upon the body either with acute nephritis or it may be with cancer.

Where there is trouble with the legs, the patient being unable to stand and confined to the bed, some psychological thinkers proffer some such explanation as this. The legs are the things we stand on, that which gives support to the body. In the symbolic pageantry utilized by the unconscious—and it must be understood that the activity of the unconscious proceeds almost exclusively through what are to us symbols—the instinctual life is our mental support. It is that which we tend to rely upon, our stability and foundation, during life. Should therefore our understanding of life fall short of what it should be for us—and obviously that standard varies with different people—so that we unduly repress our instincts to the point when the resulting sense of insecurity and anxiety become intolerable, the psyche achieves a revenge through an affliction of the supports of the personality. Thus it is that we learn, so it is said, by illness. When our supports, no matter of what nature, have been annihilated, we sometimes seek to enquire into causes and origins. When the enquiry is honestly furthered, with a sincere view to self-knowledge, and internal resistance broken down by meditation or analysis, no doubt recovery would ensue. That is to say, the disappearance of the alarming symptoms, and a return of normal function.

The solvent to these difficulties, the practical solution of the problem, consists primarily in the elimination so far as possible of fear. Of course, from the larger point of view, fear is an essential part of our make-up. Man is so puny a creature on the face of the earth, and nature is vast and terrible in her operations. How else could it be that fear eats at the heart of each of us? But this is a wholesome fear—a fear which is the beginning of wisdom. The emotion under consideration is a pathological thing—fear of the future, fear of position, a needless worrying about affairs which cannot be helped or changed, at least not by hugging a constant fear that they will change in a manner that is painful and sad. From the spiritual point of view, fears such as we have named act as a great freezer, as an inhibitor of action and of the free flow of vital energy from within. The man who is afraid to embark upon a given course of action because it may lead to failure, or whose apprehension of success and of the future generally, is hardly likely to accomplish very much. "Fear is failure" says one magical aphorism, "and the forerunner of failure. Be thou therefore without fear, for in the heart of the coward, virtue abideth not."[25]

One of the most interesting instances of the psycho-therapeutic attitude to fear and anxiety and the escape-problem as a whole was Groddeck's treatment, when he was a physician before applying psychology to his problems, of certain cases of indigestion and nervous dyspepsia. One of the psychological theorems regarding this form of discomfort is that it is due to anxiety. We all know how bad news or worry affects the digestion, from turning the food sour to taking away the appetite. But the root cause of this particular anxiety is not the problem in hand, but the anxiety which has its roots in an early conflict and is made the worse by the occurrence of an immediate problem evoking conflict and anxiety. Groddeck's treatment—almost the homeopathic principle—emphasized or comprised a diet of precisely those foods which formerly disagreed with his patient. If eggs were the cause of indigestion the diet would comprise eggs until eventually the psychic would give up attempting to evade the associations which had been linked to eggs, and the digestive trouble would in time disappear. To force the psyche to face its problems and accept them was his idea rather than that the psyche should continually baulk from and attempt to flee the symptoms it threw up in the body. The unconditional acceptance of the conflict, and the associations connected with it, was the first step towards cure. The technique is, in a word or two, an attack on the escape mechanism. Integrity cannot be won by an escapist attitude towards life. The reward of the attitude which escapes from problems and the reality of life is more likely than not to be nothing but the gnawing pain of guilt and sin.

The same method is often made use of in other forms of therapy. Amongst these, for example, is the treatment of nightmares by analysis. The terror experienced in nightmare, causing the dreamer to awaken bathed in perspiration, angered by a palpitation of the heart, and experiencing an inexplicable sense of impending catastrophe, is likewise due to some conflict or other. Its nature, being unconscious, can only be determined by the context of the dream, and by the lengthy process of confession, free association, and reductive analysis.

But if the dreamer can be trained in his waking state to realize that the nightmare is only the expression of an internal conflict, then he has proceeded halfway to the point where it will cease to bother him. He must accept the presence of such a disorder rather than attempt to escape it, because escape is not an adequate solution of a psychic problem.

This discovery was brought home to us during the war. Amongst the soldiers at the front were those who would not recognize the very obvious fact, that war was a dangerous matter and that they were afraid. This they would not accept, though underneath a veritable torrent of fear was raging, and the whole of the instinctive impulse was to bolt from the scene of battle. Those who recognized this impulse but at the same time saw that flight was impossible and that the war had to be seen through, came to no mental or spiritual harm.

It was the former type, suffering from a terrible fear but boasting that they were not in the least afraid, who became affected by shell-shock. Shell-shock—the shock experienced by the nervous system through the devastating noise of explosion, had nothing to do with their actual trouble at all. The cause was simply a cowardly refusal to face the conflict raging in the psyche. And when this became so intolerable, an actual split occurred in consciousness, so that there was a gap in memory, awareness, and in efficiency.

With the acceptance of the theory of conflict as a cause of nightmare, a subtle change gradually creeps into the nightmare-dream. The following is one rather fine example, together with the method of dealing with it.

A woman patient frequently dreamed that she was hanging from a rope in a room which had an enormously high ceiling, about fifty or sixty feet high. The rope was affixed by a hook to the ceiling, and the weight imposed upon the hook was gradually loosening the plaster around. Any moment, the hook would tear loose from the ceiling, and the body would be dashed to the ground. At this juncture of the dream, unable to face the terror of being hurled to death on the ground, the woman awoke in a frenzy of fear, screaming. The advice given in this particular case—and since the dream is a typical nightmare, the same technique may be widely recommended—was to suggest to the woman the advisability of meditating on the dream before falling to sleep at night. The suggestion was to lengthen the term of the dream so as to invite the nightmare and observe what happened when the plaster did finally break, tearing the hook from the ceiling.

Constant and deep reflection on the dream's theme before sleep was the method by which the unconscious could so be influenced as to induce a vigilant attitude even during the progress of the fantasy. The topic of meditation would also be the conscious application of the idea of non-resistance. Let the catastrophe occur, and see what happens. If the fantasy is being perched on a high cliff and at any moment there is the danger of being hurled to the ground, awaking at mid-point in a sweat of fear, then gradually train the mind to thrust out all resistance to the fall. By methods such as these resistance and repression is broken down and fear eliminated from the sphere of consciousness.

Here, some word should be said about repression[26] and the means of its elimination. A great many people have come to believe, through a very casual reading of some of the early psychoanalytic literature, that psychology countenances the removal of repression by means which are unethical and antisocial. Nothing could be further from the truth. Repression is always defined as an unconscious and automatic process. It is a process by which the personality protects itself against distasteful concepts, by thrusting them without the horizon of consciousness into the dark and forbidding region of the unconscious. Since this process begins very early in life, the unconscious is by middle age stuffed with a mass of repressed material ideas about parents and relatives, associations connected with environment, infantile beliefs and actions. Suppression, on the other hand, is a deliberate and conscious thing. It presupposes a process of conscious selection and elimination, in which one alternative is suppressed in favor of another.

It is repression, the unconscious process of thrusting things out of sight, which is the dangerous method. It is dangerous because repressed emotions and feelings lock up memory and power in the unconscious. Because ideas become associated with each other, forming definite complexes, there is, if repressed memories begin to grow by association, a splitting off of one side of the mind at the expense of the other with a consequent locking up of energy and vitality which should be available for the entire personality. The conquest of repression proceeds as with the conquest of internal conflict previously described.

There is no need to live an anti-social or vicious life, one of self-indulgence or of degradation as so many people think. To be free from a repression does not argue that one should have behaved like "a young man about town." Though that is not to say that a reasonable satisfaction of the instinctual life should be eschewed where this is at all possible. But the frank realization and acceptance of the human personality as many-sided, and a refusal to blind oneself to experience no matter of what kind, will go far towards relieving the partition erected between the unconscious and the conscious, and removing resistance and repression.

To restate the attitude expounded in this chapter, I conceive of analytical psychology as the spouse of the ancient system of magic. For psychology has succeeded in evolving a system which can be applied to almost any individual who wishes to know the several departments and constituents of his own personality. Possibly for the first time in the history of civilized thought, there is a technique which is of inestimable value to the average man. It is of supreme value to the student of magic and mysticism, who, too often, labors under several delusions of what it is that he hopes to accomplish, and in what length of time he will do so. A study of analysis will prove first of all that he cannot proceed quicker than his own unconscious permits him. This will prevent gate-crashing, and an irrational enthusiasm and desire for speed. Secondly, through the elimination of erroneous ideas as to himself, the phantasms of wish-fulfillment and insensate day-dreaming, he will have obtained a more comprehensive account of what magical and meditation systems can accomplish, and what degree of achievement in these spheres is open to him. He will be entirely less subject to delusion and deception because his attraction to magic will not have been caused by the unconscious desire to escape from the pressing problems of his immediate existence with which he finds himself unable efficiently to cope.

Moreover, he will have familiarized himself with the true extent of his own sense of inferiority. The compulsive necessity of becoming unduly aggressive because of an imagined or pathological inferiority will no longer urge him to an intolerable sense of deficiency. Being acquainted with the fundamental problem of insecurity which every thinking individual is bound to have, since man is so apparently insignificant and unimportant when compared to the vastness of the universe, he will not be liable to adopt extreme religious or scientific notions from so-called spiritual experience or laboratory experiment to buttress up his own desire for some one thing which is secure and reliable.

Analysis is the logical precursor of spiritual attainment and magical experiment. It should comprise definitely the first stage of spiritual training. Were it possible, and were there magical schools in existence, it would gratify me enormously to see magical training preceded by six or twelve months of application to reductive analysis, pursued by sympathetic physicians or lay-analysts who had long and intimate experience with clinical work. The magical schools must open a department of analytical psychology, if their own systems are to attain public prominence worthy of attention and patronage. Such schools, though offering courses of training considerably prolonged, would eventually develop such a type of individual that the public would eliminate "dangerous" from its association with magic, and be obliged to take cognizance of the soundness of its technique. This union of two systems would, for magic at any rate, build up psychological credit, and a sense of great reliability and prestige would accrue to it.

One of the greatest obstacles to success in magic, to any kind of worth-while result in the mystical sciences, is that the psycho-emotional system of its average student is hopelessly clogged with infantile and adolescent predilections which have not been recognized as such. The ego is compelled to extreme courses of action, as though by compulsion. And underneath his every activity lurks the unconscious spectre—fear. It is precisely with these monsters of fantasy that analytical psychology can deal effectively, and it is from such absurd obstacles that the magical students is a confirmed but unconscious sufferer.[27]

By associating magic with analysis, we should be able to avoid the pitfalls into which our predecessors fell so headlong. The production of genius—more specifically a religious and mystical type of genius—ever the goal of magic, should be more within our grasp than ever before, and considerably more open to achievement.

These ideas are mentioned not because a systematic union of magic and psychology will be here presented, but in the hope that this effort will spur some psychologist acquainted with magical and mystical techniques to attempt such a task. Whoever does succeed in welding the two indissolubly together, to him mankind will ever be grateful. For such a union comprises the marriage of the archaic with the modern, the unconscious with the conscious—the precursor of the birth of the Golden Flower not for any individual alone but for mankind as a whole.

Endnotes

1. Other helpful books on the subject include *Hatha Yoga* by Theos Bernard, and *Yoga: A Scientific Evaluation* by Kovoor T. Behanan.

2. Aleister Crowley adopted the medieval spelling of *magick* with a "k" to differentiate the psycho-spiritual science from stage magic. The magicians of the Golden Dawn, as well as countless theurgists before them, spelled magic without the "k." Like Regardie, we see no reason to surrender the word "magic" to the arena of the stage magician.

3. Keep in mind that this book was first printed in 1938, over a decade before Gerald Gardner published *Witchcraft Today* and started the religion of *Wicca,* which is positive and life-affirming. Regardie's reference to "such pathologies as witchcraft" refers to the medieval superstitions, hexes, and general hysteria that resulted in the Inquisition and the Salem Witch Trials.

4. Unfortunately in modern times the "pathology of demonolatry" has a following among certain individuals who call themselves Satanists. Although many self-proclaimed Satanists are merely practicing a rather juvenile philosophy created out of adolescent rebellion based on the rejection of the religious beliefs of their parents, others are simply unethical, dysfunctional sociopaths who have little or no regard for others. Satanists of the latter sort can safely be defined as individuals who worship Satan (the Christian entity of evil), invoke evil spirits, and practice harmful (black) magic towards others. Thus, Satanism is *not* a life-affirming philosophy, and it should be soundly rejected by any true seeker who wishes to evolve spiritually. For as Regardie stated in *The Tree of Life,* 241–242: "Those who employ such methods [of black magic] should be severely shunned by the Theurgist as he would a foul disease." In the Neophyte Ritual of the Golden Dawn, the candidate swears "...I will not debase my mystical knowledge in the labour of Evil Magic at anytime tried or under any temptation" (Regardie, *The Golden Dawn,* 123). It should be clear that serious, ethical magicians do not engage in Satanism or black magic.

5. The two pillars are a major part of the symbolism of the Qabalah, an ancient Hebrew mystical tradition that is the cornerstone of modern western magic and spiritual growth. For more information about the Qabalah, see Regardie's *A Garden of Pomegranates* (Llewellyn, 1988) or our own book, *The Golden Dawn Journal, Book II, Qabalah: Theory and Magic* (Llewellyn, 1994).

6. In a Golden Dawn temple, that is. Temples of other magical or esoteric groups do not necessarily have these pillars as part of the temple furnishings. (Masonic temples, however, do have two pillars.)

7. From the Neophyte Ritual. Regardie, *The Golden Dawn,* 125.

8. A Hindu esoteric text which emphasizes liberation from the lower, the cultivation of consciousness, and the awareness of the higher self.

9. From the Neophyte Ritual. Regardie, *The Golden Dawn*, 129.

10. See *The Secret of the Golden Flower*, translated by Richard Wilhelm with foreword and commentary by C. G. Jung (London: Paul Trench and Trübner, 1931).

11. In Hebrew doctrine this energy is linked to the *Shekinah*, the feminine "presence" or "dwelling place" of God.

12. Or *Geburah*. The Hebrew letter Beth has the dual sound of either "b" or "v."

13. Applying gender to something as abstract as the Sephiroth can be a tricky thing. In some schools of thought Chesed is seen as feminine and Geburah masculine. For the most part each Sephirah contains certain aspects of both sexual polarities. No one Sephirah is simply all masculine or all feminine.

14. The Buddhist doctrine of moderation—the avoidance of extremes.

15. The system referred to here is Thelema, as envisioned by Aleister Crowley.

16. From the Adeptus Minor Ritual. Regardie, *The Golden Dawn*, 237.

17. A severe mental disorder. Psychoses are commonly characterized by derangement of personality and loss of contact with reality and causing deterioration of normal social functioning.

18. See Part Two, Chapter Six for a ritual on regression.

19. From the Adeptus Minor Ritual. Regardie, *The Golden Dawn*, 237.

20. Groddeck's books include *The Book of the It* (Intl. Universities Press, 1976), and *The Meaning of Illness: Selected Psychoanalytic Writing* (Intl. Universities Press, 1977).

21. Any mental or emotional disorder, arising from no apparent organic lesion or change and involving symptoms such as insecurity, anxiety, depression, and irrational fears.

22. Chronic inflammation of the kidneys.

23. This is unnecessarily confusing. Regardie's definition of the Pillars here (the Left Pillar as the side of Mercy and the Right Pillar as the side of Severity) only applies to the alignment of the Tree of Life *as it is reflected onto the human body in magical workings*, not as it is seen in diagrams of the Tree. These Pillars are almost always described as they are seen in the diagram. That is, the Left-hand Pillar (Binah, Geburah, and Hod) is known as the Pillar of Severity and the Right-hand Pillar (Chokmah, Chesed, and Netzach) is known as the Pillar of Mercy. The two Pillars retain these these traditional titles whether one is looking at or backing into the Tree.

24. From the Neophyte Ritual. Regardie, *The Golden Dawn*, 125.

25. From the Neophyte Ritual. Regardie, *The Complete Golden Dawn System of Magic*, Volume Six, 13.

26. In psychology, repression refers to the unconscious exclusion of painful impulses, desires, or fears from the conscious mind.

27. The student of western magic must be especially vigilant against inflation of the ego.

CHAPTER TWO

THE TREE OF LIFE

There are then, roughly, the broad divisions of certain principles common to both psychology and to magic. And it will be conceded by all that the problems relating to fear, anxiety, insecurity, and inferiority, in connection with the broad divisions of the conscious and the unconscious, are fundamental to both systems. Therefore, before being able to consider any of the techniques of the methods employed by magic, it is essential that we analyze a little further this classification of the psyche into the conscious and the unconscious. While a simple outlook has certainly its advantages, yet difficulties arise demanding a further subdivision and calling for the consideration of additional factors operative within the unconscious. It is really not so simple as seems at first sight. Magic employs a somewhat more extensive view of the two primary aspects of the psyche. And it is necessary to consider at greater length the intricate nature of man, so that we may realize more or less exactly what it is that in magical experiments we are desirous of achieving.

It seems to me that the division of the psyche into conscious and unconscious is entirely too simple to prove adequate as a means of explanation. The almost over-used instance of the iceberg—with one-seventh of its mass above the surface and six-sevenths below—is all right as far as it goes. But does it go far enough?

If that division is to avail us at all in practice, that portion of the psyche which is below the surface of our normal awareness demands more insight into its nature and rather deeper analysis. There is, therefore, some wide realization of the inadequacy of this division, varying with the different schools and systems of practice. Thus in the Freudian school we meet with the primary concepts of the libido, which is defined with particular emphasis on the sexual urge. There is also the slightly broader classification of psychic activity into a triad of the *id*, the *super-ego*, and the *ego*.

In the system propounded by Dr. C. G. Jung, we meet as before with the libido, though here it is defined not as sexuality but in far more philosophical terms as the sum total of psychic energy and vitality, and its expression is through instinct, desire, and function. The faculties of the mind also are described in a four-fold pattern, operating in a positive and negative way. There are the feeling, thinking, sensation, and intuitional functions of the psyche, each capable of a passive or an active response, depending upon whether the psyche be introverted or extroverted. The unconscious itself is also conceived to have a dual aspect. That part of it which is personal and individual, and that great stream of power, archetype and image of which the former is only a part—the collective unconscious. It is a universal and uniform substratum common to the whole of mankind. We may consider it to be the historical background from which every psyche and every consciousness has proceeded or evolved. It is the primordial basis upon which each race and people and civilization evolves its own individual pattern. It is this that the mediaeval alchemists called *Anima Mundi*.[1]

While having innumerable points of contact with the above psychologies, the magical conception differs in several respects. For one thing, it prefers to use a diagram to express its viewpoint, believing that reflection upon this glyph, which for centuries has been an object of meditation, will yield illuminating ideas associated in the unconscious with its parts. Secondly, it believes that man is a more complex being than the newer schools would allow. The diagram it employs is a Qabalistic glyph called the Tree of Life. This shows the ten spheres or *Sephiroth* as they are called arranged in a geometrical pattern to form three columns or pillars. That to the left shows three spheres one above the other, and is called the Left Pillar or the Pillar of Mercy.[2] The Right Pillar or that of Severity also shows three spheres, while the central pillar is indicated by four spheres one above the other, the Pillar of Beneficence.[3] To each one of these spheres is ascribed a different characteristic of the self. That is, the diagram expresses the integral nature of man according to ten quite distinct functions. It is the unity of these ten factors which together comprise what we choose to call man.

The *id*, to use the Freudian term, is the most central core of man, the deepest level of his unconscious, being represented on the Tree by the upper-most sphere of the middle pillar. Reference to the chart (Figure 2, p. 28) will elucidate the problem enormously, clarifying my explanations. At the outset, a word or two must be added about the employment of foreign words and an unfamiliar terminology. It is, in my opinion, a regrettable fact that objections should be raised to unfamiliar and strange words. When some new language is to be learned, the alphabet is at first difficult to acquire. This happens in magic, for in most instances there are no terms existent in English to express the idea to be conveyed, and where such a term does exist it does not have the appropriate psychological or spiritual background to indicate what is required of it. It is my object, nevertheless, to co-relate such terms where they do exist with those of the Qabalistic system, to indicate that it has long recognized these concepts now being dealt with by psychology. Not only so, but it has evolved a profound technique whereby such potencies may be brought into manifest operation.

The magical correspondence of the psychological id, or *es* as Dr. Georg Groddeck called it, is the *Yechidah*—a word meaning the monad, the self, the paternal *ens*[4] of Light. It is the "essence of mind which is intrinsically pure," to adopt a definition of an Eastern religious text.[5] It is also the Buddha-nature, the realization of which is that alone which differentiates the enlightened man, the sage, from him who is ignorant and unenlightened. Just as in physics, where the electron may be considered either as an electrical particle or as a system of radiations or waves, so this *Yechidah* may be considered from two quite distinct points of view. It is the innermost kernel of the self, the deepest core of consciousness itself, unconsciousness to

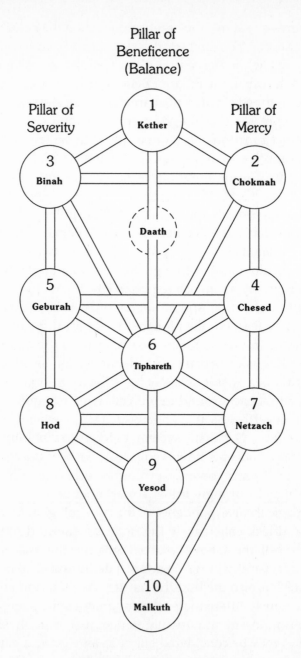

Figure 2: The Tree of Life.

our ordinary awareness—while on the other hand it is the life-flow itself, the current of libido, which is the sum-total of our vitality and our life.

Since the translation of Eastern texts has been made available, many psychologists have pounced on several Chinese terms for inclusion within the technical nomenclature of their own systems. One such term selected by Jung to have reference to a concept such as explained above in connection with the *Yechidah*, is *Tao*.[6] This term, so ambiguous to the Western mind accustomed to precision and accurate definition, has been variously translated as God, or a goal, or heaven. The sinologue Wilhelm prefers the word "meaning" and Jung employed it as having a closer association with the conception which he wished to explain, for it is precisely this factor in consciousness which, eventually, provides a meaning for life and for man. And in the diagram which is provided in *The Secret of the Golden Flower* to which Jung wrote an erudite and profound European commentary,[7] the placing of the psychic factor *Tao* is similar to the position of *Yechidah* upon the Qabalistic Tree of Life.

Though I wish to avoid metaphysics so far as is possible, certain theories demand expression. In order to retain accuracy with simplicity, it must be stated that the Qabalistic tradition posits a universal stream of life, described in terms of light, behind as it were the monad. That is to say, the *Yechidah*, so far from being an ultimate division in itself, is but one particular point or section of the universal life or the collective unconscious, and owes its separate existence to that pulsating stream behind it.

It is interesting here to record that Groddeck surmised that the unconscious, in the ordinary Freudian sense, is the precursor of reason, the brain-mind; whereas the *it*[8] produces the unconscious, the brain, and everything else that belongs to life. The unconscious is a part of the psyche, the psyche a part of the *it*. He also believed that whatever happens in or through a man, from the moment of conception to the occurrence of death, even what he reasons out for himself and does of his own free will, *everything* is directed by this unknown *it*.

If we wish to consider the self in its widest sense as consisting of so many layers of consciousness, not unlike an onion, having ten peelings or skins, then the *Yechidah* is the deepest, or central layer. Those immediately above it—and it must be remembered that this is figurative speech, and that the spatial analogue does not hold good here—are what we name the *Chiah* and *Neshamah*. These would correspond to the anima and the animus in the system elaborated by Jung.

Again referring to the Chinese mystical text commented upon at length by Jung, we will see that according to the Chinese the whole of nature is permeated by two principles, one positive or masculine, the other negative or feminine. These are named the yang and the yin.[9] These two principles are present in the human psyche, and looking at it from the widest possible point of view, we could assume that the conscious level of the mind is the yang, and the unconscious is the yin. But this division, because it is the widest generalization, is inadequate and is capable of further classification. Because within the mind there are both positive and negative elements, factors which are those of thought and feeling. This holds true also of the unconscious, and though we have referred this to the yin, within its sphere there is both a yang and a yin operation.[10] If we refer to one of the deepest levels of the unconscious, then this yang and yin operation is what Jung means by the animus and anima, and what the Qabalah indicates by *Chiah* and *Neshamah*.

It may be useful to quote definitions of these two psychological principles to provide authoritative explanations as we proceed. One pupil of Jung's, Joan Corrie, the author of ABC *of Jung's Psychology*, says the following:

> *The anima is in contact with the objects of the inner reality—the images of the collective unconscious—as the persona is in contact with the objects of external reality. The anima is an archetypal figure that might almost be described as the precipitate of man's age-long impressions of woman—not his conscious reasoned ideas, but the unconscious inherited mould into which she is cast.*

The anima is a correspondence of the Neshamah which is feminine and passive, representing the true spiritual vision of intuition or the imagination.

Here it may be interpolated that it has always been an axiom of the magical system that the being which is active physically is passive spiritually and vice versa. In many an occult work do we find some such statement as this:

> *Man is termed the positive member of the two sexes. In reality only his physical body is positive. His etheric body is purely negative.... On the other hand, while the female is commonly supposed to be the negative of the two sexes, it is really her physical body that is negative, for her etheric body is positive, and the real creative pole of the sexes.*

It will readily be conceded that every person is psychologically bisexual.[11] He is a combination of both masculine and feminine elements, and within him operate the yang and the yin. In man the feminine elements, and in the woman the masculine or positive traits, are alike unconscious. And the deepest and truest archetypes of these unconscious traits are in the anima and animus, the *Chiah* and *Neshamah*. Here, after a fashion, is the explanation of the frequently observed phenomenon of the unparalleled tenderness and love of which many a man is capable, and the harsh and cruel lengths to which certain types of women may go when infuriated or aroused.

True, therefore, to its compensating or balancing principle, the soul or unconscious of a man has a feminine bias which we refer to the anima, while that of a woman has a masculine bias, the animus. This latter is defined as a constantly changing figure, its energies in a state of continuous fluctuation. The animus is not a persistent unvarying figure as is the anima. The typical woman finds her conscious feeling expression centered in one person of the opposite sex; she is monogamous externally. But, internally, her unconscious is apparently polygamous, "for the name of her animus might be 'legion.' He represents the *logos* principle,[12] the masculine reason of her unconscious nature."

On the Tree of Life, this animus principle is equivalent to *Chiah*, the will; this word also means life, animal life. This principle is the first creative vehicle of the *es*, as its other pole is *Neshamah*, understanding and love. The will is in essence a dual principle; it presupposes a beginning and an end. For obviously to will a thing is at once to admit that you have not that thing. To desire to be a thing is to assume that you are not the thing desired. True love, however, is centered always upon one object, an object with which the lover seeks to identify himself to the exclusion of all else. It is this love which fundamentally is implied in the term anima. To love is to understand. Understanding bestows insight and intuition. This is anima.

Tao, animus, and anima, or *Yechidah, Chiah,* and *Neshamah,* constitute the innermost core of what we have chosen to call the psychic onion, the primordial principles operating in the deepest levels of the unconscious. It might be said that this is the level which is always in direct contact with the racial and universal levels of the collective unconscious—that dynamic and ubiquitous stream of life and vitality of which the *Yechidah,* together with its vehicles, comprise just one particular center of consciousness.

Before proceeding further, and since I have used the onion as a metaphor of the self, it may be wise to quote a paragraph of Groddeck's *Exploring the Unconscious*:

> We all of us fancy that we must have a core at the center, something that is not merely shell; we would like to hold within us some specially dainty kernel, to be a nut protecting the future, the everlasting. And we do not realise, cannot realise, that we have in fact no kernel, but are made up of one leaf on top of another from outermost to innermost, that, in fact, we are onions. But in the onion every leaf shares its essential nature. The onion is honest right through, and only becomes dishonest, rotten, if it tries to grow a kernel different from the rest of it, and to destroy the peel as though it were something false, something no honourable onion should acknowledge…. Everything in us is a peeling, but in every peeling is the essential nature of the whole. The self is an onion self.

This is similar to the Buddhist conception.

The triad of principles just considered, the Supernals,[13] being the more primitive part of the psyche, the ancient center which harks back to the countless epochs of the distant past, we must now turn our attention to its compensating and balancing aspect, the conscious ego. This clearly is a much more modern and recent development in the ageless history of the self—a comparatively modern evolution—a channel by means of which we have become conscious of the original primeval and fundamental unconsciousness from which we have emerged. And because of this development of awareness concerning these deeper levels of ourselves, so are we able to examine and understand them. It is by this particular evolution that we are able to make conscious the content of the unconscious. This definition of evolution is practically identical with the definitions of both psychology and magic—that is, that their objects are to expand the horizon of the mind, to enlarge the sphere or scope of consciousness itself. These methods are those of evolution itself.

In magic, this conscious ego is denominated the *Ruach*. It comprises those spheres on the diagrammatic Tree of Life which are numbered from four to eight inclusive. It is an aggregate of functions rather than an integrated and single unit—which is probably one reason why some psychologists believe that this part of us is as yet very unstable in its formation. Also that the unfavorable and faulty circumstances surrounding the childhood of most people greatly enhance the tendency to disintegration which already exists. This aggregate comprises memory, will, feeling, and thinking, clustered about the ego itself, which is the central sphere— five in number. Its life-blood is the current of thought and perception just as the life-blood of the Supernals is the libido, the current of life and energy. The Jungian concept of the ego, or conscious mind, is the persona, the personality which comes into relation with external things. It is a mask. It is the individual's mode of adaptation to the world, his character as it appears to be and as he quite often himself conceives it. It is an evolved mechanism to acquire contact with the outside world, so that by means of experiences thus obtained the *it*, or the *Yechidah*, may come to a self-conscious realization of its own divine powers and high nature.

It is in connection with this persona, this thinking *Ruach* that we would do well to reflect upon two aphorisms of the Eastern psychological systems. At first sight, it would appear that they are mutually exclusive and contradictory. In one Eastern book it is written, "The mind is the slayer of the real. Let the disciple slay the slayer."[14] This alone will be a problem to the average student. In the West, generally speaking, the universe is considered as having two large divisions, the physical and the mental or spiritual, the two latter being spoken of as synonyms. So that if the mind itself is defined as a hindrance to the perception of reality, most of us would be plunged in a rather difficult quandary.

The second is "The essence of mind is intrinsically pure." Should we desire to translate terminology, we will find I think that the Jungian Tao, or the very deepest level of the unconscious, is as near an exact definition of "the essence of mind" that we could find. It is only a popular and false misconception of psychological concepts that relegated the unconscious into a mere receptacle of the evil shadow-beings of human nature. Some have considered it exclusively as a receptacle retaining the primeval slime deposits, harboring the most violently explosive material. But in point of fact, as but little practical acquaintance with the problems of analysis proves, the unconscious does not harbor exclusively explosive motives. The unconscious stream only becomes explosive when the *Ruach*, the conscious mind, has repressed its legitimate and just activity. The taint of the *Ruach* is a self-sufficient conscious outlook. Its vice is an over-refined and emasculated attitude towards life. A river dammed somewhere along its channel is bound to flow over, and when this does occur the river cannot be blamed. Should there be necessity to erect a permanent or even a temporary dam, suitable precautions should be taken to ensure that some other channel is kept open whereby the excess waters may seek their outlet. So also with the unconscious. Itself—the essence of mind which is intrinsically pure—it is neither dangerous nor explosive. But if the individual be prevented from having access to life due to some maladaptation to environment, some failure fully to express both the yang and the yin of his nature, that repression acts as a constant source of irritation, presenting always some likelihood of a psychic explosion.

It is this false dam, the obstacle which is erected along the river's course—psychological resistance—which is the "mind" which slays or prevents the realization of reality. How many of us really understand life and the world as they really are? That is without projecting upon our perceptions, the desire of what we should like to be? Few have insight into our deepest motives, the real causes of our attraction to our friends, of revulsion from our enemies. There are not many, I surmise, who can at all times account for their actions in terms of consciousness. The majority of us are moved a great deal of the time by involuntary compulsion. It is a true saying that habits are a necessity imposed upon us by evolution to ensure the smooth functioning of the psyche. But they are necessary only in so far as they do permit the psyche to function freely. And with many it is just that mass of habits and predilections which is the barrier to the free activity of the psyche. To question people as to the purpose of their habits, a survey of their activity and why they were formed originally, is to obtain much illumination as to what is implied by the phrase "The mind is the slayer of the real." In point of fact, it is not the mind which inhibits our perceiving what is real, what is worthwhile and desirable in life. It is the *false* development of mind—that mass of prejudices, emotional biases, improperly formulated philosophies and superstitions, relics of the inheritance from misguided parents—which is here denoted.

And until we do understand its nature and perceive its extent, never shall we be freed from its dominion, or released from its compulsion. And until we have thoroughly understood our own behavior, motives, and the mechanism of our own attractions and repulsions, we have no insight.

Possibly then we should be able to perceive that underlying this conscious mind—which hitherto we assumed as the sole reality, the only criterion of judgment—is a vast area of inspiration and beauty which is the intrinsically pure essence of mind. If we could open ourselves, or become fully conscious of, this essence so that its content without distortion were capable of ascending within sight of our focus of consciousness, then should we begin to realize as never before the true nature of life and its problems. "In such a case," remarks Dr. Jung in his *Collected Papers on Analytical Psychology*, "the unconscious vouchsafes us that furtherance and assistance which bountiful nature is always ready to give man in overflowing abundance. The unconscious possesses possibilities of wisdom that are completely closed to consciousness.... It creates prospective combinations just as our consciousness does, only they are considerably superior to the conscious combinations both in refinement and extent. The unconscious may therefore be an unparalleled guide for human beings."

When this state or condition of consciousness has been arrived at, when what formerly was unconscious has been brought within the horizon of consciousness, the entire character of life becomes changed and illuminated. Previously it was a thing of fear and horror. Nearly all men, underneath, possess some sense of inferiority and insecurity. All seek in one way or another to rise above that inferiority, and to discover some rock of security to which they may feel anchored. It is when we have attained to a realization of the "pure essence of mind" that inferiority is practically banished and security obtained; and then we can deal with life and our fellows.

The ninth sphere or Sephirah on the Tree of Life is that of the *Nephesh*, which means the animal soul.[15] It is the sphere proper of the animal instincts and urges, what may in truth be called the Freudian unconscious—that which was conscious at one time or at one stage of development but which has since been lost to consciousness. It is regarded as comprising those psychic faculties which are not conscious. All the various automatic, habitual, and routine actions; all the things that we say and do "without thinking" and all the thousand things we never really "do" at all, these processes are assigned to the unconscious realm, to the principle of the *Nephesh*. To it is related the cerebellum, the hind section of the brain, and it is intimately connected with the glandular and sympathetic nervous systems. As such it is that part of our being which regulates the circulation of the blood, the pulsation of the heart, our digestion and respiration. All the promptings of desire and the urges of passion that spring unbidden within us, have their seat in *Nephesh*. This is the underworld of the psyche through which we get comparatively close to nature, to the elemental side of life. It is the undermind in which function the primary instincts of self-preservation and reproduction. It is the seat of the sex instinct itself. The Jungian concept of the unconscious might be the appropriate term for this side of life, as is held by the Freudian school, whereas the much abused word *superconscious* would be distinctly descriptive of the Supernal Sephiroth of the *Yechidah*, *Chiah*, and *Neshamah*[16] corresponding to the Jungian unconscious.

The tenth Sephirah is that of the physical brain and the active physical body.[17] Here it is that we find the receptacle in which the other principles have their abode, and the instrument through which they function. This tenth sphere, *Malkuth*, the sphere of action, we may consider as active, as yang, when compared to *Yesod*, the yin, which we may define as the seat of the impelling instincts, predatory lusts, and animal impulses. On the other hand, the *Ruach*, which is an active thinking principle, we likewise may describe as yang in relation to the yin of the Supernals, which are quiet, passive, and hidden behind the scene. *Malkuth* has innumerable other correspondences, but a consideration of these does not at the moment concern us.

It is obvious that disorders in the proper function of the higher or interior psychic principles will have their corresponding effect on the body, which, as the tenth Sephirah, is but the synthesis of the preceding nine. Any conflict between parts of the psychic make-up will accordingly present a physical disturbance corresponding in position and intensity to the exact nature of the lesion. By purely empirical methods the ancients developed a vast series of correspondences between the various parts of man's body and his psychic constituents. It is this tradition which forms in reality the fundamental basis of what is true and valid in such arts as character-reading, palmistry, phrenology,[18] and the such. For as within, so without. And what is present within the mind is bound in some way to react upon the obverse of the psycho-physical medallion.

There is another method of classifying the components of the psyche by means of a rather different view of the Tree of Life. The method just completed considered each separate sphere. But at the same time we may look at the Tree from the point of view of its levels or layers. In this event, taking the first Sephirah alone, we have what technically is known as the archetypal world. It is that underlying essence of the unconscious which is the most primordial of all, its functions reaching back into the immeasurable past. It is a stratum whose characteristic is those symbols and archetypes which were first assimilated to the simple homogeneous structure, if it may be called, of the evolving consciousness. The Hindu system calls this condition or state *Turya*[19] or ecstasy, absolute consciousness, and its experience in consciousness is of that rapturous type which the mystics of all ages have testified to as union with God. In this divine world, we contact those subtle images which the ancients called the gods. Or rather the ordinary every-day sphere of consciousness becomes invaded by a volitional up-welling of these archaic images and archetypes the first set of psychic forms, subtle, intangible, and dynamic, through which the libido flows on its outward journey from the *it*.

The 2nd and 3rd Sephiroth constitute what is called the creative world, the state of *Sushupti*.[20] It is that stratum of the primordial psychic sphere in which function the principles of the anima and animus, wisdom and understanding. Therefore its reaction upon the ego would be through a stimulation of the creative faculties, and an enhancement of its entire horizon and field of awareness. As the second state of consciousness, it has a correspondence with dreamless sleep. Yet even this description is inadequate, for dreamless though its characteristic may be, it is too vital to be defined in so passive a way. In certain philosophic literatures, it is held that *Sushupti* is a state in which even criminals commune with the higher nature, and enter into the spiritual plane. It is said to be the great spiritual reservoir by means of which the tremendous momentum towards evil living is checked. Though involuntary with such people, it is constantly salutary in effect.

The next level to be considered is comprised of the 4th to the 9th Sephiroth inclusive; it is called the formative world or *Swapna*. This is the world of dreams; it is the level of the instinctual drives and the dynamic urge to expression. Its images, the pageantry of dreams and the fantastic adventure of the night, are those supplied by the experience of the day although the dramatization of the actual dream is the exclusive content and prerogative of this plane.

Where there is an effort on the part of the higher genius or *it* to transmit noble impulses or inspiration from its own divine realm, the state of *Swapna* has to be passed through. This passage colors the tenor of the impulse, imparting to what may originally have been pure thought and transcendentalism an emotional tone or feeling which is expressed in terms of symbolism. Thus whatever ideas are impacted upon our consciousness from higher spheres are tinted with the dream symbolism of the formative world. A wide knowledge of the nature and significance of symbols, and an acquaintance with the operation of *Swapna* is necessary if the original message and its meaning are to be divined. Here we have, also, the emotional mechanism providing the drive and impulse to physical action, the endocrine glands. For the physical positions of the more important glands correspond to important centers[21] and dynamisms of this particular level of the psychic structure.

The 10th Sephirah corresponds to the active world, *Jagrata,*[22] the top layer of consciousness, the ego, that surface consciousness which attends primarily to the business of every day life. It is an evolution emergent from the dark secret levels of the unconscious and, paradox that it is, has usurped the function and rule of the source from which it has sprung. On these four different levels of consciousness, which the Qabalists have called the four worlds, the several principles of man have their operation and unceasing activity.

It is precisely with these different phases of man's psychic nature that the technique of magic deals. Here is the motive of a former suggestion that analysis should be so co-ordinated with magic as to comprise the first stage of development. For in climbing the Tree which is the formal expression to denote the realization of the Sephiroth from the bottom upwards, the first approached is the 9th, that principle of man which is called the *Nephesh.* That is to say, the next level of consciousness beneath the ordinary waking state of the active world, is the level of dreams and lurid image and picture. It is the most superficial layer of the unconscious—using this term as the composite of the formative, creative, and archetypal levels of the Tree of Life. The formative world is that of the warring instincts and unconscious conflicts, the realm of the predatory lusts and passions. It is with this particular level that the analyst must deal in the majority of his patients in order to resolve those conflicts that have their existence in that plane. If there be conflict and incessant warfare here, how can the flow of spiritual energy descend from the higher Sephiroth, or, depending upon one's point of view, ascend from the deeper levels of consciousness? If the direct result of an unresolved conflict is to tie a knot as it were in the psyche, naturally there is no free passage for the libido, which is thus thwarted and frustrated. How can access be obtained to the more primitive, diviner parts of the psyche, those archaic levels of the unconscious whose nature is entirely spiritual, where function those principles which aspire to the super-human shining heights, if the channel be dammed and the way barred by conflict? If the message or revelations from these lofty heights are changed in nature and perverted by the presence within the mind of a powerful and ugly complex, how can there be real magical and spiritual development?

Since analytical psychology confines itself, by its own definition, to an examination and a clarification of the two upper and most superficial levels of consciousness, this process must be considered the preliminary aspect of magical routine.[23] Where analysis preaches the gospel of re-education in the attitude towards life, and when we find psychological patients producing magical designs or *mandalas* of the type that Jung reproduces in *The Secret of the Golden Flower*, here we have an encroachment upon or a usurpation of the realm and function of magic, and a transcending of the limitations of the ordinary analytical technique.

Just as the technique of analysis must comprise the first stage of development, so to my mind the second stage is occupied by various elementary techniques of magic. I say elementary advisedly, for it is only those elementary techniques which the average westerner may ever feel inclined to take upon himself, being debarred from more intense application to the magical art by such limitations, among other things, as time, the necessity for a business and domestic life, etc. The more advanced magical routines[24] are for the exceptional person, and comprise the training of the human psyche to complete spiritual mastery. Splendid vision though this is, an ideal goal for the few, it is nevertheless outside the capacity of most of us who are obliged to live the ordinary life of the twentieth century man or woman.

The preliminary techniques we may consider under several headings, viz:

1. The Qabalistic Cross.
2. The Lesser Banishing Ritual of the Pentagram.
3. The formulation of the Middle Pillar and the Tree of Life in the Sphere of Sensation.[25]
4. The methods of Circumambulation,[26] and the Vibratory Formula of the Middle Pillar.
5. Ceremonial Magic.

For the moment, I shall content myself with presenting a bird's-eye view of each so that a picture of the entire scheme may be envisaged. The first method describes a formulation upon the body of a geometrical figure the effect of which is designed to call into operation the deepest levels of the unconscious. If I say at the outset that every technique of magic is intended in different ways to open the conscious ego's field of vision to the deeper, more spiritual aspects of the divine nature, there can be no possibility of misunderstanding. The procedure of the Qabalistic Cross is through the cultivation of a species of, what is called in psychology, the fantasy, of encouraging the imagination to build images through which the power of the *it* may flow unimpeded.[27]

Though the most elementary, it is in reality one of the most important phases of magical work. Indispensable to the beginner, it is of just as much value to the more advanced student. It is an axiom of magic that it is the divine will alone which is capable of conferring illumination and enlightenment, and so acting that every action of the ego has its correct place in the scheme of things. Thus it is that the Qabalistic Cross is the ideal means of placing the ego under the direct surveillance of the *Yechidah*, the divine will in every human being. It is an excellent method for rendering the consciousness porous and susceptible to the dictates of the more responsible and humanitarian levels of the unconscious.

The Lesser Banishing Ritual of the Pentagram, described as the second method, is the sequel to the former exercise. It is a technique designed to eliminate from the psychic sphere those interior elements which are undesirable. By an effort of the imagination, the student visualizes those qualities or conflicts or psychic lesions which are not required. By means of vibrating certain sonorous sounds called anciently divine names, whilst tracing certain lineal figures both in the air and within his imagination, he is enabled to project them from him. With the projection outwards, and assisted by the increased flow of libido, they may be disintegrated by him. Other forces, archetypes of the deeper levels, are formulated and invoked to assist in so difficult a task. The entire ritual, properly performed, is one calculated to lead the student slowly but gradually towards the heights envisaged by the system.

The most important routine method of spiritual development in the entire magical system is, in my estimation, the third exercise in my classification. If the student remembers the Tree of Life he will see that the Middle Pillar is a series of five spheres arranged in a single upright column. The exercise proceeds by the visualization of these Sephiroth as circles or spheres of light in various significant parts of the physical body. More accurately, they are to be realized as centers already existent in the aura, which is for this purpose defined as an egg-shape of subtle electric matter, a magnetic field which surrounds and interpenetrates the material body of man. The object of this visualization is to awaken these Sephiroth in balanced activity as a means of providing the higher genius, as the *it* may be named, with a psychic mechanism by which it may freely function within consciousness at the intent of the ego.

It will be recalled, as stated as an axiom, that certain of the psychological principles of man have their correspondence with various organs and limbs and parts of the physical body. The exercise called the Middle Pillar is a demonstration of this axiom, giving the attributions of these principles as a practical experiment to be attempted. The visualization of the Sephiroth and the measured vibration of divine names arouse the centers of this aura, or Sphere of Sensation, from their former latent condition. The effect is gradually to bring into operation the dormant and hitherto unsuspected parts of the psyche. The results of this practice evince, for one thing, an unparalleled increase of vitality and power. This induces and is succeeded by a calmer judgment, less perturbable by the affairs of the external life, though the capacity for dealing with it remains unimpaired. It produces a solution to spiritual perplexity, bringing to an end the curse of indecisiveness, assisting the mind to a more responsive and open attitude to the dictates or intuitions of the higher self.

At first, only the Middle Pillar receives attention. But as practice renders the student expert, even dexterous in manipulating his visualizations, he will find it worth while to lengthen the duration of the practice, increasing the field of his attention. Balance and equilibrium brought within achievement by the formulation of the centers of the Middle Pillar, then the Sephiroth of the two side Pillars of Mercy and Severity are added to the picture.[28] Progress is bound to be slow and gradual here, but given patience and perseverance a new sphere of power and spiritual perception will unfold itself.

As a means of giving poise to neurotic patients, and of assisting the task of analysis, the practice of the Middle Pillar may be recommended to psychologists. For by these means the conscious mind is rendered calm and still, the desirable condition to permit the ascent of the archetypes and inspiration of other levels of consciousness. During the period of attention to the Middle Pillar, dreams far more readily cross the threshold of consciousness, and as time proceeds, they seem very definitely to pertain to less superficial aspects of the psyche, to the regions which normally are very difficult to contact—the creative and archetypal worlds of the animus, the almost exclusive concern in the past of poets, mystics, and magicians.

The fourth routine exercise, the Vibratory Formula, is fundamentally an extension of the Middle Pillar visualization. Its technique proceeds in a way similar to the earlier exercise. But here we confront a rationale of a different order. The theory here is that by awakening a power or level of consciousness within man's own sphere it is possible to contact the corresponding force in the external world or a similar level of perception and experience in the collective unconscious. Its intent is not only the development of the individual by rendering him conscious of his other principles, but to transform him into a willing vehicle and instrument of the universal mind, of that great and uniform substratum common to the whole of mankind. It is within the power of man, by these methods, to associate himself with the almost omnipotent vitality and spiritual value of those divine powers which as an aggregate comprise the universe. It is the first step towards what is colloquially termed adeptship,[29] that path by which man is translated into a voluntary co-worker with nature in the task of evolution.

The final exercise is magic proper—the art of ceremonial magic. By now it should be abundantly clear that not all magic is ceremonial; that not necessarily does it proceed by way of ceremony or ritual. Nor does it always require the usual paraphernalia of robe, candle, incense, and lodge-room. There is much in magic which is not too dissimilar with the methods of meditation. That is to say, it follows an interior route, and is a means of dealing with the psyche by way of the actual psychological instruments of psyche without reference to any external object, symbol, or piece of equipment. It is the technique of an equilibriated introversion.

Just as the exercises described above comprise the second stage of magic as analysis is the first, so ceremonial magic as a distinct method is the third. I will iterate that charlatans and misguided enthusiasts have done only too much to confirm general opinion in the belief that magic is sheer quackery, but the earnest student who has applied faithfully these fundamental principles, will, by his enriched nature, bear testimony to its value, both therapeutic and spiritual.

Ceremonial magic has been misunderstood by overzealous beginners principally because there has been no general understanding of the principles here laid down as rudiments of the work. Except in the rare cases of those born with a definite flair, it is quite impossible to succeed in ceremonial magic until a great deal of development has been obtained. And by development, I imply the awakening or formulation within of the Sephiroth of the Tree of Life. Development implies the arousing of the dormant power of the psyche. Above all else it means the ascent into consciousness of the light and love and wisdom of the higher genius, the *Yechidah*. Until that light shines above and through the student, and the magical power is operative within, ceremony must remain what it is for most people: a thing of habit and custom—a set of observances perfunctorily to be performed, celebrations in which there is no trace of virtue, of value, of power.

The divine power once awakened, and the light of the higher self pouring through the mind, then ceremony appears in an entirely different guise. It becomes a magical engine for the harnessing and directing of the power and consciousness of the psyche. Ceremony may be realized now as a means of mobilizing the hitherto unknown factors in man's constitution, and employing them for various ends, which depend entirely on man himself and the extent of his knowledge and spiritual development. Here is no place to utter portentous warnings about the use and abuse of magical powers and spiritual knowledge. Within the psyche itself is a sentinel which never sleeps.

It is a guardian of the moral law whose punishment is so dire and devastating that there is no appeal save by expiation of crime. From the dicta and judgments of this inner self there is no escape, except through the admission and the acceptance of the abuse, followed by a grim determination for ever to avoid a similar deed.

Endnotes

1. The "Soul of the World."
2. Once again, Regardie's description is unnecessarily confusing, and we feel impelled to point out once more that his definition of the Pillars here (the Left Pillar as the side of Mercy and the Right Pillar as the side of Severity) only applies to the Tree of Life *as it is reflected onto the human body in magical workings*, not as it is seen in diagrams of the Tree. The Left-hand Pillar (Binah, Geburah, and Hod) is known as the Pillar of Severity and the Right-hand Pillar (Chokmah, Chesed, and Netzach) is known as the Pillar of Mercy.
3. Also known as the Middle Pillar, the Pillar of Mildness or the Pillar of Balance, alluding to its aspect of moderation between two extremes.
4. "The One."
5. It is our opinion that the Freudian *id*, in its more restricted definition, corresponds to the Qabalistic *Nephesh* rather than the *Yechidah*. See Part Two, Chapter Six.
6. A Chinese term for "way." It refers to the one absolute reality which is said to have brought forth "Ten Thousand Things." It is the union of yin (female energy) and yang (male energy).
7. The Collected Works of C. G. Jung, #13, *Alchemical Studies*.
8. The word *it* is the English translation of the Latin word *id*, which Freud used in his theories. (The German translation is *es*.) To avoid confusion we have italicized the word *it* throughout the text to indicate where Regardie was referring to the Freudian *id*.
9. On the Qabalistic Tree of Life, yang energy can also be attributed to the masculine right-hand pillar called *Yachin*, while yin energy corresponds to the feminine left-hand pillar of *Boaz*.
10. This is similar to the Golden Dawn teachings concerning the sub-elements— that each element contains a mixture of the other elements as well.
11. Again, a mixture of the elements.
12. *Logos* is Greek for "word." It represents the creative principle.
13. The Supernals are the three highest Sephiroth of Kether, Chokmah, and Binah. These three are considered to be on a higher level than the rest of the Sephiroth.
14. From *The Voice of the Silence* by H. P. Blavatsky.
15. To clarify, the Ninth Sephirah is *Yesod*, to which the *Nephesh* is attributed.

16. To clarify, the Supernal Sephiroth are *Kether, Chokmah,* and *Binah,* to which the *Yechidah, Chiah,* and *Neshamah* are attributed.

17. There is another part of the soul/psyche that is sometimes overlooked. This is the *G'uph.* Centered in Malkuth, the *G'uph* is closely tied to the physical body and the total range of all psychophysical functions. It is a low level of the subconscious that communicates with the brain about the current condition of the human body.

18. The study of the shape and protuberances of the skull in the belief that they reveal character and mental capacity.

19. Regardie freely interchanges Eastern and Western terms here. It is important that the reader not confuse the terminology between the two traditions. The four worlds of consciousness according to the Hindu tradition (from highest to lowest) are *Turya, Sushupti, Swapna,* and *Jagrata.* The last three of these worlds relate to three planes of existence (causal, astral, and physical) and are said to be the source of the mantra AUM: "A" refers to Jagrata, "U" refers to Swapna, and "M" relates to Sushupti. The silence that succeeds each intonation of AUM refers to Turya, the highest state of consciousness. Turya is described as conscious dreamless sleep or meditative sleep.

    In the Western tradition, the Four Worlds of the Qabalah as placed upon the Tree of Life are *Atziluth* (containing Kether), *Briah* (composed of the Sephiroth of Chokmah and Binah), *Yetzirah* (including all Sephiroth from Chesed to Yesod), and *Assiah* (consisting only of Malkuth). Atziluth is the divine world of archetypes, Briah is the creative world of archangels, Yetzirah is the formative world of angels and the astral realm, and Assiah is the active, material world.

20. The state of mind in dreamless sleep.

21. These are known as the Chakras. See Part Two, Chapter Eight.

22. Complete awareness of the state of mind.

23. This is excellent advice. We should point out, however, that not all psychotherapists are sympathetic to magic. It is important to find a therapist who is open-minded enough to realize that one's magical or spiritual path is not "part of the problem."

24. Such as evocation, astral projection, or skrying in the spirit vision.

25. The "Sphere of Sensation" is the aura.

26. The term "circumambulation" is not accurate here. Circumambulation refers to "walking around" as in walking around the temple. It would be more accurate to describe this process as "circulation" or "circumagitation" of the light. However, Regardie has derived the misuse of the word "circumambulation" from original order manuscripts—see *The Golden Dawn,* page 347, line 7.

27. One of the tragedies of Western culture is the depreciation of the human faculty of imagination. Rather than celebrate it as the creative power of genius that is responsible for all human invention, Westerners tend to belittle this gift as a childish diversion.

28. Some advanced Middle Pillar exercises are given in Part Two, Chapter Ten.

29. Spiritual mastery.

CHAPTER THREE

THE QABALISTIC CROSS AND THE PENTAGRAM RITUAL

S ome years ago, the principles of this exercise of the Qabalistic Cross were published in my book *The Tree of Life*, and I repeat the rubric as follows:

1. Touch the forehead, say "**ATOH**" ("Thou art").
2. Bring the hand down and touch the breast, say "**MALKUTH**" ("the Kingdom").
3. Touch the left shoulder, and say "**VE-GEDULAH**" ("and the Glory").
4. Touch the right shoulder and say "**VE-GEVURAH**" ("and the Power").[1]
5. Clasping the fingers on the breast, say "**LE OLAHM AMEN**" ("forever, Amen").

The words employed are in the Hebrew tongue. Hebrew is so employed because the magical system first attained prominence in Europe since it was adopted by some Jewish philosophers whom we call Qabalists. Apart from this usage of Hebrew words, there is not the slightest implication of Hebrew theology or philosophy. The gestures themselves are a variance of the ordinary Christian Cross, making use of the last few phrases of the Lord's Prayer. That it is utilized in magical work is due to the fact that it constitutes an ideal method of equilibriating the personality and raising the mind to the contemplation of higher things.[2]

The first name in the invocation is *Atoh*. This is a Hebrew word meaning "Thou," the second personal pronoun. To explain this in the simplest possible way, may I say that there is some justification in metaphysics for this usage. The reader who has studied some philosophy will have noted reference to a triad of concepts—such as the thinker, the thing known, and the act or result of cognition. The ancient authorities of the Qabalistic philosophy conceived that the deepest or most spiritual principle in man, which they argued was man's highest notion of divinity, was just such a triad of a thinker, knowledge, and the act of knowing. To each one of these principles or functions of the higher self, they therefore attributed a personal pronoun as a symbol. The thinker, the *Yechidah* itself, manifestly was "I." "Thou" was referred to the thing known. And the third person "he" was referred to the activity of the thinker—though all three were considered an indissoluble unity. But bearing in mind at all times the concept of the middle way by which the extremes of the opposites may be avoided, they chose as the word to express the higher self in this slight ritual the second pronoun "Thou."

The other words employed are names of Sephiroth on the Tree of Life. *Gevurah* or "Power" is that center numbered five on the diagram. *Gedulah* or "Mercy" is the fourth.[3] These two are the centers represented by the two lodge room pillars, the two opposites encountered in everyday life. It is of these two centers that speaks the ritual in junction already quoted about unbalanced severity being cruelty and oppression.

Malkuth is the tenth Sephirah. It is translated by the word "Kingdom" inasmuch as the ancients considered that man's nature was a kingdom of inconceivable extent, a kingdom of vast and wide complexity, one having over it a divinely ordained ruler, the *Yechidah*. The last phrase of the ritual is of little significance, save as it completes the gesture. The word Olahm means "forever." But it can also mean "world" or "universe." We would assume that it is so placed as a peroration because within the miniature universe which is man, there are innumerable elements and principles in constant activity, the entire ten Sephiroth of the Tree of Life.

If the reader will bear these brief explanations in mind, the description of the rubric which follows will be seen to have more significance than otherwise might be the case.

Atoh is a reference to the higher genius, the *it*. *Malkuth* refers to the body, this with the *Yechidah* being the dual expression of the living human organism, the two expressions of the yang and the yin, using these latter terms in their widest connotation. *Gevurah* and *Gedulah*, the two extremes of power as the highest aspects of the ego, signify the two modes of that ego's capacity for action and reaction. The final gesture, closing on a point which is between these two extremes indicates the voluntary decision of the evolving psyche to seek a balanced position, the Middle Way, a place which partakes of both the opposites and yet which is not subject to their equal but opposing pulls.

It has been emphasized that the fundamental task of both analytical psychology and magic is to attempt to bring into operation the higher genius—or to bring into full working consciousness the content of the hidden and buried unconsciousness. We should remember the parables of the archaic philosophical religions whose fundamental tenet was that within man was a spirit, a dynamic center of consciousness which, because of its contact and association with matter, had been plunged into a profound sleep, a state of somnambulism. The problem is: how may this slumbering level of the primeval consciousness be awakened within us? By endeavoring to extend the horizon of consciousness, to enlarge the field of awareness so as to embrace what previously was unconscious is obviously a logical method. To become aware of all our actions, our thoughts and emotions and unsuspected motives, to regard them in their true light as actually they are and not as we would like them to be or as we would wish the onlooker to perceive them. It requires, to take this step, an extraordinary degree of honesty and courage, both indispensable virtues to the student of psychology and magic. The more of this suppressed and forgotten material stored in this at one time unknown or dormant side of our nature that can be raised into the clear light of the day, by exactly so much do we awake from that inert stupor into which we have in the past been plunged. And also, by just that much do we liberate ourselves from the compulsion to nature's instinctual commands, and become freed from what Levy Bruhl has called the *participation mystique*. It is a phrase coined to express that peculiar unity with nature which primitive man felt and enjoyed, that participation in the unconsciousness of nature which only became disrupted as the evolution of mind made itself apparent, a slinking serpent within the peaceful Garden of Eden.[4] But mankind, despite thousands of years of evolution, has not yet freed itself as a whole from this subjection to the unconsciousness of nature whereby it moves and feels without deliberation and without conscious volition. Here and there we do find an individual who has realized the snare and burden in which he has lived, and attempted accordingly to release himself from the bonds in which he had been bound.

Any system, therefore, which recognizes these deep unconscious levels of awareness and vitality, insisting moreover upon that recognition, assists in the evolution of mankind. The Qabalistic Cross, so called, considered as a preamble to more serious and difficult work, indicates just this awareness of other levels of consciousness, and the necessity of bringing them into operation within the human psyche. Not only so, but it recognizes that these newly awakened levels of power and consciousness may be deeply disturbing to the novice who attempts this voyage of discovery. Therefore, what is essential is that not only should they be awakened, but that they should be recognized and equilibriated in a balanced disposition. This also it is the object of the Qabalistic Cross to accomplish.

One more word before proceeding to a description of the technique of its performance. The tradition holds that these words should be vibrated and not merely enunciated. That is to say, the student must discover for himself that method of humming or of pronouncing these words which will assist in the production of a vibration. Some find that these words uttered in a shrill voice is best adapted to the requirements. Others, including the present writer, have found through experiment and frequent test that a moderately deep pitch, slightly higher than the ordinary speaking voice, is most suited to produce the desired vibration. Each syllable should be evenly vibrated, no one being accented at the expense of another. The test of the vibration, strange though it may seem, is that it should detonate in the palms of the hands and the soles of the feet.[5]

When vibrating a word forcibly, but not necessarily loudly, a tingling sense should be felt in every cell and nerve of the body, and it should seem particularly that in the hands and feet every atom and cell has become alive and is in a state of rapid vibration. Little more than this can be said in explanation without actual demonstration. But it is such a simple matter in which to attain proficiency that no difficulty should be experienced. The metaphysical theory involved here is that by means of vibration, the actual formation of the body-mind system may be changed and renewed.[6] That is to say, the proponents of the system urge for a consideration of the fact that within a period of seven years the body has undergone a complete biological change and, during that time, has renewed its entire cell structure. It has ejected old and deceased organisms, and by means of the metabolic process, has built itself a new cell organization. The vibratory technique, therefore, hastens the expulsion of dead tissue and unwanted molecules and particles so that new ones being absorbed into the system, whilst attention is devoted to expanding the field of consciousness, a purified body is produced through which that higher consciousness may more readily function. It is principally a question of tactics. One could on the one hand content oneself solely with the task of widening the field of consciousness, altogether to the exclusion of bringing the body system within the scope of this purifying process. Or, on the other hand, the entire time and attention could be given solely to the production of certain obscure bodily changes—as do some oriental hatha yogis, to the exclusion and at the expense of desirable factors of consciousness. Magic, very sanely, combines the advantages of both points of view, eliminating the dangerous and harmful features common to the others. Always in a salutary way is the path between the two extremes indicated.

When actually performing the Qabalistic Cross it is well to face the east, the place of the rising of the sun. This takes advantage of a prevailing symbolism which identifies the *Yechidah* with enlightenment and wisdom, a spiritual concept always determined by and defined in terms of light. It is from the east that the light arises. Standing motionless, with the eyes closed should that render the act of reflection easier, endeavor to contemplate the nature of the *Yechidah*, that it is by definition, the quintessence of light, life, love, and liberty, and that these are the qualities of the essence of mind which is intrinsically pure.

One very essential point constantly requiring recollection is that in the magical symbolism, as well as in that of psychology, as has been demonstrated, the various psychic principles have a spatial co-relative in the human body. That is, certain principles correspond to or have a special affinity with certain organs or limbs of the body. This certainly is a fact within everybody's experience. Emotion is almost always associated with the heart, reason with the head, passion with the genitals. The magical tradition simply classifies and considerably extends this list of affinities.[7]

Whilst considering the Yechidah, recognizing that it represents freedom and that its nature is light itself, the student should endeavor to visualize just above the crown of his head a spherical form of light. The diagram on page 73 (see Figure 4) will indicate its likely position. The symbolism places this above the head because, in the first place, since the Yechidah is the root of man's consciousness, it is a principle of whose presence the majority of us have never become really aware. This is not to deny its existence, but only to affirm our previous ignorance. Moreover, magical symbolism, which incidentally is of the same type as that employed by the unconscious, also affirms that this divine genius, being the highest principle within of which we still have no awareness, has not yet fully incarnated within us. That is to say, it is a potency which overshadows us—a principle which the race will be able to realize fully only some thousands of generations hence. The consensus of experienced opinion has it, therefore, that this overshadowing, no matter whether actual or only metaphorical—does assuredly exist, and that the psychic correlative of an overshadowing is a center just above the crown of the head. Fantastic this certainly may sound at first. But I cannot make any attempt to justify it or to defend it. And were I called before a tribunal of intellectual criticism, I would only recommend that the practice be followed as a definite scientific experiment, and the results experienced.

Let therefore the student consider his higher and divine genius, the core of his unconscious, as of the nature of wisdom and love and light, visualizing its sphere of activity as having an affinity with the region immediately above the head. After some seconds of this quiet recollection, let him raise his hand above his head, then lower it to the forehead and vibrate the first word *"Atoh"* as though formally to affirm the presence of that genius. The hand employed should then be brought in a straight line down to the region about the diaphragm. Vibrate the word *"Malkuth."* As this is done, let the mind dwell on the fact that as the hand descends, so does a stream of light descend from above, a steady brilliant ray of light permeating him through and through. A shaft of light is thereby formed which extends from the crown of his head to the soles of his feet. Strictly speaking, *Malkuth*, the last Sephirah, is referred to the feet. For convenience's sake, however, we touch the breast or solar plexus with the mental recognition that it is the region of the feet that actually we have reference to and to which the shaft of light is directed. This forms the first half of the exercise. Some seconds pause should take place here, in order to visualize and feel as strongly as is possible the presence of a brilliant ray of light.

Then, shifting the attention from the central pillar of light to the left shoulder, let the student consider that here is a reservoir of enormous power, and vibrate the word *"ve-Gedulah."* A ray of light should be commenced here in the imagination, and visualized to penetrate the breast until it reaches the right shoulder, when the remaining word *"ve-Gevurah"* is vibrated. Thus is formulated the horizontal shaft or the cross-bar of this cross of light.[8]

The first gesture traced a light-beam from head to foot, while the second one traced the ray from shoulder to shoulder. Interlocking the fingers on the breast, and vibrating the final word *"le-Olahm Amen,"* the student should endeavor to see a cross of light actually standing within him. None but very few may hope at once to succeed in feeling this, in obtaining the pulsing sensation of a cross of light vibrating within. It will require persistent and regular exercise before this sensation makes itself apparent. It is a significant development, marking a definite stage in growth. Some little preliminary practice in the art of visualization may be necessary, as well as in acquiring the ability of giving utterance to the names so that the sound appears to vibrate in a given spot. When this is acquired a name can be vibrated in the head, the palms of the hand, in the thighs or feet, or elsewhere at will. As skill is obtained, and the sense of the cross of light becomes more marked and definite, the opening practice can be extended. That is to say, prior to visualizing the center of light above the head, the student should endeavor to expand the sphere of his consciousness. By this, it is meant that he should try to imagine with eyes closed that the body grows and grows until the height increases enormously. Let him formulate in his own mind that the physical form heightens to such an extent that the head gradually touches the ceiling, goes through the roof, and finally that the semblance of a vast figure with head in the clouds of space is obtained, the feet resting securely on earth. In fact, from this exalted point of view, the earth seems but a small globe beneath the feet. Having obtained this sense of expansion, and it may be accompanied by a heightened sense of consciousness or of ecstasy, then let him visualize during the first vibration that the ray of light descends from the heavens upon his head, penetrating him and eventually illumining the region of his feet which are set firmly upon the earth. The sense of expansion is a definite one, rendering the performance of the gestures of the Qabalistic Cross a much more vital and significant experience.

The reasons given for the necessity of this astral expansion lies in the fact that the ancient mystical systems hold that the transcendental nature of man, the essence of mind, is infinite in nature, a positive void of which no quality can be predicated. As one Eastern scripture puts it:

> Learned audience, the illimitable void of the universe is capable of holding myriads of things of various shapes and forms, such as the sun, the moon, the stars, mountains, etc. ...space takes in all these, and so does the voidness of our nature. We say that the essence of mind is great, because it embraces all things, since all things are within our nature.

The instruction to expand consciousness, or to formulate the astral form as of gigantic proportions standing solitary in space, containing within itself all the forces and worlds of the entire universe, is a literal fulfillment of the above metaphysical postulate. Likewise, in some of the few Hermetic fragments that we inherit, there is similar advice. In fact, it states the technical process so excellently that I am moved to reproduce it here:

> Increase thyself to immeasurable height, leaping clear of all body, and surmounting all time, become eternal and thou shalt know God. There is

nothing impossible to thyself. Deem thyself immortal and able to do all things...become higher than all Height and lower than all Depth...to be everything at the same time in earth and sea and heaven. Think that thou art as yet begotten, that thou art in the womb, that thou art young, that thou art old, that thou hast died and art beyond death: perceive all these things together...and thou shalt know God. But if thou shuttest up thy soul in thy body, and abasest thyself and sayest 'I know nothing, I can do nothing, I am afraid of earth and sea, I cannot mount to heaven, I know not what I was or what I shall be;' then what hast thou to do with God? (Corpus Hermeticum xi. [ii]).[9]

Something of the sort can be seen in the writings of Plotinus.[10] In any event, metaphysical or psychological or nonsense, only constant practice will determine whether it has validity and value, or whether these are simply delusions of unbalanced minds. The final test must be a pragmatic test; it is that of science itself.[11]

It will now be seen why it was stated above that this practice is essential to all magical work. In fact it should precede or form part of any series of mental exercises upon which one may embark. Inasmuch as it does endeavor to ally the personality with the true sources of life, permitting them in any event a species of open channel to enter into consciousness, no words can underestimate or exaggerate its importance. This is not to suppose that at once will the casual performer of the Qabalistic Cross become aware of the secret self of the unconscious, "the flame which burns in the core of every man." That is certainly not the implication for he who runs may not read. What is implied is that continuation in the way of regular practice brings with it a recognition of the transcendental self. Or, to put it in another way, a bridge is formulated between the conscious and the unconscious, permitting the mind to be made porous to diviner things. Gradually and almost imperceptibly, the student will become aware of the inspiration of that higher genius. The principal error on the part of earlier writers on magic—and my earlier literary efforts are also included within the scope of these strictures—was that constantly they spoke of ecstasy and divine illumination and transports of spiritual delight.[12] These experiences may be true of the more advanced or evolved student. For the average individual they can have but little meaning. What actually does occur is that there is a gradual connecting up of one level of consciousness with another.

This links on to another, and so forth. Until finally, the everyday waking consciousness becomes permeated with an awareness of divine creative faculties which have fertilized its intolerable barrenness. This awareness marks the end of that interior sense of sterility and frustration. Here we have, in a word, the rationale of such mystical phraseology as "union with God" the "spiritual marriage," "alchemical nuptials," etc. There is, to state it differently, a gradual engaging of the clutch. By this method there is no violent grinding of gears. There is only an imperceptible and slow change-over to another speed, or rate of vibration as it is called, to another mode of functioning. The every-day wake-a-world consciousness becomes more refined and sensitive, aware of new possibilities, displaying an understanding of and an insight into life and experience which it never had before. A wide tolerance is developed. And an all-inclusive sympathy for and concern in man's problems is manifested where formerly there was self-centeredness and disinterestedness in anything that did not touch upon personal problems. These are tests, experiential facts open to all, facts which are of value only to him in whom that insight awakes by dint of persistent effort. For no one else has it the least validity.

The Qabalistic Cross provides the preamble as well as the peroration to another exercise. This is named the Lesser Banishing Ritual of the Pentagram. The rubric of it is as follows:

1. Perform the Qabalistic Cross.

2. Face east. Stretch out right hand holding a dagger.[13] Trace a banishing earth pentagram.[14] Vibrate the word "**YHVH.**" (Pronounced "Yod-heh-vav-heh").[15] (See Figure 3, page 59.)

3. Still holding out hand and dagger, turn to the south.[16] Trace another pentagram in precisely the same way and vibrate the word "**ADNI**" ("Ah-doh-nai").[17]

4. Then turn to the west and trace pentagram. Vibrate "**AHIH**" ("Eh-he-yeh").[18]

5. Turn north. Trace pentagram and vibrate "**AGLA**" ("Ah-ge-lah").[19]

6. Return to the east. Extend arms in the form of cross.

7. Say: "**Before me Raphael.**"

8. **"Behind me Gabriel."**

9. **"On my right hand Michael."**

10. **"On my left hand Auriel."**

11. **"For before me flames the Pentagram,"**

12. **"And behind me shines the Six-rayed Star."** [20]

13. Repeat the Qabalistic Cross.

The function of this ritual, though capable of extension in several other directions, is pre-eminently one of banishment.[21] Its aim is to eliminate from the sphere of the mind those qualities or sensations which the critical ego deems unnecessary. Its rationale is that a system of vibration may act upon the human organism in a purifying and strengthening way. Every molecule, every cell, astral, mental, and physical, is affected by this ritual, since the basis of every psycho-physical activity of man is grounded in these centers of energy and spiritual force. These microscopic points, or monads, are the minute sensitive points of spiritual consciousness—each of them a *Yechidah* or *it* to its own particular system or small universe. In the reality of their existence and function is based the deepest sense of man's individuality, and the basis of matter also. Mind and body are not two separate things but dual manifestations of one and the same unknown unit.

The result of the celebration of the Qabalistic Cross, the vibration of the divine names, the formulation of the four pentagrams, and the invocation of the archangelic forms in the four quarters, is that gradually coarser elements are ejected from the sphere of sensation. To take their place other particles, more sensitive and refined, of a higher grade of spiritual substance, are attracted to the personal sphere and become infused into the character and nature of the physical and psychological constitution. The nature of these newly-acquired particles is such as not to impede the free flow of libido or of power and inspiration from the underlying levels of the unconscious to the superficial awareness of man. In this way, a very real purification takes place, enabling the influence of the higher genius to penetrate the refined and porous brain to diffuse throughout the personality a more profound insight, and a keener zest and appreciation of life, and it bestows a greater ability to cope with it.

The ritual itself is not a simple movement, but is composed of several phrases. The first is that of the Qabalistic Cross already explained. The second consists of the tracing of a limiting circle, marked at each of the four angles or cardinal quarters by a pentagram. Third, the invocation of the archangelic guardians. Fourth, the repetition of the opening gesture.

Having expanded consciousness, and visualized himself as a towering cross of light, let the student face the east of his room,[22] stretching before him his right hand. It is customary to employ a straight-bladed dagger with a cross hilt, but this is relatively unimportant for the novice; the fingers alone being quite adequate to the work. To trace the pentagram bring the outstretched arm over to the left side, to a point in front corresponding to just about the middle of the thigh. Move the arm upwards to a point which would correspond to the top of the head. Descend on the right to about the middle of the right thigh. This movement will have traced a large inverted "V," about three feet high.

Move the outstretched arm over towards the left to slightly above the left shoulder. Then carry it horizontally to a point just above the right shoulder and then diagonally downwards to the point originally started from. Difficult and complex it may sound, but in practice it is very easy. If a five-pointed star is drawn on paper, it will be seen at a glance what the import of the above directions are. They have been delineated at length above because, incredible as it seems, the writer has found some individuals performing the most outrageous gestures in the belief that they were tracing pentagrams. The only point to remember is to make a fairly large figure, about three feet high, and above all that it should be a well proportioned pentagram, and not a deformed or eccentric one. Some little practice may be required to achieve this, especially in making the final diagonal so as to complete the gesture exactly where the initial ascending line began.

This is all straight-forward enough. But this is the mere physical aspect of the exercise. In practice something more is demanded of the practitioner. While tracing these pentagrams with his arm outstretched, his visualizing faculty must be active and alert. He must endeavor to imagine these four pentagrams as flaming figures of a

bluish-golden hue similar to that
produced by igniting methylated
spirit.[23] After completing the physical tracing of the figure, he should
be able to perceive by the mind's
eye, with the eyes closed, the pentagrams flaming quite vividly in
front of him. Naturally this requires
much practice. And save for him
whose faculty of visualization is
already very well developed, it is,
unfortunately, a faculty not easily
come by. Only exertion and continual practice will develop this.

Figure 3:
Lesser Banishing Pentagram.

Thus the first stage of the ritual is the visualization of the pentagram while actually tracing it with finger or dagger. When the
commencing point of each pentagram has been returned to, let the
student pause, and, imagining a central point in that figure, bring
up his arm to that center, stabbing or charging it energetically with
outstretched dagger. It is at this juncture that the divine name
should be vibrated, slowly and evenly. It suffices to vibrate each
name but once. Each of these four names associated with a pentagram in a different cardinal quarter has to be vibrated in precisely
the same way as was directed for those names connected with the
Qabalistic Cross. It should be endeavored to feel them operating
within. Also visualize that as they are vibrated, the power of the
name travels out through the pentagram's center to the end of that
particular cardinal quarter. This procedure is to be followed in each
quarter, the only variation being the different name employed.

It will be noted that each of these names is comprised of four letters each.[24] In the mystical system of the ancients each was attributed
to one of the four elements or the four modes of activity comprising
our make-up,[25] and the ritual has direct effect upon these. It would
take too long and serve no good purpose to dilate upon the reason
why these names were supposed to be effectual, and why certain
names were associated with certain quarters and not to others.[26] Suffice here to say that the tradition has found them effectual for the

purpose under consideration, and the experimental work of modern students has confirmed this psychological association. The student desirous of delving more deeply into the subject, wishing to discover the system by which symbolic names are attributed to certain quarters or to the Ten Sephiroth, will find much material in *The Tree of Life* and *My Rosicrucian Adventure*, as well as in *The Golden Dawn*.

The last pentagram having been traced in the north, the student returns, still holding arm with dagger outstretched, to the east where he started from.[27] With his arms extended to form a cross, and being aware about him of the four pentagrams vitalized by the vibration, he now commences a further phase of the ritual. Here is demanded of him the visualization of the vast archangelic figures standing behind each pentagram, as though the latter were a sort of flaming shield supported by those magical or telesmatic images.[28]

Some word or two needs to be expressed about archangels and angels. Most readers, unfamiliar with the nomenclature and general tenets of the magical philosophy, may feel inclined to baulk at this juncture. The postulate, however, is quite a logical one. For the philosophy of magic conceives of one root source from which all life sprang, one fundamental life current, infinite and omnipresent, expressing itself in diverse ways. This we can call if we wish, God, libido, the collective unconscious—depending upon what system of religion or metaphysic we subscribe to. Within this universal life are archetypal images—nodal points which act as termini or power stations through which, as it were, the root life-stream flows and is diluted or transmuted so as to be assimilable or available to a lower form of life. These primordial archetypes of the collective unconscious are the psychic "forms into which repeated ancestral experiences have molded the typically human mode of apprehension." Generally speaking then, these primordial archetypes, man's first definition of the manifold forces of nature, comprise what in magic we mean by gods and archangels and angels.

One very clever expositor, referring to the manner in which the ancient magicians conceived of these archetypes or magical images, expresses the idea thus:

> They took each factor in Nature and personified it, gave it a name, and built up a symbolic figure to represent it; just as British artists have by

their collective efforts produced a standard Britannia, a female figure with shield charged with the Union Jack, a lion at her feet, a trident in her hand, a helmet on her head, and the sea in the background. Analysing this figure as we would a Qabalistic symbol, we realize that these individual symbols in the complex glyph have each a significance — in fact, an occult glyph is more akin to a coat of arms than anything else … A magical figure is the coat of arms it represents. These magical figures are built up to represent the different modes of the manifestation of cosmic force in its different types and on its different levels. They are given names, and the initiate thinks of them as persons, not troubling himself about their metaphysical foundations…. An angelic being, then, may be defined as a cosmic force whose apparent vehicle of manifestation to psychic consciousness is a form built up by the human imagination.

When facing east, therefore, and vibrating powerfully the name *Raphael*, the student should attempt to build up in his imagination, or to visualize a vast angelic figure, conceived of in the traditional conventional style, of vibrating yellow and mauve hues. The whole figure, the visualization complete, will be gracious and slight and airy, and the mauve which touches up and brings out the vivid pale yellow will cause the robes to flash and shimmer, giving the impression of shot silk. It may also appear that a gentle breeze is wafted from behind the figure.

In the south, the archangelic form to be imagined will have a predominance of flaming red, touched here and there by vivid flashes of emerald green. In the hand of the figure will be seen an uplifted sword of steel, while little tongues of fire will lick the browned earth about the bare feet. An intense radiation of heat should be sensed from *Michael*.

Watery characteristics will mark the nature of *Gabriel* in the west, and blue offset by orange will be its color. A blue chalice of water will be held aloft by the telesmatic figure, which will sometimes seem as though it were standing in a rushing stream of clearest water. Sometimes, it may seem as though there were a small waterfall behind the figure, pouring cascades of water into the temple or room.

In the north, the angel *Auriel*[29] will appear to be standing on very fertile ground, grasses and wheat being about the feet. Sheaves of corn will be held in both the outstretched hands, and on the whole, the prevailing colors will be a mixture of citrine, olive, russet, and some little black.[30]

The technique of here employing these telesmatic or magical figures of the archangels, once the appropriate names have been vibrated and some realization obtained of the presence of the correct type of spiritual power flowing through the figure, is to imagine that the emanation from the archangel penetrates and cleanses the personality. That is to say, in the east from behind the archangel *Raphael* should be felt a gentle wind or breeze which, permeating the entire body, blows from it every trace of impurity. From *Michael* in the south, warmth at first of gentle degree should be felt, increasing in intensity to a powerful heat which burns and utterly consumes every blemish which troubled the personality. This purging should be felt as consecrating one to the service of the higher self. The same technique should be applied to *Gabriel* in the west, except that one is purified with water, while in the north one is invested with the stability and fertility of *Auriel*, archangel of the earth.

Of course this sounds a most complex and complicated procedure to pursue. But with practice, the entire exercise will be found to be easy. First of all, the student should recognize that a wise man knows how to limit himself. He will limit himself at the start to obtaining mastery of the mechanical part of the ritual without reference to the initiated technique. That is to say, his aim should be to commit the ritual to memory so completely that at any particular quarter there is no groping for the appropriate names. Then each phase should be studied separately until skill and ease are achieved. He should apply himself to familiarizing himself with the sense of expansion of consciousness and visualizing the descending ray of light which formulates itself into a vast radiant cross within him. A certain degree of accomplishment gained in this exercise, and already being skilled in the tracing of perfectly geometrical pentagrams in mid-air, the next task is to obtain about him a clear formulation of the blazing pentagrams, vivified by the vibration of the appropriate divine names being hurled through them. Application to the technique of purification by means of again expanding consciousness, whilst surrounding himself with the colossal magical figures of the archangels comprises the next important stage. The final task is to visualize, before performing the Qabalistic Cross again, a pentagram of fire burning on the breast. Seen on the back is a hexagram, its ascending triangle being red in color, and its descending triangle of blue, both triangles to be interlaced.[31] I hope the student will not be frightened by this mass of directions, for he can be assured that the exercise is not nearly as obscure or terrifying as it sounds. Practice will make perfect, and the realization of the goal to be acquired will provide sufficient confidence to enable him to pursue the practice still further until complete mastery is achieved.

In this way, his mind being made quiescent, and his body and emotional apparatus purified, the consciousness of the hidden grades or levels of his being may gently and gradually ascend and manifest to his perceptions, thus assisting him in his inward growth, in the conquest of ignorance and the acquisition of self-knowledge.

Before closing this chapter, one final set of directions remains to be communicated with regard to this practice. Once skill has been acquired in performing accurately and effectually this Lesser Banishing Ritual of the Pentagram, the student may endeavor to perform the entire ritual in his mind. Seating himself comfortably in his chair, facing east, he should endeavor, without so much as rising or without any audible vibration of the words, to expand the form of his sphere of sensation and bring down the light of the higher self upon him. He ought also to be able to imagine himself as standing, moving forward to the east and tracing the pentagrams without moving the physical arm, silently or mentally vibrating the appropriate magical words. Likewise with the archangels. The mere determined effort to visualize them and mentally pronounce their names will call up the figures, and evoke the type of force which should flow through them.[32]

My sole caution is against attempting what obviously is an advanced practice until literally months have been spent working away at the physical performance of this exercise. The writer knew some people who neglected to take this piece of sound advice. Their work became very careless and slapdash, and whatever advantage was to be obtained from the ritual was never forthcoming.

This astral ritual is, as I have said, an exercise to be undertaken only when a good deal of mental stability and control has been obtained—results which follow from persistent application, two or three times a day for many weeks or months, to an enthusiastic and vigorous performance of the Lesser Banishing Ritual of the Pentagram.[33] Sudden spurts of enthusiasm followed by prolonged bouts of inactivity avail nothing in magical work. In fact, such an attitude towards the subject is indicative in itself of, if not neurosis, then of a very powerful conflict raging in the unconscious. It indicates that the opposites are still operative within the mental sphere, and that the Golden Flower of stability and equilibrium has not yet begun to blossom. The student would do well to become fully aware of the conflict, determining to be affected neither by violent enthusiasms nor by equally violent depressions. Above all, he should perform quietly and patiently the Banishing Ritual. Let him continue steadfast, with courage and equanimity, in the daily celebration of his chosen work.

Endnotes

1. For some reason Regardie has switched the natural order of the Qabalistic Cross. Here he has the student touching the left (Gedulah or Chesed) shoulder followed by the right (Geburah or Gevurah) shoulder. In the Golden Dawn manuscripts, including those published by Regardie himself in *The Golden Dawn*, and in his book *The Tree of Life*, the Geburah (right shoulder) always comes before the Gedulah (left shoulder). "The Power" always comes before "the Glory." In the Christian Cross performed by Roman Catholics, the left shoulder is touched first, but this still does not explain why Regardie suggests it here and nowhere else in his writings. We have no explanation for it. We suggest that the reader follow the traditional order of the Qabalistic Cross as presented on page 166 of *The Tree of Life*, page 53 of *The Golden Dawn*, or in Part Two, Chapter Nine of this book.

2. The cross itself is a universal, pre-Christian symbol. It is our belief that people have been crossing themselves, in one form or another, since the beginning of civilization.

3. The more common name for this Sephirah is Chesed, which means "mercy." Its other title, *Gedulah*, means "glory" or "greatness."

4. The serpent is often a symbol of wisdom. On the Qabalistic Tree of Life, the Serpent of Wisdom represents the paths that connect the various Sephiroth. In the story of the Garden of Eden, the serpent suggested that Adam and Eve eat fruit from the Tree of Knowledge. This means that they became sentient thinking beings who were set apart from "the unconsciousness of nature."

5. A tingling sensation can also sometimes be felt in the face.

6. Scientists are now becoming aware of what magicians have known for centuries—that all matter is vibratory energy. There is a physical phenomenon known as *"harmonic resonance"* which means that if one object starts to vibrate strongly enough, another object nearby will begin to vibrate or resonate with the first, if both objects share the same natural vibratory rate. The magician vibrates a god-name in order to effect a harmonic resonance between the deity as it exists within his own psyche and as it exists within the greater universe. The aim is to have the psyche "resonate" with the divine. Not only does this lift the consciousness to a higher, more purified level, it accelerates the purification of the body through the expulsion of old dead cells.

7. In magic, such lists are called Tables of Correspondence. They can be found in several books, such as Crowley's *777* (Samuel Weiser, 1982), which is based upon Golden Dawn manuscripts), and Bill Whitcomb's *The Magician's Companion* (Llewellyn, 1993).

8. Once again, Regardie has switched the natural order of the Qabalistic Cross here. "ve-Gevurah" (right shoulder) should precede "ve-Gedulah" (left shoulder).

9. Libellus XI. (ii), "A Discourse of Mind to Hermes." See Scott, *Hermetica,* 90–91.

10. Plotinus was a leading Neoplatonist of the third century C.E. He strove to combine Greek logic and rational philosophy with mysticism and transcendental experience. His major work, the *Enneads,* was compiled by his student Porphyry.

11. For this reason it is important that the student keep a diary and record the results of all meditations, exercises, and rituals.

12. In addition to giving a mistaken impression of what spiritual growth *is,* it has also resulted in many seekers assuming that their meditations yield contact with "Secret Chiefs or Illuminated Masters from the Inner Planes." Thus they mistake initial contacts with the higher self, along with corresponding images of *personal growth meant for themselves,* as important messages for all humanity, and they come to think of themselves as avatars or messiahs. This unfortunate tendency is an anathema to the Great Work.

13. This should be a special dagger that is only used for the purpose of banishing. In actuality, no such implement is needed, and the magician may simply use his index and middle fingers to trace the pentagram just as effectively.

14. Although the figure traced is the same as the Banishing Earth Pentagram, in the LBRP it should be referred to as the *Lesser Banishing Pentagram.* This is because it is traced in all four directions, alluding to the four quarters (sub-elements) of Malkuth: Air of Malkuth, Water of Malkuth, Fire of Malkuth, and Earth of Malkuth.

15. YHVH is transliterated English for יהוה, which is called the *Tetragrammaton* or "Four-lettered Name." It is considered the ineffable name of God. Each letter of the name is also attributed to one of the Four Worlds of the Qabalah: Yod = Atziluth, Heh = Briah, Vav = Yetzirah, And Heh Final = Assiah.

16. Keep the hand or dagger extended as you turn from the east to the south, west, north, and back around again to the east, drawing the appropriate pentagrams as you go. Visualize a ribbon of light extending from the center of the

first pentragram in the east to the center of the second pentragram which will be drawn in the south. The four pentagrams are thus connected to each other by an astral ribbon of the same color creating a magical circle, whose end must be linked with its beginning point in the east.

17. The transliterated form of the word *Adonai*, meaning "Lord."

18. The transliterated form of the word *Eheieh*, meaning "I am."

19. This word is a notariqon—an acronym for the Hebrew sentence *Atah Gibor Le-Olahm Adonai*, which means "Thou art great forever, my Lord." The first letter of each word is used to make up the word *AGLA*.

20. The positioning of a hexagram behind the magician alludes to an advanced magical working in which the magician visualizes the Golden Dawn's Banner of the East within his aura. There are several variations of lines 11 and 12 given in many books; their differences are very slight. The version given here is consistent with that described in Regardie's *The Golden Dawn*. Another version states, "*For around me shines* the Pentagram and *within* me shines the six-rayed Star." The total number of points formed by the four pentagrams (4 x 5), and the single hexagram (6) is 26, the number of Tetragrammaton and of the Middle Pillar. Another version is "*For about me flames* the Pentagram, and *in the column shines* the six-rayed Star." This latter version, adapted by Crowley, is the one that we prefer. It can be found in Regardie's *The Tree of Life* with the word *stands* substituted for the word *shines*. The column here alludes to the Middle Pillar, and is a reference to the magician who stands in the Pillar of Balance. It also alludes to the unification of the macrocosm and the microcosm by a hexagonal column of light between a hexagram above and a hexagram below. (In this version the total number of points on the four pentagrams and the two hexagrams is 32, the number of the Paths of Wisdom, the holy name AHYAHWEH (the combination of *Eheieh* and *YHVH*, the macrocosm and the microcosm. One of the unpublished papers from the AO (an offshoot of the Golden Dawn) suggested that line 11 could be either "And behind me shines the Six-rayed Star," or "and behind me shines the Hexagram of Light." This same paper states that a thirteenth line could be added if the magician so desired: "And above my head the Glory of God." Whatever version the magician chooses is a matter of personal preference.

21. Specifically the banishment of negativity, unwanted energies, or neuroses.

22. Most texts describing the LBRP state that the magician is to start in the east and finish in the east. We now feel it might be better to have the magician start and finish in the center of the room, facing east. He can move to the east to trace the first pentagram and then continue around the circumference of the temple. He would only need to stand in the center of the room whenever performing the Qabalistic Cross and the Invocation of the Archangels.

23. The pentagrams could also be visualized in flaming white light. White light has a tendency to be seen on the astral as bluish light by clairvoyants.

24. Each is a "tetragram."

25. The element of fire corresponds to our will and feeling faculty, water to our creativity and intuitive faculty, air to our intellect and thinking faculty, and earth to our faculty of sensation.

26. See Part Two, Chapter Nine for an explanation of why these names are used in the Pentagram Ritual.

27. Or the center of the room. Refer to Endnote 22.

28. A telesmatic image is an image constructed according to a predetermined set of correspondences. This image is then consecrated and charged to achieve a specific purpose. And the charged image becomes a sacred icon— a living symbol of the force it represents.

29. The archangel of earth. Also called Uriel. (Raphael, Michael, and Gabriel are the archangels of air, fire, and water, respectively.)

30. These four colors are the usual colors given for the Sephirah Malkuth, which has the element of earth generally assigned to it. These are also the colors of elemental earth in the King Scale.

31. These last two lines refer to visualizations in steps 11 and 12 in the LBRP. (Refer to Endnote 20.) Regardie's suggested visualization of a pentagram on the chest and a hexagram on the back results in a total of 31 points on the five pentagrams and the single hexagram, the number of the divine name *Al* (אל).

32. This practice will eventually become second nature to the magician. For an example, if the magician is having a "rough day at the office" he can imagine himself at home, performing the LBRP in full regalia in his private temple space. All of this can be performed astrally and with great effect toward cleansing negative influences from the magician's psyche.

33. During this time the student should refrain from invoking and concentrate solely on banishing.

CHAPTER FOUR

THE MIDDLE PILLAR EXERCISE

I t is my confirmed belief that several weeks at the very least of patient application to the Lesser Banishing Ritual of the Pentagram should precede any effort to perform the Middle Pillar. For one thing, it will have trained the student in several little tricks of routine and magical technique quite apart from the intrinsic virtues of the exercise, which is to purify and cleanse the entire sphere of personality to the end that the higher self may manifest through a purified body and mind. If the exercise has been labored at for two or three months, performing it two or three times during the course of each day, the student will approach the further stages of magic well-prepared, quite able to cope with and accommodate the increased vitality and power which will pour through him.

It will be realized how necessary analysis is as a preliminary routine to magic. The student should have arrived at a fair understanding of himself, his motives, and the mechanism of his mind, and integrated himself more or less thoroughly so that no dissociation or serious neurosis exists within the psyche. For the presence of a powerful complex of associated ideas in the unconscious, or a marked dissociation splitting off one part of the psyche from the other, will have the effect of short-circuiting the flow of energy generated or released by the Middle Pillar. An explosion in the form of a complete nervous breakdown, or even of the destruction of mental stability, will be a likely result. Many instances have been known of unprepared students contracting fatal physical illnesses through attempting work of this nature, though this is more true where Eastern exercises have been unwisely attempted. Some of these unfortunates, when the dissociation was rendered complete, have succumbed to chronic melancholia or taken their own lives. These warnings are not intended to be portentous or terrifying, but only to impress upon the student the solemnity of these undertakings, a journey of self-conquest than which nothing could compare in importance or seriousness.

To my mind, the exercise described as the Middle Pillar is the groundwork of all actual developmental work. It is a process which is the basis of magic. That this has been but seldom realized is obviously at the root of the futile attempts to do ceremonial and perform ritual, of which the general public hears every now and again. Even students of magic of many years standing have been guilty of negligence in this respect, and also in failing to recommend it to their successors. The name of the exercise is taken from the position of the central Sephiroth on the diagrammatic Tree of Life (see Figure 2, p. 28). This exercise concerns those centers numbered one, six, nine, and ten. It also includes the shadowy center drawn in dotted lines, placed between three and four.[1] For various reasons I cannot go into detailed metaphysical explanations as to the underlying philosophy of this shadowy Sephirah, though students who desire more information about it will discover the elaboration of this theme in my *Garden of Pomegranates* and *My Rosicrucian Adventure*. Suffice to say here that it arises from a consideration of the process of evolution on the one hand, and the two pillars previously referred to, on the other. The ancient philosophers who developed this system believed that as man evolved, that is to say as he developed sufficient control over his emotions as to be able to remain poised in a detachment from the dual pull of the opposites, so there developed within him a new faculty of discrimination and spiritual discernment. Psychologically this idea has been verified. For it has been said that as the over activity of the superficial mind, the flitting from one thing to another, prevents creativeness, so equally does inertia, dullness and the unwillingness to move. If fact, any of the two extremes or opposite modes of behavior or thinking are characteristic of the unevolved man. As was said by one magician "The Secret of Wisdom can be discerned only from the place of balanced power"[2]—that is from between the two temple pillars. Poise at a third point, which neutralizes to some extent the violence of the swing of the psychic pendulum from one extreme to the other, is the result of cultivating equanimity, representing an equal capacity to be either at rest or active, interested or withdrawn at will, and not from emotional compulsion.

This central point between the two symbolic pillars of the opposites, the place of balanced power from which the working of the opposites may correctly be viewed, is the implication of *Daath*, which is the name of this shadowy Sephirah. Rightly it is shadowy, and the word is used advisedly for in the majority of us who have not cultivated the difficult art of avoiding the opposites, the development of this new principle has proceeded with the utmost slowness. It is a new factor of adaptation or equilibrium, especially between the two broad divisions of consciousness—the ego on the one hand with its desire for adjustment to modern life with its refined and non-natural conditions, and on the other hand with the superficial levels of the instinctual life, concerned with primitive things, of self-assertion and the unbridled gratification of its every whim and caprice. It is this new factor of adjustment which comprises the principal impetus to what has been variously called in the east the Golden Flower, and in mediaeval Europe the growth of the Red Rose upon the Cross of Gold.[3] It is the Stone of the Philosophers, the medicine of metals.[4]

To the four central Sephiroth plus the shadowy *Daath* as the fifth, are attributed divine names—which, as in the former exercise, are to be vibrated powerfully in conjunction with the imaginative formulation of various images.

Let me expatiate upon these divine names by stating that they may be considered as the keynote or vibratory rates of various degrees or grades of consciousness. In their prolonged investigation into the hidden knowledge and the secret side of man's nature, the ancients who were as empirical scientists as our psychologists today, came to associate various sound-values or rates of vibration with various parts of the body, and also with particular types of

magnetic force and strata of consciousness. No religious or metaphysical theory need attach to the employment of these names. The
system rests entirely upon its own merits. The simplest way of
regarding them is, as explained above, as vibratory rates. Again,
they may be considered as key notes by means of which access is
obtained to the consciousness of the different parts of our being,
the existence of which hitherto we have been kept in ignorance.[5]

With each of these five centers there is associated a divine name
to be used as a vibratory formula. The attributions as we have
received them, together with the traditional name of the Sephiroth,
are given below with the names of the principles active in the
human psyche. The numberings are those that appear on the Tree.[6]

1. Kether—*Yechidah*
   "**AHIH**" (pronounced "Eh-he-yeh")

   Daath—*The Link*
   "**YHVH ALHIM**" ("Ye-hoh-voh E-loh-heem")[7]

6. Tiphareth—*Ruach*
   "**YHVH ALOAH ve-DAATH**" ("Ye-hoh-voh El-oah ve-
   Da-ath")[8]

9. Yesod—*Nephesh*
   "**SHADDAI AL CHAI**" ("Shah-dai EI Chai")[9]

10. Malkuth—*Body*
    "**ADNI HARTZ**" ("Ah-doh-nai ha-Ah-retz")

The divine names and the names of the Sephiroth should naturally be committed to memory, as also the following scheme of their
position or relation to parts of the human frame (see Figure 4, p. 73).

Kether, the first Sephirah, is a center of light, and in the
Qabalistic Cross, it is attributed to a center posited slightly above
the crown of the head. It refers to that higher genius or *it* which,
not yet fully incarnated within, broods above, a silent watcher. It
is for each of us the source of inspiration and freedom and
enlightenment. It is life itself.

Daath, the shadowy Sephirah, which develops in the course of
evolution as we learn the domination of our mental and emotional
propensities, is situated at the nape of the neck. Its position is at a
point on the spine just below the occiput, about one or two inches

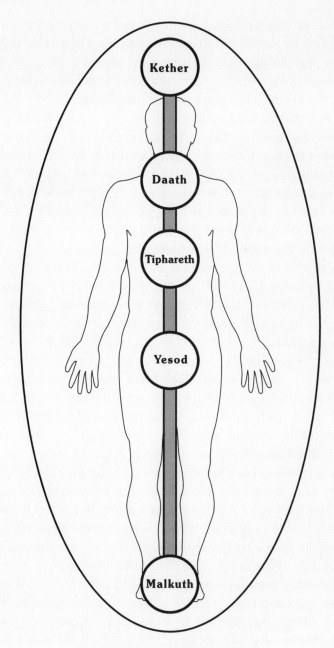

Figure 4: The Middle Pillar.

above the larynx, and its diameter may be imagined to be about four inches in extent. It is conceived to be a symbolic link, self-induced and self-devised, between the higher genius on the one hand, and on the other, the ego, the conscious self referred to that group of characteristics clustered around *Tiphareth*.

On the Middle Pillar, *Daath* connects the higher faculties to the ego, *Kether* to *Tiphareth*. This latter Sephirah is resident in the neighborhood of the heart, and its sphere extends from the diaphragm or solar plexus more or less to the spine. Its center may be imagined to be the lowest point of the sternum or breast-bone to which the ribs are attached, its diameter being about six inches.

Below *Tiphareth* is *Yesod*, a center which is referred to the region occupied by the generative organs, and its size should be visualized as of the same dimensions as *Tiphareth*. The final center is *Malkuth*, referred to the feet, and it will be found by experience that the ankles comprise the periphery of a visualized sphere about four inches or so in diameter, the center being the sole of the foot.

The method of working this practice called the Middle Pillar is to stand upright, hands to side, eyes closed, breath being inhaled and expired steadily. Above all the mind should be quiet, calm, and still. When familiarity with the exercise is obtained, it may be performed sitting or lying down. These preliminary conditions being fulfilled, let the student begin by transferring his attention to that region immediately above the crown of his head, where he should endeavor to visualize a sphere of white brilliance. To accomplish this may take some little while. Several attempts may be required before any realization of this center occurs. But when it has been obtained, let it be regarded with a certain sense of devotion, and contemplated as being the spatial correlative or correspondence of the vital core of his being. This devotional attitude should enliven it considerably, and the sense of light and power, the first avenues of sense by which this higher phase of consciousness may be grasped, should increase wholly beyond anticipation. At this juncture let him vibrate three or four times, slowly, the name *Eheieh*.[10] This is a Hebrew divine name meaning "I am" (or more accurately "I will be") a statement which in reality is all that one can truthfully say of the self. Every other characteristic and quality belongs not to its own intrinsic nature but to the vehicles and sheaths of consciousness through which it functions.

Steadfast in the contemplation of this source of power and enlightenment, he should endeavor to feel that an all-penetrant beam of brilliance is emitted downwards towards the nape of the neck. Here it widens, expanding to form a brilliant center similar to, though smaller in diameter than, that above the head. Applying the same vibratory technique here, while realizing that this is not his divinity but its conscious link or point of contact with his ego, the student should again feel the radiation of power and vitality. So marked and powerful should this become at this juncture that even in the palms of his hand will the vibration of energy be felt as almost of a physical nature, and quite possibly a prickling sensation will be noticed in the head and neck. A quite indescribable sense of poise and mental quiescence should also be experienced— no inconsiderable attainment, no small acquisition in these days of hurried business life and social fluttering.

After several vibrations of the appropriate name, again the beam of light should descend to the heart or region of the solar plexus, and from there a warmth and a quite different sense of power will gently radiate as though from an interior sun. Here too, a name should be slowly vibrated in such a way, which can only come through practice, as to detonate precisely in the physical area being contemplated and not in another. It must be felt to vibrate in the region between the diaphragm and the point opposite to it on the spinal column.

Pass in contemplation from the heart to the center of the generative organs. Visualize the sphere of light and vibrate the name, employing the same technique as before and noting carefully the reaction in consciousness. Some minutes having been spent arousing this center and vitalizing in with power, pass downwards to the feet where the magical center will be found to awaken quite easily. In point of fact, it will be discovered that the mere contemplation of *Kether*, the center above the head, will by reflex action bring into operation the *Malkuth* center, these being the two poles, height and depth, of the Middle Pillar.

This very briefly is the technique. Little can be said which the zealous student will not be able to discover through application to it. If the student spends about five minutes in the contemplation of each Sephirah on the middle column, the exercise will take approximately twenty-five minutes to half an hour. And surely there is no one so busy today who cannot devote at least one half hour a day to the task of self-mastery, to the cultivation of spiritual insight, and in the quest of his own divine nature.

My own plan of personal instruction, one developed some three years ago, was to perform this exercise sitting beside that student I had decided to teach. The principle involved was that of induction. I assumed that by bringing into operation the centers within my own sphere of sensation while sometimes, though not invariably, holding the hand of the student, the unawakened centers of the latter would react and revolve out of sympathy, or by reflex. It amounted, in a word, to a sort of initiation, and powerful it may become too. And I discovered that whereas the average student took some while before stumbling upon the best means of producing the desired results by the Middle Pillar, those few students whom I had initiated in this way were capable of performing the exercise immediately after in a highly successful way, even when away from my presence and atmosphere.[11]

When seeking for the ideal technique of initiation, to perfect a rite of initiation from a purely individualistic point of view, one of the methods I hit upon was the combination of the Middle Pillar formula with an actual ceremony. That is to say, by ceremonially invoking a spiritual force by means of the appropriate pentagram or hexagram ritual, vibrating congruous divine names, and performing the Middle Pillar in a room or temple thus powerfully charged by the manifestation of this spiritual force, the result was all the more effectual and definitely realized in consciousness.[12]

A simple ceremony which invokes the divine and archangelic currents of elemental force, using invocations composed of ecstatic passages from various sacred scriptures, is almost ideal for the purpose.[13] Not only does this method succeed in providing a neophyte with an introduction to the light of his own higher genius and to the realm of magic, but it is a supreme technique of self-initiation.[14] Various changes may be rung on a simple theme. And according to the student's own ingenium and spiritual aspiration, so will he devise several methods of employing the techniques I have described above.

There will be some who will propound belabored theories as to suggestion—that because I consciously or otherwise suggested to these students that there were magical centers existent within their own system, their unconscious accepted the suggestion and produced the looked-for result. Others, yet again, will murmur the magical word "telepathy"—arguing that I projected, though not necessarily deliberately, certain ideas or sensations from my mind into that of the receptive student who thus was influenced against his own better judgment or skepticism. With none of these am I wholly in accord, though in each of them may be some germ of truth. None of them answer the facts of experience. And I can only suggest that these people would do far better to apply themselves zealously to a little experimental work rather than waste time in vain explanations and baseless theories.

Some will note that this exercise corresponds in some ways to the yoga chakra system.[15] There is, assuredly, correspondence. But there are several very important differences and variations. The first, a minor difference, is the number and position of the centers involved. But this does not require discussion. What is fundamental, however, is the entirely different approach. The yoga technique commences its meditations from the lowest chakra and works upwards to the Sahasrara above the head. On the other hand, in the western system, the Middle Pillar starts from the highest and works downwards. In a word, the Western ideal is not to escape from the body but to become involved more and more in life, in order to experience it more adequately, and in order to obtain a mastery over it. The ideal is to bring down godhead so that one's manhood being enriched may thereby be assumed into godhead. Always does this system begin from the real center of working— the higher genius which, by definition, is in contact eternally with whatever infinite deity there may be. That is to say, through the *Yechidah* we have immediate access to all the dynamic inspiration and spiritual power of the collective unconscious.

By the magical hypothesis, the higher genius corresponds within man to the possible relationship of God to the universe.

That is to say, man being the microcosm of the macrocosm, a reflection of the cosmos, is a universe within himself, a universe ruled and governed by his own divinity. So whatever magical work is undertaken must always be in accordance with the dictates and under the surveillance of that higher genius. And since, at first, there is no immediate method of realizing whether any particular magical effort has the approval, to state it simply and naively, of the higher self, the sole course of action must be for the student to place himself in alignment with that genius. This is done by invoking it at the outset of any magical operation, and trusting to be made a vehicle of wisdom and understanding.[16] The first movement of the Middle Pillar—as also the Qabalistic Cross, which is a quick method of obtaining the same result—achieves precisely that. For since the source of life and love has always been conceived of as light, the preliminary step is to perceive that brooding brilliance above which is the emanation of, or the direct center through which manifests, that higher genius, or with which the latter is in especial sympathy. And the remaining steps are deliberately to open one's manhood as it were to the descent of divinity—to bring down the light into the personality. Here it must be emphasized lies the vital distinction between the yoga chakra system of the Hindus and the magical exercise of the Middle Pillar. At first such a descent is characterized by an increased sense of power and vitality. Gradually this widens to emotional quiescence and control with a mental poise, followed by a gradual broadening and enhancement of the entire mental horizon.

There is yet another highly useful application of this formula. It is to the art of healing that I refer.[17] Formerly when I employed massage and magnetic healing in my professional work I found the Middle Pillar and the spiritual energy that it generates and makes available of inestimable value.[18] Cases of nervous exhaustion, catarrh, constipation, incipient consumption, pleurisy, and many another will respond in an incomparable manner to this combination of massage and the willed communication of power. That is to say, using effleurage and friction, especially on the spine, as the principal massage technique one should place oneself en rapport with the higher self by the contemplation of the center of light above the head. By silently vibrating the divine name appropriate, one is enabled to tap a tremendous source of healing power which is infinitely greater than that which ordinarily one has at one's disposal as an average human being. This magnetic or spiritual power flows through one steadily and powerfully. Directed by a calm will, and assisted by a clear visualized idea of the result desired, it may be communicated like an electric current through the arm and hands to the finger tips. Thence it enters the patient's body as the palms of the masseur's hands glide over the surface being treated. It requires some little practice to retain awareness of this divine Light while engaging in so strenuous a physical effort as deep massage, but it is not an impossible one. It is a great help if the visualization of the sphere above the head is attempted whilst walking, for example. When this can be done, then its employment for the purposes of healing is quite simple. I can commend it unequivocally, both to physicians and psychologists. It is my hope that analysts will take over the technique for use in their own consulting rooms. Let them adopt it in its entirety as the one ideal method of inducing the right state of mind appropriate to free association and the cathartic confession. Should its present form be considered unsuitable, I reiterate that it has possibilities which render it worthy of being remodeled in the light of present-day psychological knowledge to suit modern contingencies.

There are several little physical helps which greatly enhance the degree and amount of power which can be made available. Correct breathing, especially, is one of them. There could hardly be a better adjunct than breathing in a rhythmical manner. The latter in itself, quite apart from the Middle Pillar, is supremely efficacious in producing quiet and calm. The entire system is stilled and strengthened as the lungs slowly take up a rhythm, and keep to it indefinitely.

First of all the student should train himself in the method of breathing correctly—that is to say, in the method of filling his lungs with air from the very bottom. He should combine abdominal with both diaphragmatic and costal breathing. The act of inspiration, if carefully observed, consists of these three phases. First the abdominal part of the lungs are filled, then that underlying the diaphragm, and finally as the shoulders are slightly lifted the thorax itself becomes filled. They are so continuous as to appear an undivided act. In this way, every cell of the entire lung surface comes into contact with the oxygen inhaled, which is thus passed into the bloodstream. Most of us usually breathe very insufficiently, only a fraction of the cellular surface of the lung coming into contact with the inhaled air. Thus there is always a large quantity of residual air in the lower reaches of the lungs. There is always a large surface of the lung area which is not employed; and a quantity of carbon dioxide and cells in an impoverished state of health are ever present.

This method of breathing introduces a far greater content of oxygen into the lung, destroying therefore, by combustion, toxins and undesirable elements, and also producing a better state of health. There are many individuals who, because of conflict and neurosis, have attempted to flee from life. They have attempted to evade a full contact with the stream of vital experience, and this psychological attitude of evasion has reacted upon the bodily functions. One of these particularly affected is that of breathing, the lungs falling into the habit of functioning at about half their proper capacity. The circle is a vicious one. For inadequate breathing by itself induces an enfeebled state of health, perpetual exhaustion, catarrh, and many another ill. Likewise, this constant state of ill-health reacts upon the mental outlook, confirming and strengthening the escapist attitude towards life because the individual is now only half alive, incapable of reacting to the pleasures and joys of life. For mind and body, as so often reiterated in these pages, are not two distinct units. The functions of the one interlap with and interpenetrate the functions of the other. More accurately they should be regarded as the two functions of one entity, two methods whereby it may acquire experience. Too much therefore cannot be said of the necessity for cultivating the lungs to operate at full capacity. This cultivation cannot be too often stressed, for life is power, and power is life and consciousness, indispensable in the path of magic which leads to the knowledge of the higher self.

The proper method of deep breathing having been acquired, the cultivation of a rhythmic breath should be the next step. The most suitable and simple method is the four-beat rhythm. If the student will inhale very slowly, mentally counting one, two, three, four and then exhale to the same beat, he will discover that this undoubtedly is the best rhythm for inducing that state of calmness and peace which is so necessary for meditation and reflection. And, in passing, let me add that the state of quiescence sought after is one not of passivity and negativity. It is one of alertness and eagerness. What one should cultivate is a quiescence in which every mental faculty is alert, waiting to be used. A tranquility characterized by a sense of enormous power and capacity is the state to be aimed at, one in which there is the maximum of awareness and inner poise.

Success in the technique of the rhythmic breath is an unmistakable symptom which cannot fail to be recognized when it arises. There is first the sense of peace, satisfaction and quiet joy, without the least cessation of one's mental capacity. Next follows a sense of vibration felt all over the body, as though every cell and molecule were acting in unison and moving, as it were, in a single direction. The result of this vibration is to transform the lungs and the entire body into a single storage battery, generating and storing electricity and power, transmuting them into will and faculty. Hard upon this, if the rhythm be persisted in, comes a quiet ripple over the diaphragm or solar plexus—a difficult symptom to describe, because it produces no perceptible physical or recognizable change, though the sense of the rhythm is none the less distinctly felt. When this occurs, and when one becomes aware of a single vibration through the body, and a gentle vibration or sense of luminosity and lightness in the brain, the student may be assured that he has achieved success in this particular practice.

This state gained, the Middle Pillar should be proceeded with, and the names could be silently vibrated in tune with the rhythmic inhalation and exhalation of the breath. The sense of the brilliance above which I prefer to think of as the "lamp above the head," or as others have called it "the candle of vision," becomes much more perceptible and marked. Very often it develops into an awareness of a whirling sphere of fiery light radiating peace and illumination into the mind and body. Little more need be said, for I have no desire to provide material which may act upon suggestible minds. There are people so constituted as to be able to produce symptoms of any described kind with the least application, and with practically no spiritual effect upon themselves or their mental or moral nature, and certainly no progress in that path which leads to the knowledge of the higher self. Silence with reference to symptoms and results is therefore most desirable.

Endnotes

1. This is *Daath*, which is not a Sephirah, but rather a conjunction of Chokmah and Binah.

2. From the Neophyte Ritual. See Regardie, *The Golden Dawn*, 129.

3. The symbol of the Rosicrucians. Rosicrucianism is a form of mystic or esoteric Christianity whose teachings embrace the Hermetic sciences.

4. The Philosopher's Stone is an alchemical symbol of true spiritual attainment. The search for the Philosopher's Stone is the search for truth and illumination.

5. Along the same lines, each letter of the Hebrew alphabet has a musical note attributed to it. Thus each divine name in Hebrew can be sung or played on a musical instrument. See the Appendix: The Musical Qabalah.

6. In this list, Regardie has given the name of the Sephiroth of the Middle Pillar next to their corresponding part of the soul. Beneath that he has provided the divine Hebrew name that is to be intoned or vibrated in the exercise. Thus Kether, which is equated with the *Yechidah*, is activated in the aura by vibrating the divine name "AHIH" (which is the transliteration for *Eheieh* אהיה), and so on.

7. Daath has no divine name of its own, so in the exercise of the Middle Pillar, it "borrows" the divine name for Binah which is the highest Sephirah that is close to Daath. (Since Daath is usually considered a passageway to the Supernals, Binah would be the Sephirah at its point of termination.) Although Regardie states here that YHVH is to be pronounced as "Yeh-hoh-voh," we see no reason it should be pronounced differently from the way it is pronounced in the LBRP—as "Yod-Heh-Vav-Heh." The term *Jehovoh* or *Jehovah* is simply a transcription of the Four-lettered Name YHVH—the letters of which were merely considered as stand-ins for the actual name of God, which was unknown and unpronounceable. We believe that the divine name *YHVH Elohim* should be pronounced "Yod Heh Vav Heh El-oh-heem" in all Golden Dawn rituals.

Some modern magicians believe that the divine name given for Daath (and for Binah) should not be pronounced as YHVH Elohim. They argue that YHVH was never vocalized by devout Jews who thought it was too holy to pronounce. Whenever it occurred in writing, the words *Elohim* (god or gods) or *Adonai* (lord) were always spoken as a substitute word for YHVH. Thus some magicians contend that the compound word YHVH Elohim is a mistake, and that what was intended was that the spoken word "Elohim" be substituted for the written word "YHVH" in Binah and in Daath. (The second word in the compound name YHVH ELOHIM was considered by Jews as a reminder that the holy name YHVH is never spoken but rather vocalized as "Elohim.") While this argument may be true for devout Jews, it is not valid for practicing magicians in the tradition of the Golden Dawn. There are several examples of Hebrew mystics vocalizing the various permutations of the Tetragrammaton for specific ritual work with the Sephiroth. This points to the differences between orthodox Jewish practice and the esoteric practice of western Hermetic magicians.

8. For the same reason indicated in the above endnote, the divine name here should be pronounced "Yod Heh Vav Heh El-oh-ah ve-Dah-ath."

9. The "ch" in *Chai* should be pronounced like the Scottish word "lo*ch*."

10. Another common suggestion is to vibrate the name several times until it fills the mind completely, and no other thoughts remain. One other method is to pronounce the name as many times as there are Hebrew letters in the name.

11. This type of Middle Pillar initiation can also be used to charge talismans. Regardie used this technique to charge one of our medallions. (For more on this, see Part Two, Chapter Ten.)

12. One very potent combination of such rituals is the LBRP, succeeded by the Rose Cross Ritual, and followed by the Middle Pillar Exercise. The RCR can be found on page 306 of Regardie's *The Golden Dawn*.

13. See Regardie's Revised Middle Pillar Ritual for ⑤=⑥ in Part Two, Chapter Ten.

14. Regardie strongly advocated the idea of self-initiation, particularly in those cases where it was not possible to find a local temple of duly qualified initiators.

15. The eastern *chakra* system is fully described in Part Two, Chapter Eight.

16. According to Golden Dawn tradition, the highest must always be invoked first—the highest divine name, followed by archangels, angels, and finally elemental rulers and spirits. (In principle this can be compared to a military chain of command. If you want something to get done, you must contact the highest ranking officer, who then delegates the work down to officers of lower rank.)

17. Some Middle Pillar healing techniques are given in Part Two, Chapter Ten.

18. Regardie was both a chiropractor and a Reichian therapist. Deep massage is an important part of Reichian therapy, designed to break down rigid muscular tension (armoring) that affects both body and psyche. Chiropractic medicine uses the manipulation of the spine to relieve physical pain. It is easy to see how one system can be used to complement the other.

CHAPTER FIVE

CIRCULATING THE LIGHT AND THE FORMULA OF VIBRATION

The formula of the Middle Pillar has many and varied uses. It serves as an excellent prelude to any type of spiritual work. For those whose penchant or principal interest is the art of meditation as the supreme means of placing themselves in alignment with the higher self, no better opening to that meditation could be found. It also serves, as suggested above, as the only worth-while preparation for serious magical work. It is that technique which generates the magical power which by its presence spells success in the routine of ceremonial or ritual magic. Those who have not applied themselves to this practice—or have not stumbled upon its essential core by accident, as very often happens—are certainly not those who have in any way proved the efficacy of the art of ceremonial. They believe that the ultimate factor which confers success is any one of a thousand things save this particular preliminary one. We read in some authoritative tomes that the factor in question is the whirling dance, or music played by violin or harp, the mystical circumambulation or the mental spasm sometimes caused by invocation or adoration. In practice, however, should any of these routines succeed in producing the requisite and longed for result, it is, as it were, in spite of themselves. That is to say, they are purely secondary and subordinate techniques. Their method is hit or miss, and does not rest upon a sound basis of attainment nor upon a sure understanding of magical principles. The practice of the Middle Pillar is the introductory or preparatory means of aligning the personality with the inner self, of identifying and unifying all the levels of the true consciousness which we, in our complacency and blindness, choose to call the unconscious.

Reverting back to the technical side of things, there is yet another development of the Middle Pillar which requires description. Having been awakened from latency into some degree of activity, it is necessary that the power that the centers generate should be circulated through the invisible or psychic system. Failure to do this is, in my estimation, one of the most potent sources of nervous trouble and disturbance experienced by dabblers in occultism, who have experimented with various amateur or incompletely delineated methods of awakening the psychic centers. The energy thus awakened streams back and forth from the center. But unless some method is devised for distributing it and thus relieving the pressure, the center itself will in the course of time suffer derangement through over-stimulus, and there is bound to ensue some serious disturbance to the nervous and psychic system. Nervous breakdowns have been common-place amongst those who have unwisely attempted these things on insufficient knowledge, and neuroses have reaped a timely and bounteous harvest among students of the occult.

With every one of the five centers active and throwing power into the mind and body, and there is a clear awareness of an actual column extending interiorly from the crown of the head to the soles of the feet, an entirely different technique must now be pursued. The student should return to the contemplation of his Kether, the lamp of invisible light above the head. Imagining this center still to be in a state of radiation, let him will that its energy circulates through the system in this wise. It descends from the head towards the left shoulder. Passing through the entire length of the left side of the body, the magnetic current strikes the sole of the left foot. Thence it passes over to the right sole,[1] upwards through the leg and thigh and body to the right shoulder, eventually returning to *Kether*.

Possibly this may sound fantastic to some readers. Impossible and incredible to others. But the fact remains that it can be done and simply too. It requires, above all, to be attempted in the spirit of honest investigation and tried again and again until the current of energy responds to the firm command of the will, thus following the course directed. Once clearly commanded, the current flows in that direction quite automatically and on its own momentum. The mind, naturally, must be calm and concentrated, not prone to wander off into pleasant excursions on the day's events.

In this way, a great deal of the power generated is circulated through every particle of the body, so that each of these cells feels alive as never it has felt before. This, be it remembered, quite apart from the enhancement of the general field of consciousness. What I have described may be called for clarity's sake the formula of Circulation Number One.

It is now necessary to circulate the stream of power in yet another direction. The object is to ensure that no single area of the sphere of sensation be omitted from its vitalizing and cleansing passage. Once again returning to the vision of the light above the head, this time imagine and will that the current of spiritual power descends from *Kether* in a forward direction. That is to say, it passes downward in front of the face, descending through that region along the neck and chest, down the thighs to the feet. When it strikes the thighs, the stream turns backward along the soles of the feet, along the calves at the back, ascending the spinal column and neck until, once more, it reaches *Kether*. Both this formula and the preceding one should be repeated several times, until they become quite simple. The process should be accompanied by the rhythmic breath, so that the descending current coincides with the exhalation of breath, while the ascending current accompanies the inhalation. It is really very easy, and it is only the description of it which sounds involved and complex. This formula we will call Circulation Number Two.

The third formula of circulation is rather different. The two preceding methods will be discovered to have produced wheels of power spinning around the periphery of the aura or sphere of sensation at right angles, as it were. The third formula is more akin to the motion of a spiral. Having returned on each of the former occasions of circulation to the contemplation of *Kether*, imagine the upright column of brilliance, corresponding to the Middle Pillar, formulated through the center of the body. Pass now to the visualization of *Malkuth* emanating its inherent power of stability and equilibrium and fertility. Perhaps the easiest way to conceive of the motion of the third formula is to imagine the act of swathing or bandaging a leg. You wrap the gauze tightly around the lower part of the limb, gradually ascending the leg in closely wound spirals. This, simply, is the technique of the formula under consideration. You should imagine a ray of power coming out from the right side of *Malkuth*, moving over to the left foot. Here it descends under the legs, and comes up on the right a little higher up the spiral. Repeat the same movement again and again, until eventually you feel the distinct sensation of a whirling of spiritual power which gradually rises from the feet to the thighs, its spiral-current still fairly close and connected, over-lapping those immediately below. From the thighs, the whirling or spiral proceeds up the trunk tightly enwrapping or enswathing it with a bandage of pure white light. This continues, until once more the current returns to rest in *Kether*. This completes the formulae of circumambulation, as the method is sometimes called.[2] These circulatory movements will be referred to again later, and the student is asked to pay special attention to them.

The Chinese yoga instruction, *The Secret of the Golden Flower*,[3] has a sentence or two which is very apposite to this technique of the mystical circumambulations:

> *Therefore when the Light circulates, the powers of the whole body arrange themselves before its throne, just as when a holy king has taken possession of the capital and has laid down the fundamental rules of order, all the states approach with tribute.... Therefore you only have to make the Light circulate; that is the deepest and most wonderful secret. The Light is easy to move, but difficult to fix. If it is allowed to go long enough in a circle, then it crystallises itself; that is the natural spirit-body. This crystallized spirit is formed beyond the nine Heavens. It is the condition of which it is said in the Book of the Seal of the Heart: silently in the morning thou fliest upward.*

To summarize the practice, the Middle Pillar consists of several phrases. There is the preliminary establishment of a rhythmical intake and exhalation of breath. The formulation of the five centers on the Middle Pillar, each one separately. And finally, the several formulae for the distribution of the power thus generated.

As one becomes more and more familiar with this process with the passage of time, the practice being continued daily, little artistic flourishes as it were may be introduced to enhance its efficiency and assist the process of interior development. Some caution, naturally, is needed. Common sense is essential. The student does not wish to generate or open himself to more power than easily he can accommodate. This would prove, if not dangerous, then quite useless. For one thing, it would impede his own development and progress.

The additions referred to are the colors of each center to be visualized whilst vibrating the name. This notably changes and stimulates the reaction of the Sephirah. Care is needed, and that is why it is recommended that for months the student should not apply himself to this color scheme, contenting himself exclusively with the visualization of the light-centers as white in color. *Kether* is of pure white brilliance, and the rays that it emits and radiates upon the personality are of the same hue. Lavender-blue is the color that is traditionally associated with *Daath. Tiphareth* is gold, whilst *Yesod* is purple or puce.

It is when we approach the consideration of the *Malkuth* color that we experience some difficulty. Tradition gives us several scales of color all of which are of equal efficacy. The sphere of *Malkuth* is divided by two diagonals into four sections; citrine at the top, black at the bottom, with russet and olive occupying the two side sections.[4] More simply, it is sometimes useful to visualize this Sephirah solely as a jet black sphere, or yet again as of a dark green color. The student must suit himself here, finding out by practice which visualization produces the best results.

When he has pursued such a practice for many months, let him extend the scope of his efforts to the formulation not only of the Middle Pillar, but the Sephiroth of the two side columns as well. By doing this, he formulates within the Sphere of Sensation the three pillars of the complete Tree of Life.[5] The technique and the procedure to be followed is precisely that delineated with regard to the Sephiroth of the Middle Pillar. The only gap in the student's knowledge are the divine names of the Sephiroth of the two side pillars, and these I give below together with the appropriate colors.

When there is much time at the student's disposal, and when he has won sufficient confidence in his ability, an additional aid is to employ the archangelic names in addition to the divine names with the several centers. For example, when visualizing *Tiphareth* as a glowing golden sphere, he will slowly vibrate three or four times the Name *Yhvh Aloah ve-Daath*.[6] Then he will pause while concentrating on the sphere. He will connive to realize in full consciousness the implications of this sphere—its attributions with regard to astrological planets, its spiritual qualities, and its relation to his own divine consciousness. This meditation performed, let him commence to vibrate in the same way and the same number of times the archangelic name of *Raphael,* again extending the meditation to realize that the latter name means divine healing. It implies that light which descends with "healing in its wings."[7] And so on for the remaining centers.

Below are the names attributed to each Sephirah of the Tree of Life, their archangels, the appropriate region of the body in which they are to be visualized, and the color of the visualization:

1. Kether	Ahih	Metatron[8]	Crown of head	White
2. Chokmah	Yoh[9]	Raziel[10]	Left side of brain	Grey
3. Binah	Yhvh[11]	Tzaphkiel[12]	Right side of brain	Black
Daath	Yhvh Alhim		Nape of neck	Lavender-blue[13]
4. Chesed	Al[14]	Tzadkiel[15]	Left shoulder	Blue
5. Gevurah	Alhim Gbor[16]	Kamael[17]	Right shoulder	Red
6. Tiphareth	Yhvh Aloah ve Daath	Raphael	Heart	Gold[18]
7. Netzach	Yhvh Tzabaoth[19]	Hanael[20]	Left hip	Green
8. Hod	Alhim Tzabaoth[21]	Michael	Right hip	Orange
9. Yesod	Shaddai Al Chai	Gabriel	Genitals	Puce[22]
10. Malkuth	Adonai ha-Aretz	Sandalphon[23]	Feet	Mixed colors[24]

It will be noticed that the attributions of *Daath* are deficient in an archangelic name. This is because the sphere is, in reality, no part of the traditional Tree of Life. The latter consists of ten spheres only, and it was with these ten spheres that the ancients occupied themselves and provided the necessary correspondences. The philosophy appertaining to *Daath* is almost entirely a modern one. But there is another mediaeval system which, attached to this Qabalistic system, provides us with an invocation of the element spirit. A great deal of research on this was done by Dr. John Dee and his skryer Edward Kelly, both of whom called it the Angelic or Enochian system. My experience confirms that the archangelic names contained in one of these very potent magical invocations are very sympathetic to the nature of *Daath*, which is described as a link between the ego and the higher self. These names may very logically be attributed to *Daath* and be used with it. They are Elexarpeh, Comananu, and Tabitom.[25] The method of vibrating these archangelic names is to split each one into syllables, each one receiving the maximum amount of vibration. Let care be taken so that the vibration detonates solely in *Daath*.

The Middle Pillar as already described, together with the for-mulae of circulation, constitutes the first half of this particular for-mula. The other half is denominated The Vibratory Formula of the Middle Pillar. To perform it properly presupposes a great deal of familiarity with the results to be obtained from the Middle Pillar and the complete Tree of Life exercise. It, however, proceeds a stage further. The former exercise devoted itself solely to awakening the centers considered as psycho-physical symbols or co-relatives of various principles operating within the psyche.

The Vibratory Formula, so called, envisages another goal. Its object, once the interior Sephiroth have been established and some awareness obtained of the principles they represent, is to ally or con-nect up those psychological principles to their replicas in the collec-tive unconscious.[26] The traditional magical theory is that since man is a reproduction in miniature of the universe, his own interior consti-tution must be modeled on the pattern of the larger universe of the collective unconscious. Just as the individual unconscious is not, as we have seen, a simple unit but comprises several constituents, so also the collective unconscious. Moreover, the tradition holds that by awakening any principle within, or by becoming conscious of any factor operative within the psyche, it is possible by an extension of the sphere of its operation to tap the corresponding aspect of that cen-ter or psyche in the collective sphere. The deeper levels of the collec-tive unconscious bear to the individual unconscious the same relationship as do the deepest levels of the latter to the conscious thinking ego. That is, they comprise the root and hidden sources of life, integrity and illumination. It is the equilibriated realization of these sources of life which make the difference between the enlightened man and the ignorant one. And these roots are the sources of life upon which the whole of existence in all its aspects depends.

Since magic has as its avowed intention the discovery of the higher self, and then to associate that higher self with the rest of the spiritual nature in a mood of co-operation, one way of accomplishing this co-operation is to connect deliberately the levels of the individual unconscious with the different planes of the collective unconscious. The result of the acceptance of the existence of the personal unconscious acts as a solvent of the habitual resistances to its free operation. Therefore, co-operation with that part of nature, the higher self, is the implication of that acceptance. Likewise the acceptance of the collective unconscious in the manner described, with the realization that the whole of life is an indissoluble unity, accordingly raises that conscious co-operation to a higher and much more deliberate level. It removes evolution from the purely personal alignment with nature, to a realization of the divine object of individual existence. With it comes the intuition in full consciousness how best that object may be fulfilled in relation to all other men and to life as a whole.

If I describe its technique, some understanding perhaps of its purposes may be divined. It presupposes, as said, some familiarity with the Middle Pillar. It demands, moreover, that the Middle Pillar should be in active formulation as an interior column of brilliance at the particular moment when the Vibratory Formula is to be employed. The student, then, begins to visualize in the atmosphere before him the name of that particular Sephirah which represents the level of consciousness he proposes to deal with.[27]

I must here interpolate that traditionally the letters of the Hebrew alphabet were employed for the purposes of this visualization. But I see no reason why the ordinary person should be obliged to burden himself with the necessity of studying Hebrew for this purpose. In the case of the serious student who wishes to make a profound study of the Qabalah from a purely magical point of view, and wishes to engage in the full ceremonial and ritual aspects of this tradition, I should be the first to insist that Hebrew be made a part of his curriculum. It would enter into every department of magic, in its wider implication, that he would touch. For the average student, however, English or Roman letters may be just as well employed. And I recommend that in the visualization only the consonants corresponding to the appropriate Hebrew characters of a name be employed, not the vowels. That is why in the rubric of the Pentagram Ritual, and in the table of correspondences above, I have spelt the divine names in consonantal form only.[28] The pronunciation of them is provided elsewhere.

The name visualized in Roman letters in the air, let the student imagine that he has drawn these letters into the lungs by means of a deep inspiration of air. The names should be visualized in flames; in flames corresponding in color to the Sephirah being employed. That is to say, if it be the fifth Sephirah, the name should be visualized in scarlet and vivid red flame. But if the seventh Sephirah is being considered, the name ought to be formulated as in an emerald green of surpassing brilliance and clarity.

The name having been inhaled into the lungs by means of an inspiration, it should be silently and powerfully vibrated, the entire attention being concentrated upon this to the exclusion of all else. While in the lungs, the white light of the Kether ought to be felt descending upon the name, consecrating it to the service of the higher self. Then the name should be visualized, whilst the breath is retained, as descending from the lungs via the Middle Pillar to the feet.[29] Here it should be again vibrated very powerfully. When the entire Tree of Life within is pulsating sympathetically to this vibration, the name rises rapidly once more to the lungs where once more it is subjected to a silent vibration.

The exhalation of the breath accompanies an audible vibration of the name. It also accompanies a gesture to be made which consists of two movements. The first is the placing of the left foot about six to twelve inches forward. The second is the raising of both hands to the side of the head, on a level with the eyes, and then flinging them forward as though to project a force emanating from within. As the arms are flung forward, the exhalation and powerful vibration aloud of the name takes place. This gesture is called the Projecting Sign.

The visualized name should be perceived as going forward in space until it strikes as it were against the confines of the universe. Here it gathers power, from the infinity of the void, as it were, whence it commences to surge backwards in the mind's eye upon the student.

Some seconds after the projection and audible vibration of the name the student should bring his left foot sharply back, and after dropping both hands to the side, raise the forefinger of the left hand to his lips. This is called the Protecting Sign, or sign of silence. It is the traditional gesture of the Egyptian god Harpocrates—one of the symbols employed to represent the holy child that grew from the union of the two opposites. It thus represents the growth, silent and unseen, of the Golden Flower. Whilst employing the sign of silence, the student should contrive to imagine that the name which has been projected by the first sign to the outer limits of space, surges back upon him, penetrating him through and through. His whole being should be flooded with a divine light, and a sense of ecstasy should overwhelm the mind and vision.

Standing quietly in this sign, the practitioner should meditate upon the spiritual value involved in the nature of the name he has used. There should dawn upon his mind by direct perception an understanding and a wide sympathy with that spiritual power to which he has opened himself and which now flows unimpeded through him. It is often accompanied at first by a complete blank-out of every faculty of the mind, so that for at least some seconds one is lost utterly to oneself. It seems that in that brief moment we are swung forcibly across the gulf of the abyss into another and diviner region by the vibratory momentum of the power of the name. It is a distinct recognition of, and participation in, that type of experience which has variously been called mystical and religious. It is a rare and holy event for the individual ceases, it may be for but a single instant of time, to be a man. He is caught up in a diviner sphere, and is enwrapped by the transcendental folds of the descending tongues of the spirit. For but a moment or two only— for the very nature of consciousness, with its feeble instrument the brain, is such as to be unable to endure for very long this white heat of ecstacy. And then once more the ego, dazed and stunned by so awe-inspiring and terrific an experience, recovers its equilibrium, resumes its normal function, and asserts itself once more. But the nature of that consciousness is never the same afterwards. It has changed in that an impression of higher things is left, a sense of exaltation and of expansion. It dimly understands that godhead has descended into its sphere, and that it has been raised into divinity.

It must be understood that this technique is applicable to any of the names belonging to the ten Sephiroth. And moreover, it must also be clearly understood that the vibration should be repeated several times as described, and that the three formulae of circumambulation or circulation must be employed with this Vibratory formula as they were with the Middle Pillar.

One authority on magic describes the effect thus:

> *It is a sign that the student is performing this correctly when a single vibration entirely exhausts his physical strength. It should cause him to grow hot all over or to perspire violently, and it should so weaken him that he will find it difficult to remain standing. It is a sign of success, though only by the student himself is it perceived, when he hears the Name of the God vehemently roared forth, as if by the concourse of ten thousand thunders; and it should appear to him as if that Great Voice proceeded from the Universe and not from him. In the above practice all consciousness of anything but the God-Name should be absolutely blotted out; and the longer it takes his normal perception to return, the better.*[30]

My own personal experience of this formula while confirmatory, is not quite so drastic as the above description would make out. Two or three little hints may be given to the student which may be helpful. The first of these, is with regard to breath-capacity. Shallow breathing renders the Vibratory Formula null and void, or at any rate of little value. It seems to confirm the yoga theory of a certain relationship existing between the breath and consciousness. The western system as such does not countenance or employ the yoga theory whereby the rate of breath is slowed down in order to restrain the motion of the mind. But from the physical point of view, which is valid in its own sphere, those lungs which are capable of filling to their fullest capacity, and are capable of retaining the breath for over thirty seconds, are more likely to be useful for this formula than weak and puny lungs.

Another important point is that the experiment should be performed in as nearly an empty room as possible. Or, where this is not practicable, all heavy furniture should be cleared as far from where the student stands as is compatible with the size and arrangement of the room. The reason for this is simple. The sharp pang of ecstasy, the dizziness induced by full inhalation and prolonged retention, and the enormous power which this Vibratory Formula generates are so tremendous that until the student accustoms himself to it by frequent repetition, he may find himself incapacitated for a second or two. The perspiration by the way induced by this practice is a peculiar one, being very similar in consistency and odor to that generated by Pranayama[31] of the Yoga system.

The incapacity experienced is such that he may, while lost to himself, stumble forward and fall. If, during the practice, the fall is to be encouraged, then it is as well that it should be on to a carpet or something soft. It would spoil the effect of the practice were the student to break up the induced state of consciousness by casting his eye about anxiously and with fear in order to avoid doing himself a physical injury by hitting some piece of furniture.

When the practice however has been repeated some dozen times or so, the entire psychic and physical system becomes accustomed to the severe strain imposed upon it without manifesting any sign of weakness. The student will find himself enabled to make the Sign of Silence without falling or stumbling, even though the surge of power within him may feel unbearable, and the ravishment of ecstasy too intolerable to stand. But "Wisdom says be strong. Then canst thou bear more joy. Be not animal; refine thy rapture."[32]

Repetition and becoming accustomed to the mental and spiritual phenomena induced by the formula makes the ecstasy more bearable and enables one to become strong in that spiritual joy, and capable of resisting the physical symptoms of weakness.

There are innumerable other techniques which are included under the comprehensive term magic: divination, clairvoyance, astral projection, godforms, and many others. The only matter requiring some few words here is that of ceremonial. But the principles underlying this are so simple that the student who has understood the psychological principles laid down earlier in the book will have no difficulty in understanding its function. The purpose of ceremonial is that of all magic—the awakening of the interior man, the aligning it with the consciousness and powers of the universe about him. Its method, though, seems to the novice slightly different from the others. Actually, however, its procedure is identical with the other techniques, except that it brings them down to the physical plane. That is to say, instead of performing a series of purely introverted exercises, ceremonial magic devotes itself to enacting on the physical plane a series of psychic events. That is to say, it combines, according to its own principles, the benefits of introversion with those of the extraverted temperament.

We have seen that the ten Sephiroth represent different principles in man. The former chapters have described various methods of dealing with these constituents and with bringing them into operation. Ceremonial magic would apply itself to this problem of the manifestation of interior psychological principles in this way. It would take a room or temple, and so arrange it as to represent either the Tree of Life as a whole, or some particular aspect of a portion of it. The philosophy of the diagrammatic Tree is explained in various Qabalistic works, and an understanding of that would determine the arrangement employed. Certain stations would be set up in the temple, with officers placed there to represent the activity and operation of a certain Sephirah. Thus a ceremony, if it has been arranged by individuals who were thoroughly conversant with magical principles and with the basic principles of the Tree of Life, would be a celebration in dramatic form of the powers of these ten Sephiroth.[33] The celebration of it physically, with each officer aware of the Sephirah represented and knowing how to bring the power of that Sephirah into operation either by the Vibratory Formula or by the assumption of the traditional godform ascribed to that Sephirah, will have made available an enormous amount of power. The penetration of this spiritual force into the sphere of sensation, and its reaction upon the consciousness of all present, is likely to produce a result in consciousness similar to, but much more concentrated and powerful than, the effects of the magical methods above described.

Little more need be said, but each student can work out the idea more completely. A great deal more material on the subject of ceremonial magic may be found in my *Tree of Life* and *The Golden Dawn*. But for the moment, my remarks may be limited to the above. And I must again emphasize what has been reiterated through the entire length of these pages. Ceremonial magic will avail the student nothing, and be of no practical use to him at all, until he has applied himself with great sincerity and application to the simpler practices delineated above. The Pentagram Ritual, the Qabalistic Cross and the Middle Pillar comprise the simple steps to spiritual development. It is only when these steps have been taken, and skill in their performance achieved, that he may feel it right and proper to approach that great edifice of ceremonial magic which is like a ladder, the bottom rung of which is rooted upon the earth so that all may climb quite easily. Its heights, however, are lost in the clouds of spiritual attainment where none may go until he has accomplished all that is possible here and now, and until he has integrated himself through and through. As has so often been stated here, I consider that analytical psychology must be regarded as the first part of that onward journey to the heights at the end of the distant plains. Not until the mind and the emotional system have been cleansed and unified by the cathartic process of psycho-therapy, can the full spiritual benefits of magical work be reflected into the mind of man.

Endnotes

1. This appears to be derived from a Golden Dawn formula known as the "Four Revolutions of the Breath" (see Regardie, *The Golden Dawn*, 347).

2. Once again, the term "circumambulation" is not appropriate here. It would be more accurate to describe this process as "circulation" or "circumagitation" of the light.

3. A Chinese Book of Life.

4. These sections refer to Malkuth as the physical realm, containing the four elements of fire, water, air, and earth. When Malkuth is considered as the primary Sephirah of elemental earth, these divisions represent the sub-elements (fire of earth, water of earth, air of earth, earth of earth).

5. See Part Two, Chapter Ten for a complete ritual of this sort, titled "The Tree of Life Exercise," also called "The Rite of Three Pillars."

6. Meaning "Lord, God of Knowledge."

7. From the Neophyte ceremony. See Regardie, *The Golden Dawn*, 125.

8. This name may have a Greek etymological base. Possible translation: "near Thy throne."

9. More often the divine name for Chokmah is given as *Yah*.

10. "The Herald of God."

11. According to Golden Dawn tradition, the divine name for Binah is YHVH *Elohim* (transliterated as *YHVH Alhim*). This name is also used for Daath. The archangel *Tzaphkiel* is also used for Daath.

12. "Beholder of God," or "the contemplation of God."

13. The color of Daath is usually listed as either lavender or gray-white. The Golden Dawn ascribed certain colors to the Sephiroth and the paths in each of the Four Worlds of the Qabalah. The usual colors assigned to the Sephiroth are related to the world of *Briah*, while the paths that connect them are given colors that correspond to the world of *Atziluth*. The color that Regardie suggests using for Daath here (lavender), relates it to the world of *Atziluth*. This implies that Daath as a bridge or energy conduit has more in common with the paths of the Tree than with the Sephiroth.

14. "God."

15. "Righteous of God."

16. Elohim Gibor, "God of Battles," or "Almighty God."

17. The "Severity of God." William Gray erroneously stated that the root of this name was *khab*, which meant "to suffer, to feel pain, or make war." However, prominent Golden Dawn scholar Adam P. Forrest has pieced together the true origin of this name. According to Forrest, the original Archangel of Mars was *Samael*—a name that MacGregor Mathers changed to Zamael in order to avoid confusion with the Qliphotic *Samael*. When the Qabalists began to assign Archangels to the Sephiroth, someone attributed a list of Planetary Archangels to their corresponding Sephiroth, and the martial *Samael* was naturally assigned to Geburah. At some point this list was copied into Greek. In late Greek writing, the letter Sigma (the first letter in *Samael*) came to be drawn in the shape of a "C." Still later, when the Greek list was copied into Latin, the copyist made the error of transliterating the Greek name of CAMAHL as *Camael* rather than *Samael*. Even later, someone (perhaps a member of the Golden Dawn) back-transliterated Camael as כמאל and thus was *Camael* (or *Khamael*) born. And although it originated as an error in translation, it does help magicians distinguish between Samael, Archangel of Evil, Zamael, Archangel of Mars, and *Khamael*, Archangel of Geburah.

18. Yellow.

19. YHVH Tzabaoth, "Lord of Armies."

20. This should be *Haniel*, and not be confused with Anael, the Archangel of Venus. *Haniel* means "the Grace of God," or "One who sees God."

21. Elohim Tzabaoth, "God of Armies."

22. Violet.

23. This name may have a Greek etymological base. Possible translations: "Lord of the extent of Height," "Co-brother," or "the sound of sandals."

24. The colors of Malkuth are citrine, russet, olive, and black.

25. Although Regardie's reasoning is valid, we suggest that students not mix Hebrew and Enochian here, particularly if they are unfamiliar with the Enochian system. Use the Hebrew divine and archangelic names associated with Binah as per Golden Dawn tradition.

26. This is verified by a passage in the manuscripts of the Golden Dawn, particularly a section of Z.1: The Enterer of the Threshold, The Symbolism of the Opening of the 0=0 grade of Neophyte (Regardie, *The Golden Dawn*, 346): "This is the secret traditional mode of pronouncing the Divine Names by vibration.... The Method described is called "The Vibratory Formula of the Middle Pillar."

27. The technique of vibrating a divine name while visualizing it flaming in the air is known as the *expanding whirl of vibration*.

28. That is, the transliteration of these names.

29. The technique of vibrating a divine name while visualizing it inside the heart or chest cavity is known as the *invoking whirl of vibration*.

30. Aleister Crowley, *Magic in Theory and Practice*, 379.

31. The eastern discipline of breath control. Many of the exercises in yoga are designed to extend the student's capacity to take in and process oxygen, which changes the blood's pH level. Practitioners of pranayama are said to have increased health, emotional balance, and vitality.

32. From the second chapter of Crowley's *Liber Al vel Legis*, 51.

33. See our book *Experiencing the Kabbalah* for an example of this type of dramatic ritualized presentation called "The Tree Walk."

Part Two

The Balance Between Mind and Magic

Chic Cicero
Sandra Tabatha Cicero

*A further analysis of the relationship
between psychology and magic.*

CHAPTER SIX

PSYCHOLOGY AND MAGIC

"We have more knowledge than our ancestors, but not more understanding."[1]

Israel Regardie defended the idea that analytical psychology and magic were two halves of the same coin at a time when few dared suggest such a thing. The one is incomplete without the other. In fact, a large percentage of ancient magical knowledge is being rediscovered and renamed by today's psychologists for modern times. Regardie considered self-knowledge and self-acceptance gained through analytical psychology as important preludes to the divine self-knowledge and spiritual realization attained through magic. When *The Middle Pillar* was first written, few espoused these ideas. Today, however, a growing number of psychologists are coming boldly within reach of embracing them. And many magicians are already using the jargon that psychologists considered germane to their profession only.

Today civilization looks to science to solve the major problems of humanity. In the early days when psychology was a young science, its disciples thought they were entering a time of a new renaissance when their efforts would provide "joy, zest, and richness of life" to fellow human beings—when the mental health of the average citizen would steadily improve. This did not happen. All the efforts of psychologists to understand the human mind and why we do things has not helped us put an end to violence, war,

despair, global pollution, or overpopulation—which are all problems of human thought and behavior. As one modern psychologist
admits, "There is a widespread belief that psychology has so lost
contact with real human experience that there would be no point in
asking it to solve major human problems."[2]

After Sigmund Freud and his peers arrived on the scene, the
clinical model of modern psychology methodically discarded any
notion that the human soul was spiritual in nature.[3] Why is the science of psychology incomplete without magic? Because it doesn't
go far enough—it analyzes human thought, motivation, and
behavior, but not the human soul. It is "soul-less" and sterile. You
won't find the best descriptions of the human condition in a book
on psychology. Look instead to literature, art, poetry, and in certain
passages of the world's holy books:

> It is to the literary world, not to psychological science, that you go to
> learn how to live with people, how to make love, how not to make ene-
> mies, to find out what grief does to people, or the stoicism that is possi-
> ble in the endurance of pain, or how if you're lucky you may die with
> dignity; to see how corrosive the effects of jealousy can be, or how power
> corrupts or does not corrupt. For such knowledge and such understand-
> ing of the human species, don't look in my Textbook of Psychology...try
> Lear, and Othello, and Hamlet. As a supplement to William James read
> Henry James, and Jane Austen and Mark Twain. These people are
> telling us things that are not on science's program.[4]

Not only is modern clinical psychology detached from the
humanities, it is divorced from spirituality. Throughout history,
humans have forfeited tranquility, comfort, and sometimes life itself
for spiritual motives. Spirituality is important to our health and well-
being—it is so much a part of us that trying to understand human
beings without it is like trying to study fish and omitting the fact that
they live in water. Unfortunately, many psychotherapists have done
just that, persuading themselves and their clients to believe that this
spiritual portion of them either does not exist or is irrelevant.

Psychology and spirituality should not be separate entities. It is
time to tear down the artificial walls that divide them. The various
schools of magic and their extensive teachings comprised an enormous body of wisdom that was the forerunner of modern psychology. The ancient art of magic can give back to the modern science

of psychology that which it has so unwisely neglected—a systematic practice for addressing the spiritual factor in humans, in a manner that is in accord with modern psychological principles. One of psychology's founding fathers, Carl Gustav Jung, was aware of this even if some of today's psychotherapists have forgotten it—a sign hanging above Jung's office door read: *Avocatus Atque Non-Avocatus Deus Aderit* ("whether or not he is called, God will be present").[5] Since the goal of both magic and psychotherapy is the well-being of the individual, it is only natural they become re-acquainted with one another. Contemporary psychology must transform itself to include a more holistic approach wherein the physical, psychological, and transpersonal aspects of the individual are all seen as interconnected, and humanity's need for healing, spirituality, and guidance is respected.

If psychology can be compared to a dictionary of words in a specific language (the human psyche), magic can be compared to a book of poetry that makes those words come alive with meaning and relevance in our lives (psychological/spiritual evolution).

Now that we have reprimanded modern psychology for its shortcomings, we can explore some of the monumental contributions it has made to the understanding of the human mind. From there we will explore how psychotherapy and magic can come together to the meaningful enrichment of both and, more importantly, for the benefit and welfare of the individual.

Psychotherapy

Psychotherapy is the treatment of mental disorders with methods that revolve around the interpersonal relationship between therapist and client. A large portion of this entails helping clients explore their own ideas about themselves. The earliest form of psychotherapy, called *psychoanalysis*, began with Austrian psychologist Sigmund Freud (1856–1939). Freud discovered that the corporeal symptoms of patients suffering from hysteria often disappeared after seemingly forgotten material was brought into the realm of consciousness. From this Freud conjectured one of the most fundamental theories of modern psychology—that within the human psyche there exists a powerful segment known as the *unconscious* which influences all of our actions, yet functions with material or content that cannot be recalled or remembered by normal processes. He regarded the unconscious as a extensive portion of the mind that housed instinctual drives and the forgotten residue of unwanted life experiences or thoughts. Freud named this "forgetting" (or the prevention of undesired ideas from entering the conscious mind) *repression*. Repression is one of a number of defense mechanisms:[6] unconscious reactions employed to satisfy emotional needs, balance opposing objectives, decrease anxiety resulting from unwanted thoughts, or change reality to make it more bearable. The cornerstone of Freud's psychoanalytic therapy was the conscious recollection or recognition of repressed memories and experiences. The basic tools of this therapy were free association[7] and dream interpretation.

In recent years other forms of psychotherapy, including behavior therapy, hypnotherapy, and group therapy, have become popular. In many cases psychotherapy is not only employed for the treatment of mental disorders, but for less severe problems. Therapists often assist people in breaking unwanted or compulsive habits (smoking, overeating, etc.).

Freud's Triad of the Psyche

Freud developed the theory that the conscious mind is only a small part of our mental composition, and our motivations are caused, for the most part, by factors that we are unaware of. Freud postulated that psyche is divided into three distinct factions: the *id*, the *ego* and the *super-ego*. According to Freud, the id is the division of the psyche that is completely unconscious and functions as the origin of instinctual impulses and demands for instant satisfaction of primal needs. It is the reservoir of unconscious drives, ruled by the pleasure principle and instant gratification. The *ego* is that portion of the psyche which is conscious, most directly governs thought and behavior, and is most concerned with outer reality. The ego mediates between the id, the super-ego, and the stipulations of reality or society. The *super-ego*, primarily unconscious, is that which is created by the internalization of moral standards from parents and society—it is the conscience and the ego ideal—a moralizing faculty which monitors and censors the ego. Because of society, parental guidance, and peer pressure, humans experience a process of repression from the day of birth. Thus the id and the super-ego are usually in conflict in most people, since as Freud thought, repression was necessary in order for humanity to live within the bounds of civilization.

Human beings, according to Freud, are motivated by vital animal instincts—primarily the sexual drive which he called the libido. Other principal elements of psychology uncovered by Freud were the ideas of the Oedipus complex and infantile sexuality.[8]

Freud's tools for exploring the human psyche included hypnosis, dream analysis, and a new technique that he termed "free association." The goal of Freudian analysis was to release repressed memories and provide an increase in self-knowledge that would release trapped energies and result in a more satisfying existence for the patient.

Jung and Spiritual Psychology

The works of Swiss psychologist C. G. Jung (1875–1961) can be seen as part of the apex of the occult revival of the late nineteenth century. Using the new vocabulary employed by Sigmund Freud, Jung described that knowledge of the human psyche which mystics and magicians had gathered since ancient times. What had once been veiled in occult jargon and symbolism, and thus viewed as superstition and nonsense by the public at large, was now for the first time expressed in such a manner that psychologists and other intellectuals sat up and took notice. Jung's exploration of psychology in conjunction with his study of the paranormal made his theories the crucial link between psychology and magic. However, his interest in occult matters was one of the primary reasons for his ultimate break with Freud.

The difference between Freud's and Jung's approaches to psychology was primarily Jung's view that the human psyche was a whole organism and Freud's belief that it was not. Freud extrapolated a rather disorderly picture of the psyche wherein autonomous components of the mind battled for dominance. Jung saw the psyche as being complete in itself from birth, the various elements of the psyche attempted to work harmoniously together, and their natural inclination was toward unity. While both men recognized two basic halves of the psyche (conscious and unconscious), Jung further divided the unconscious into two levels—personal and collective. In addition, Freud was more concerned with his patient's past, while Jung emphasized the patient's future development.

Whereas Freud referred to his method as *psychoanalysis*, Jung preferred the phrase *analytical psychology*.

Heilsweg

The psychology which Jung very gradually developed was described by him as *Heilsweg*, a German word which meant "sacred way" and a "method of healing." Jung's idea of the psyche was based on a separation between the *conscious* and the *unconscious*—the personal unconscious being a small tributary of the greater river of the *collective unconscious*. The pilgrimage of the "self" symbolized the bringing of unconscious content into the light of consciousness. Heilsweg was a method for differentiating the self from the collective unconscious that was the blueprint of individual existence. It was a way of *individuation* or the process by which a person becomes self-realized—a separate indivisible unity or "whole" which contains all aspects of the self. This was a radical departure from Freud's view that people are enslaved to the drives of the id and super-ego which pressure them into conforming with society-sanctioned patterns of behavior. According to Jung, the ego's formation of an identity was not only the beginning of true "personhood" but also the commencement of a natural polarity between the general and the specific.

Several stages marked the process of Heilsweg or individuation. The first stage was the confrontation with the *shadow*—those unconscious aspects of the self which have been buried or ignored by the conscious mind. This begins with the dissolution of the false self, the mask, or the outer persona.

> The persona is a complicated system of relations between individual consciousness and society, fittingly enough a kind of mask, designed on the one hand to make a definite impression upon others, and, on the other, to conceal the true nature of the individual.[9]

Next, the individual encounters his "soul image," the *anima* or the *animus*. The final step is the manifestation in dreams, visions, or fantasies of appropriate archetypes—primordial images such as the wise old man, or the Great Mother, images that appear as themes in religion, mythology, and folklore.

The process of individuation contains many particular aspects which collectively might be termed "outer psychology." This category includes Jung's separation of introverted and extroverted personality types as well as his organization of types in accordance with their conjunction of the faculties of sensing, thinking, feeling, and intuition.

All of Jung's ideas were of vital importance to modern understanding of the human psyche. However, the most notable contribution of Jungian psychology was the concept that individuation was a *spiritual excursion* and it is highly significant that this pioneer of psychology phrased his ideas in spiritual terms. Thus it is no surprise to find that Jung's system complements the mystical Qabalah in so many ways.

The Nature of the Psyche

Jung's definition of the *psyche* included not only that which we call the soul but also the intellect, the spirit, and the totality of all psychic processes. The psyche is as real as the body is real—all psychic phenomena are real, since the psyche is indistinguishable from its manifestations. The psyche expresses itself in images that are full of meaning and purpose—it creates reality every day. It has its own peculiar structure and form.

> For the psyche as it presents itself—as it is experienced by us—is inseparable from our physical being. But this by no means implies a biological 'dependency.' The psyche deserves to be taken as a phenomenon in its own right; there are no grounds at all for regarding it as a mere epiphenmenon, dependent though it may be on the functioning of the brain. One would be as little justified in regarding life as an epiphenomenon of the chemistry of carbon compounds.[10]

The psyche consists of many parts, but there are two primary divisions that are interrelated—consciousness and unconsciousness.

Unconsciousness

The unconscious is not simply the absence of consciousness. It is that division of the mind containing elements of psychic makeup, such as memories or repressed desires, that are not subject to conscious perception or control but that often affect conscious thoughts and behavior. The *personal unconscious* is that unknown part of the individual human mind that is older than the conscious part of the mind. It is the primal portion from which consciousness arises. This unconscious (equivalent to Freud's super-ego) is unique to the individual, and it contains suppressed, forgotten, or subliminally perceived contents originating from a person's life. Whereas the mind can be trained, the unconscious cannot. It is a creative and autonomous psychic entity that is beyond subjective control.

Jung concluded that the *collective unconscious* does not include personal characteristics distinctive to one's individual ego but rather the sum of what is inherited from the biological and psychic structure common to the human race. They are those acts and mental patterns that are universally shared by all humanity. The primordial images of the collective unconscious are the result of thousands of years of human struggle and experience.

> *Every great experience in life, every profound conflict, evokes the accumulated treasure of these images and brings about their inner constellation. But they become accessible to consciousness only when the individual possesses so much self-awareness and power of understanding that he also reflects on what he experiences instead of just living it blindly. In the later event he actually lives the myth and the symbol without knowing it.*[11]

Consciousness

Consciousness is that component of waking awareness perceptible to a person at any given instant. It is a state of being mentally awake and observant, of having an awareness of one's environment and one's own existence, sensations, and thoughts. Consciousness is therefore the function which sustains the relationship between psychic content and the ego. Many mistake consciousness with mere "thinking," when consciousness actually includes feeling, will, fantasy, and all other facets of waking life. Sentience is one of humanity's defining attributes as stated by Jung: "Man's capacity for consciousness alone makes him man."[12] Elsewhere Jung states:

> *And yet the attainment of consciousness was the most precious fruit of the tree of knowledge, the magical weapon which gave man victory over the earth, and which we hope will give him a still greater victory over himself.*[13]

Jung believed that the most important objective for any individual was the attainment of harmony between the two halves of the psyche, the conscious and the unconscious. In this manner, man would achieve the "greater victory over himself" (see Figure 5, p. 112).

The Shadow

> *If the repressed tendencies, the shadow as I call them, were obviously evil, there would be no problem whatever. But the shadow is merely somewhat inferior, primitive, unadapted, and awkward; not wholly bad. It even contains childish or primitive qualities which would in a way vitalize and embellish human existence.*[14]

The shadow represents the sum of all personal and collective psychic elements which, due to their incompatibility with the selected conscious demeanor, are refused expression in life and consequently unite into a somewhat independent splinter personality (a type of alter-ego) whose unconscious inclinations run opposite those of the conscious. It is our "dark brother" who is a hidden but undeniable part of our total psyche. The development of the shadow coincides with that of the ego—aspects that the ego rejects are repressed and have little or no outlet in a person's conscious life. The shadow often behaves to counterbalance the conscious—which can be positive or negative.[15]

Very much an archetypal figure, the shadow personality often appears symbolically in dreams as being the same sex as the dreamer. In addition, an individual will sometimes project his shadow, i.e., his own unwanted subconscious characteristics, onto another person.

In keeping with his views on the unconscious, Jung proposed that there are actually two forms of the shadow, the *personal shadow*, composed of the individual's cast-off psychic content, and

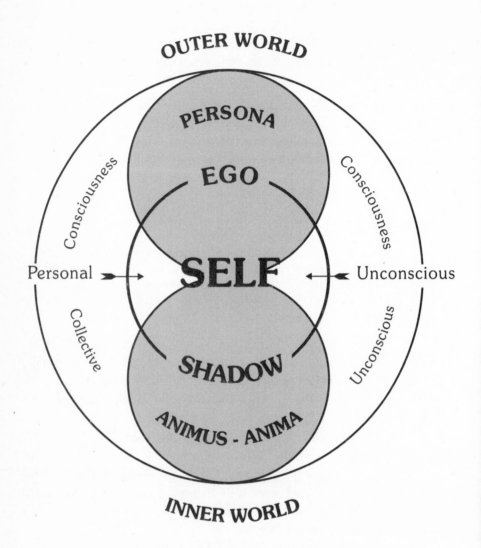

Figure 5: Jung's Model of the Psyche.

the *collective shadow*, which embodies all the collective repressed memories of humankind.

Confronting the Shadow

Everyone carries a shadow, and the less it is embodied in the individual's consciousness life, the blacker and denser it is. If an inferiority is conscious, one always has a chance to correct it. Furthermore, it is constantly in contact with other interests, so that it is continually subjected to modifications. But if it is repressed and isolated from consciousness, it never gets corrected.[16]

Throughout our lives, we are constantly having to suppress one attribute or another. Thus the shadow can never completely be assimilated into consciousness. However, it is essential that the most conspicuous aspects of the shadow be raised to consciousness. Instead of rejecting the shadow, its counterpart, the ego will be invigorated by it.

If the shadow is not reckoned with, it runs the risk of becoming a vast dark forgotten expanse which blocks one's inner creativity from being fully available to the conscious mind. This is why some people strive with Herculean strain to keep a tight lid on their shadows, concealing their private "demons" with a thin veneer of moral perfection. The spiritual fortress they construct around themselves is nothing more than a synthetic buttress held in place by force and ever in danger of structural failure should the wind change direction. "Mere suppression of the shadow is as little of a remedy as beheading would be for a headache."[17]

It is for this reason that confronting the shadow is the first step in Jung's method of individuation. To do this means taking a starkly critical and objective look into the nature of one's own being. Unconscious content is usually experienced in projection upon something that is outside of us. In the case of unwanted psychic content, some people will readily project their shadow onto someone else. Thus, we have a tendency to shift the blame onto an appropriate scapegoat— "the other guy did it," or as a comedian once insisted, "the Devil made me do it!" It is extremely difficult for some analysands to accept the fact that they do indeed have a deep, dark side. The therapist, who tries to bring the shadow out into the open, often meets with enormous resistance because the client fears that the artificial structure he has carefully constructed to protect his ego will come crashing down. This is in fact the point at which many analyses fail and the client, incapable of facing his unconscious self, stops the process cold and withdraws into his comfortable old self-deceptions.

All of us must face our shadow side. This is especially important for magicians who seek to delve into the inner recesses of the human psyche—the mind of the microcosm. No spiritual progress can be made without it. We must discover the distinct characteristics of our shadow (as opposed to other parts of the psyche such as the ego), and recognize it for what it is—a natural part of ourselves and nothing to be ashamed of or feel guilty about. Guilt and shame often cause one to repress the shadow in the first place, allowing a small undesirable trait to grow into a huge unresolved conflict, compulsion, or neurosis. In some ways, the shadow is like a neglected and resentful child who, if shown kindness and understanding, can learn to play with the other children. Objective understanding of ourselves will make it easier to face the shadow and other parts of the psyche as well.

REGRESSION EXERCISE

Examining the events of one's childhood is a prerequisite for determining how the shadow developed. An excellent method for recalling childhood memories is the following Regression Exercise:[18]

Perform the LBRP. Perform the four-fold breath. (Breathe in the count of four. Hold the breath to the count of four. Exhale to the count of four. Keep the lungs empty to the count of four.)

Sit in a comfortable position or lie down, eyes closed. Spend a few minutes inducing relaxation and rhythmic breathing. Visualize yourself within your present surroundings.

As you continue the four-fold breath, see yourself going backwards in time. As you inhale to the count of four, think of last spring. Hold the breath for four counts and think of last winter. Exhale to the count of four and imagine last fall. On the empty hold to the count of four, think of last summer. Continue the exercise in this fashion going backwards into time, from spring to winter, fall, and summer, ever backwards, keeping pace with the four-fold breath.

You may decide to go back in time in five-year intervals: five years, ten years, fifteen years, twenty years, etc. At any one of these intervals, stop and visualize yourself at that particular point in time. Observe how you looked, how your surroundings looked, the people around you at that time, how you felt about yourself, and how you saw your world. Examine significant events that occurred which shaped your view of the world and of yourself.

When ready to end the exercise, use the four-fold breath to visualize time moving forward again. (Inhale—spring, full hold—summer, exhale—fall, empty hold—winter.) Move time forward again until you arrive at the present. End the exercise with the LBRP. Always record your observations.

You should practice this exercise several times, deciding before-hand what time in the past you wish to examine further. If you become quite proficient in this technique, you can go back one year at a time, all the way back to birth.

∼

TRAUMA RELEASE EXERCISE

Sometimes traumatic experiences or memories are responsible for creating parts of the shadow personality. In such cases, a trauma release exercise can help the analysand "let go" of the calamitous experience and begin to heal. The technique for this is as follows:

Have the person lie on their back. Place your right hand on their forehead, and your left hand at the back of their head. (A breathing technique to further relaxation is helpful at this point.)

Next, guide the person to slowly visualize the traumatic event in the reverse order it happened, to a time before it occurred. In other words, emphasize that the details of the event will look like a video tape running in reverse and in slow motion.

Then have the person run this mental tape in its natural order, forward in time, until arriving at the initial point when the event began.

Guide the person to repeat this backward and forward motion until they no longer feel an emotional connection to the event.

At the close of the session, have the person take a long deep breath as they reflect upon any stress or concerns, hold the breath for a few seconds, and then release it, letting go of any residual tensions. Repeat this three times.

(It is usually recommended that the person do this exercise a number of times on their own over a period of a few weeks to be certain that it is effective. It can also be done entirely solo if preferred.)

~

Anima and Animus

The second step in the process of individuation is defined by the encounter with the animus or the anima. The *anima* is the embodiment of the reflective feminine nature of man's subconscious, while the *animus* is the personification of the creative masculine nature of a woman's subconscious. Both are "soul images" which usually manifest themselves in anthropomorphic form as "fantasy lovers" in dream and imagination. Animus and anima have a direct relationship with the persona or mask—if the persona is emotional, the soul image is rational, and vice versa. They are two of the most important archetypes, often influencing how we respond to members of the opposite sex. People often search out, and are attracted to, someone who symbolizes the attributes of their own psyche.

> *Every man carries within him the eternal image of woman, not the image of this or that particular woman, but a definitive feminine image. This image is fundamentally unconscious, an hereditary factor of primordial origin engraved in the living organic system of the man, an imprint or "archetype" of all the ancestral experiences of the female, a deposit, as it were, of all the impressions ever made by woman.... Since this image is unconscious, it is always unconsciously projected upon the person of the beloved, and is one of the chief reasons for passionate attraction or aversion.*[19]

We must learn to discriminate between interior and exterior manifestation of the anima and animus, just as we must distinguish ourselves from our shadow. Whereas the conscious recognition of the shadow brings forth the knowledge of one's own dark side as it relates to a person's own sex, so does the recognition of the animus or anima provide the means for understanding the contrasexual portion of the psyche. It is precisely this lack of discrimination that leads a person to repeatedly seek out a certain kind of mate—a "bad boy" or "nasty girl" type who will inevitably treat them poorly. This is exactly how some individuals, in failing to differentiate between their own soul image (and secret inner desires) and a prospective mate, project the inner image outward and consequently fall into bad relationships time and time again. Sometimes the animus and anima can be symbolized by parental figures, leading some people to try to find a companion who resembles their father or mother in some way. While attempting to find "the perfect mate," externalization of the soul image leads some to look outside of themselves for the perfection and beauty that lies within. This is true for most people who choose a mate who represents the subconscious portion of the psyche. And since no human mate can fit perfectly into the transferred image, after time the carrier of the projection displays his or her own character traits, resulting in frustration and discord in the relationship. If a person could only recognize the soul image within as a part of their own inner self, they would stop attributing their flaws to their mate and retract the projection. Any psychic energy that has been bound up in the projection would be freed for other, more progressive pursuits.

The encounter with the soul image usually takes place later in life, after the dynamics of youth, reproduction, and the priorities of the outer world have been satiated. Confronting the soul image is an indication that the second half of one's life has commenced. Once the contrasexual soul image has been brought to consciousness, however, it may not be possible to "lose ourselves completely" in the love of another, for we have now found the object of that love within us. This brings with it the realization that we are in fact complete within ourselves, and we do not need a slavish love to a projected illusion in order to prop us up. Instead we are enabled to develop a deeper love and a conscious devotion to our partner.

The proper role of the soul image is that of the *psychopomp*, guiding the soul around impasses on its way toward spiritual transformation. It is the mediator between the conscious and the unconscious. Whereas the persona is the reconciler between the ego and the outer world, the soul image is the reconciler between the ego and inner world. Once fully realized and integrated, the soul image can bring incredible enrichment into consciousness and a vital expansion of the true self.

Archetypes

The third step in the process of individuation is the manifestation of archetypes. An archetype is an idea, mode of thought, or god-form that has manifested from the inherited experiences of humankind—from the collective unconscious.

> The concept of the archetype…is derived from the repeated observation that, for instance, the myths and fairytales of world literature contain definite motifs which crop up everywhere. We meet these same motifs in the fantasies, dreams, deliria, and delusions of individuals living today. These typical images and associations are what I call archetypal ideas. The more vivid they are, the more they will be coloured by particularly strong feeling-tones…They impress, influence, and fascinate us. They have their origin in the archetype, which in itself is an irrepresentable, unconscious, pre-existent form that seems to be part of the inherited structure of the psyche and can therefore manifest itself spontaneously anywhere, at any time.[20]

According to Jung, once the soul image has been integrated, next comes the manifestation of the major archetypes of spirit and matter. These include the "wise old man" as the spirit principle in man, and the "great mother" as the principle of matter (or nature) in woman. Here we are dealing with the primal roots of the psyche of either sex back to its origins, and the ancient god-forms from which they derive. Both the "wise old man" and the "great mother" can appear in a multitude of figures from all world mythologies. They are the sky gods, earth mothers, heroes, heroines, magicians, priests, priestesses, prophetesses, harvest gods, and fertility goddesses of all pantheons. These ancient archetypes are transcendent energies that can bring much wisdom and spiritual growth.

Jung referred to archetypal figures of the psyche as *"mana*[21] personalities."* This is a particular archetype or group of archetypes that the individual psyche most strongly expresses or manifests. A person who has mana is said to have power and influence over others, but also runs the risk of becoming self-centered and mega-lomaniacal. This is because these great universal archetypes produce a potent attraction which can in some instances entice the individual into identifying him or herself with the archetype, creating a type of self-aggrandizement or ego-inflation. Such is the path of many modern-day messiahs, self-appointed gurus, and power-mad spiritual leaders.

> *An inflated consciousness is always egocentric and conscious of nothing but its own existence. It is incapable of learning from the past, incapable of understanding contemporary events, and incapable of drawing right conclusions about future. It is hypnotized by itself and therefore cannot be argued with. It inevitably dooms itself to calamities that must strike it dead.*[22]

All of us surrender to such arrogance during this process of individuation, however, the creative energies that are stimulated in the psyche by the appearance of archetypes can be fully accessed only after one has *humbly* acquired the ability to discern the difference between him or her self and *them*. On the road to self-growth, we must not mistake personal insights into our own inner workings as messages from God to his new chosen prophet. We must work to clarify our relationship to spirit and nature as represented by the gods/archetypes. These potent and eternal forces are a part our our psyche that are meant to empower and inspire us. Magicians regard archetypes as various forms or images of divinity that teach us about ourselves and our place in the divine universe. The conscious recognition of the psychic elements that comprise the mana person-ality archetype brings the first real sense of authentic individuality.

Accessing Archetypes

Although textbooks on psychology provide few examples of arche-types for the reader to explore, various textbooks on magic are often replete with such prototype figures. Many are readily found in the cards of the tarot. Meditation on these images, as well as a host of tarot exercises that can be found in such books as Madonna Compton's *Archetypes on the Tree of Life*, Gareth Knight's *Tarot and Magic*, Paul Foster Case's *Book of Tokens*, or our own book *The New Golden Dawn Ritual Tarot*, can be used to identify and connect with various archetypes that inhabit the psyche.

Several archetypes, in the form of gods and goddesses, are correlated to the spheres on the Tree of Life, according to their nature and characteristics. War and fire gods are assigned to Geburah, goddesses of love and pleasure to Netzach, etc. A small selection of deities from several pantheons are listed in Chapter Ten. Meditation on these figures can aid in understanding the archetypal beings that one may encounter in the process toward true self-awareness.

It is important that the student not fall into the trap of the *psychologization of magic*[23] that is a result of misunderstanding Jung's theories. To the pop "psycholo-occultist" the archetypes, deities, and symbols are simply creations of the human mind—they have no existence beyond the individual human being. Pop psychology sometimes gives the impression that humans create, work with, and discard archetypes as easily as an old pair of shoes, in a kind of superficial mental role-playing game. This view does not do Jung's theory justice, since *archetypes exist eternally and independently* of any individual. To truly understand this, one must be willing to accept the spiritual (magical) side of human existence—we are part of a cosmic ecosystem, so to speak.

Self-Realization

Throughout the process of individualization, unconscious content has been gradually raised into consciousness. Combined with the dissolution of the persona and the decrease in the sovereign power of the conscious mind, this new awareness brings with it a state of psychic imbalance. Magicians refer to this time as "the dark night of the soul." This intentionally created imbalance works to remove any mental impediments which stand in the way of further psychic growth. If the conscious mind is able to absorb and develop the psychic content emerging from the subconscious, then this state of balance induces the independent, intuitive activity of the unconscious to create a new equilibrium and the result, as Jung put it, is "the victory over the collective psyche." Then and only then is the median between the conscious and the unconscious to be found. This is the archetypal image of the *self*, and *self-realization* is the final step on the path of individuation.

The emergence of the self is a transformation of the psyche which involves a whole new outlook toward life. This is no easy process. Primal impulses from the subconscious will still assail us, but no longer will we totally identify ourselves with them, or flee from them. We must do our best to understand them, and we should not let the resulting tension between the waking consciousness and the unconscious process disturb our daily routine in any way. Our ability to withstand this tension and persevere through a state of psychic imbalance is what will lead us to a new psychic equipoise.

Consciousness and unconsciousness complement each other to form the greater principle of the self. Not only is the self at the center of these two halves of the psyche, it is also the circumference which surrounds them. According to Jung, the only content of the self that we can know is the individuated ego. Endeavoring to know more, we run into the boundaries of our own knowledge. The self is transcendental. It can only be felt and experienced— never wholly understood by the rational mind.

> It 'is strange to us and yet so near, wholly ourselves and yet unknowable, a virtual center of mysterious constitution…. The beginnings of our whole psychic life seem to be inextricably rooted in this point, and all our highest and ultimate purposes seem to be striving toward it. This paradox is unavoidable, as always when we try to define something that lies beyond the bourn of our understanding….'[24]

It is obvious that Jung is bordering on the mystical here. Jungian psychology differs from other systems in that it presents ethical objectives that have much in common with magical goals. The discovery of the self might well be described as the completion of the Great Work, or the creation of the Philosophers' Stone. The expansion of consciousness, through the elevation of heretofore unconscious material, is a form of spiritual illumination. This does not mean that the individual who experiences illumination or self-realization will spend the rest of his days in blissful meditation, but rather that he will *gradually* gain a more true understanding of himself and his connection to the divine.

The goal of Jungian psychology is the creation of psychic wholeness. It is not by any stretch of the imagination limited to the treatment of mental illness. Treatment today is often sought out to cure a feeling of pointlessness or to find new purpose and direction in life. As we approach the twenty-first century, humanity is besieged by a collective neurosis and spiritual erosion. But the cure will not be found in adherence to rigid church dogmas or cold, detached methods of psychology. Countering the disorientation of modern humanity will require a combination of spiritual awareness, mystical experience, fundamental ethics, and sound psychotherapies. A method for self-realization which encompasses magic and psychology, such as the Middle Pillar exercise, is part of the answer.

The Symbol of Unity

The psyche that has received the benefits of self-realization is expressed in a glyph called the *uniting symbol*. This is a symbol which portrays the union of all parts of the psyche, yet its synthesis transcends all of its separate components. It represents the restored equilibrium between the conscious and the unconscious. The uniting symbol portrays a balanced psychological state that we wish to achieve. In Eastern societies, the uniting symbol often takes the form of a drawing called a *mandala*, or "magic circle," said to be a balanced glyph of the cosmos. The most important uniting symbol in the West is the Qabalistic Tree of Life.

Reich and His Theories

Wilhelm Reich (1897–1957) studied medicine and Freudian analysis at Vienna University. He spent two years doing postgraduate work under Professor Wagner-Jauregg. It was during this time that he formulated two of his most recognized theories. The first was the concept of "physiological armoring"—muscular tension or physical rigidity that had the same effect as a neurosis, that is, it serves as a mechanism for the repression of unwanted psychic content. The second is the idea that *schizophrenia* is a "bottling up" of energy within the autonomic nervous system.

Reich believed that psychic problems caused muscular tension and any successful therapy had to treat both sides of the disturbance—mind *and* body. His remedy was to develop a psycho-analytical treatment combined with deep, often painful, massage which would break down the physical armament, and in turn liberate the psyche from the neurosis.[25] This represented an assault on the psychic problem by using physical manipulation. He called his method of treatment *vegetotherapy*, or as it is sometimes known as "non-verbal psychotherapy." The goal of this treatment was not simply to relax the muscles, but to bypass all verbal or intellectual defense mechanisms, to reconnect the exterior ego with the interior reality, and release that material which was being repressed.

In 1936 Reich began a series of experiments that resulted in his theory of *orgone* energy. This was a type of life force energy that Reich thought was vital to good health and which permeated all life. Some have compared it to the "astral light" of ceremonial magicians. Reich thought that muscular tension blocked the free flow of orgone energy in human beings—and that his vegetotherapy liberated the flow of orgone.

His research got him into trouble, both in Nazi Germany and later in the U.S. where he built a machine that was said to extract orgone from the atmosphere and project it into the human body. Nevertheless, the theories of Reich are thought by many people to be an important conjunction between psychotherapy and magic.

Transpersonal Psychology

Coinciding with an interest in magic, today there is also increased attention being paid to transpersonal or depth psychology, a trend initiated by Jung and and further examined by psychologists such as Roberto Assagioli (1888–1975). The word *transpersonal* means that which transcends the personal or the individual. Transpersonal psychology takes a more spiritual approach to the human dilemma, and does not reject the idea of the soul—rather, it embraces it. A true system of transpersonal psychology must examine the highest aspects of the unconscious and take a philosophical as well as pragmatic approach to human evolution.

Seeing that psychoanalysis was an incomplete system, Assagioli developed his own form of therapy and called it *psychosynthesis*. Psychosynthesis accepts the idea of the soul, the libido, and the imagination as essential aspects of the human being. It also includes the use of symbolism and allegory to initiate alchemical change and psychic integration.

> *May I emphasize the fact that the elements and functions, coming from the superconscious, such as aesthetic, ethical, religious experiences, intuition, inspiration, states of mystical consciousness, are factual, are real in the pragmatic sense...because they are effective...producing changes both in the inner and the outer world. Therefore they are amenable to observation and experimentation, through the use of the scientific method in ways suited to their nature; also they can be influenced and utilized through psycho-spiritual techniques.*[26]

Assagioli defined the parts of the psyche (see Figure 6, p. 126) as:

1. The *Collective Unconscious*, a surrounding psychic "membrane" which permits constant and active interchange between all parts of the psyche and with the general psychic environment. It is the common primordial symbols, images, and metaphors of all humanity—the part of the soul that is shared. Archetypes of the collective unconscious include extremely primordial god images such as the Mesopotamian Apsu and the Greek Chaos.

2. The *Higher Self*[27] or the true transpersonal self which is above and is unaffected by the thoughts from the mind-stream or the sensations of the body. It is that pure consciousness, the core of the self, that underlies all other aspects and functions of the psyche as well. All personal energy and consciousness issues from this source. Archetypes of the higher self include omnipotent sky gods such as the Babylonian Marduk, the Greek Zeus, and the Hebrew Yahweh.

3. The *Conscious Self* or "I" is the ego or point of self-awareness. It is the seat of personal identity that we organize our field of

awareness around. Its function is to coordinate the vast amount of interior and exterior information that we acquire and to act as an intermediary between our internal and external realities. Experience is processed by the ego through various functions such as the emotions, the senses, the intellect, and the imagination. To carry out these duties, the ego relies on discrimination, reason, and certain defense mechanisms that often conflict with other aspects of the psyche, sometimes posing obstacles to growth and healing. Archetypes of the ego include all deities who have "walked between the worlds" of life and death (conscious and subconscious), such as the Sumerian Inanna and the Egyptian Osiris.

4. The *Field of Consciousness*, which contains the ego, is the incessant flow of observable images, feelings, thoughts, sensations, and impulses. Archetypes of this region include several groups of deities with a variety of attributions: wisdom (Enki, Thoth, Hermes); love (Hathor, Aphrodite); war (Horus, Ares); pleasure (Bes, Pan); etc.

5. The *Higher Unconscious* or *Superconscious* is the transpersonal level of the unconscious—containing higher intuitions, inspirations, latent psychic functions, and spiritual energies. It is here that the higher self expresses itself in various forms through archetypes. The ordinary person is usually unaware of these forces and archetypes until they are brought to light during the process of self-realization. Archetypes of the superconscious include the first gods of a pantheon, such as the Greek Titans or the Norse Giants.

6. The *Middle Unconscious* is an inner region similar and accessible to that of the waking consciousness. This contains all things in our field of awareness that we are not normally aware of, but that we can become aware of. It is an unconscious matrix that underlies the conscious mind where the mental activities are "incubated" before their birth into consciousness. Archetypes of the middle unconscious include all deities who are associated with prophecy and oracles, such as the Greek divinities Apollo and Gaea.

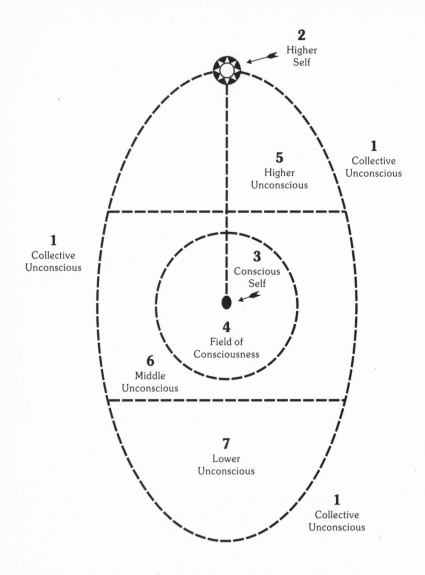

Figure 6: Assagioli's Model of the Psyche.

7. The *Lower Unconscious* contains fundamental drives, primitive urges, inferior dreams, and complexes. This is the personal unconscious which is the storehouse of hidden memories, repressed psychic content, and the shadow personality. This part of the psyche is accessed by working with hypnosis, trance, and imagery. Archetypes of the lower unconscious include all underworld deities, such as the Sumerian goddess Ereshkigal and the Greek divinities Hades and Persephone.

If we were to add anything to Assagioli's model it would be the body, or manifest psyche, which must be considered in a holistic psychology. Mind and body are interrelated extensions of one another. Just as physical discomfort can affect the mind, the mind, through focused visualization, can affect the body. Archetypes of the manifest psyche include all earth deities, such as the Egyptian Geb, the Babylonian Ninhursag, and the Greek Demeter.

Assagioli's division of the psyche is remarkably similar to the Qabalistic model of the soul. Like Jung, he saw the pressing need for all human beings to achieve a balanced inner integration and true self-realization, and he outlined a system for achieving this goal in four stages:

1. *Thorough knowledge of one's personality.* This includes a frank analysis of all parts of the psyche, both conscious and unconscious, including the shadow. Psychoanalysis is the method used by the therapist for this objective. (In magic and alchemy it is the first half of the equation *solve et coagula*—dissolve and coagulate.)

2. *Control of the personality's various elements.* After having discovered all parts of the psyche, we must take control of them. According to Assagioli, one of the most effective ways of achieving this is a method called disidentification,[28] which aids in the dissolution of harmful complexes whose newly freed energies can be controlled and used toward more positive ends. Dispelling these complexes requires the methods of objectification, critical analysis, and discrimination. (In magic, the shadow aspects of the psyche are collectively called the

evil persona—they must be recognized, subjugated to the magician's higher spiritual will, and their energies transmuted and employed for the completion of the Great Work.)

3. *Realization of one's true self: the discovery or creation of a unifying center.* The intermediate link which, if focused on and identified with, allows for the integration/unification of the lower and higher selves, and freedom from selfish interests and personal limitations. A point of connection between the individual and the divine self, which is reflected and symbolized in that point.[29]

4. *Psychosynthesis: the formation or reconstruction of the personality around the new center.* Once the unifying center is found, the next step is to gradually and systematically build a new "ideal" personality around it in an organized, purposeful manner and with clear, achievable goals in mind.[30]

Practical psychosynthesis commences with the construction of this new personality. This process involves the active utilization of all available energies and the transmutation of unconscious and previously latent forces—development of those aspects of the personality which are weak or insufficient. It is accomplished through techniques of auto-suggestion, affirmation, visualization, and by the systematic training of the less developed functions of imagination, will, and memory. Finally, all the various psychological energies and functions must be coordinated as the new personality achieves a stable organized form.

There are many levels in this process of transmutation and self-realization, and as stated earlier, they are not always entirely pleasant. It is a multi-faceted process which includes several stages—the elimination of impediments which block the flow of energies between the superconscious and the lower realms of consciousness, evolvement of latent or dormant higher functions (memory, will, imagination, etc.), and stages where the ego must yield to the work of the higher self and withstand the stresses and unavoidable discomfiture that the process requires.

In magic, this is the spiritual discipline of the Great Work and reunification—the second half of the *solve et coagula* formula of alchemy. It represents our goal to "become more than human," or in less mystical terms, to become the best possible human being we can be, evolving to our fullest potential.

Various methods and tools are employed in psychosynthesis, just as they are in other transpersonal psychologies. In psychosynthesis, the focus is always on a holistic approach to treatment, and all techniques used are subservient to the health, well-being, and psychic integration of the individual. The keeping of a diary, dream analysis, free association, hypnosis, group analysis, psychodrama, relaxation, meditation, music therapy, autosuggestion, humor therapy, chromotherapy, disidentification, visualization, development of the will, utilization of the symbols and metaphors, transmutation and sublimation of sexual energies, and development of the imagination are but a few of the methods used to obtain self-realization.

One of the goals of psychosynthesis is to integrate the superconscious, as much as possible, into the conscious and unconscious realms. Numerous metaphors for this process of self-realization and self-integration can be found in the language of the alchemists. What spiritual alchemy describes as the transformation of lead into gold is simply another way of describing the transmutation of the mundane into the spiritual, discord into harmony, and the personal into the transcendent.

Imagination and the Transconscious Self

With the lines between psychology and magic becoming increasingly transparent, we arrive at a new more transcendent interpretation of consciousness. The connecting link between all parts of the self is the *transconscious self*.[31] Composed for the most part of the processes of imagination, intuition, and will, the transconscious is a reconciling intelligence with a unique nature. It has the ability to move through, communicate with, and cause change on all levels of the psyche, and it is capable of a wide range of powers associated with communication and transformation. The imagination is the essential aspect of the transconscious self. It is a potent medium for the processes of inspiration, transmutation, integration, and transcendence. The transconscious imagination operates as a single organized mechanism, purposefully flowing between all portions of the psyche with a unifying objective. Its vast creative resources are a primary influence in the development of music, dance, literature, and other art forms.

The transconscious imagination expresses itself in two ways, the intuitive imagination and the creative imagination, which relate respectively to the natures of the reflective anima and the creative animus. Together, these two archetypes coalesce into the partly androgynous archetype of Hermes,[32] the messenger god, who symbolizes the transconscious imagination as the psychopomp, the guide, healer, and protector of the soul. The language of the soul (and the imagination) is revealed in symbol, image, and allegory. Therefore in all mythologies the many figures, places, and situations are metaphors for different archetypes, as well as different aspects of the psyche and transformative experiences. Thus does Hermes, representing the soul guide and the transconscious self, communicate to all levels of the psyche through symbol and myth.

The imagination is one of the most important tools of magic. A focused imagination is employed by magicians for everything from the consecration of talismans to healing. Concentration on a visualized image or symbol is the key to this type of working. In healing, the source of the infection or injury is often visualized as being dissolved, or the sick individual is "imaged" as being free from the disease. The exploration of the unconscious realms usually begins with the "image" of descending into a basement, a cave, or the underworld. Superconscious levels are often contacted by visualizing the climbing of a steep mountain—or climbing the branches of a mystical tree.

Properly used, the imaginative faculties of the transconscious self can be used to activate the latent faculties of the psyche and bring renewed health and well-being to the entire mind/body system.

The Tree of Life

The Qabalah is the mystical system of the medieval Jews; its exact origins are buried in antiquity. Its primary symbol, the Tree of Life, is said to be a glyph of the essence of God, the origins of the cosmos, the soul of man, and a model of how to live in accordance with the divine plan. It is also the most important symbol used by magicians and other practitioners of the western esoteric tradition. For our purposes, we will focus upon the Tree of Life as a "uniting symbol"—an image of the individuated psyche.

The Tree itself is composed of ten Sephiroth (spheres or emanations) which are listed in order and are pictured in Figure 2 of Chapter Two, p. 28: *Kether*—the Crown, *Chokmah*—Wisdom, *Binah*—Understanding, *Chesed*—Mercy, *Geburah*—Strength, *Tiphareth*—Beauty, *Netzach*—Victory, *Hod*—Splendor, *Yesod*—Foundation, and *Malkuth*—the Kingdom.

The Parts of the Soul

To the Qabalists the human soul is divided into three principal portions which overlap in some instances (see Figure 7, p. 132). These are the *Neshamah*, the *Ruach*, and the *Nephesh*. The highest of these, the Neshamah, encompasses the Sephiroth of Kether, Chokmah, and Binah. It corresponds to the highest aspirations of the soul and what Assagioli described as the *higher unconscious* or *superconscious*. The greater Neshamah is further sub-divided into three parts: the *Yechidah*, the *Chiah*, and the *Neshamah*.

The *Yechidah*, centered in Kether, is our true *divine self* (comparable to Assagioli's *higher self*), the root essence of our spiritual nature. It is that part of us that is nearest to God, the most perfect level of the self. The Yechidah is the supreme undifferentiated quality of mind that is pure, unexpanded consciousness. It simply is—"I am that I am."

The *Chiah* or life force, located in Chokmah, is the highest active principle in the human soul. It is our divine will, our inquisitive urge to become more than human. Symbolized by the masculine soul image of the animus, or the figure of the Supernal Father, the Chiah is the source of our powers of action.

The sub-division of the *Neshamah* (as distinct from the greater Neshamah), is the intuitive soul located in Binah, although it lends its name to the other Supernals as being generally descriptive of the soul's greatest aspirations. It is also the most approachable of the three Supernal parts of the soul. The Neshamah in

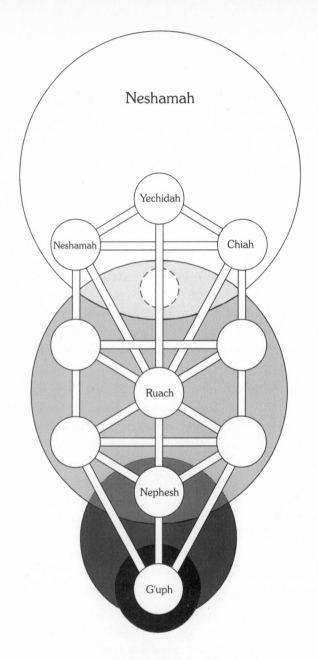

Figure 7: The Divisions of the Soul.

Binah is symbolized by the feminine soul image of the anima, as well as the Shekinah, the Supernal Mother, or the Gnostic Sophia. It is the source of human perception, comprehension, and spiritual understanding.

The Neshamah in Binah initiates delineating ways in which the self can be defined as being unique to the individual as well as limitless in archetypal manifestation. It is the understanding of how the divine manifests itself through a multitude of archetypal forms, and how it can express itself more fully as the process of self-realization continues to unfold. The Neshamah carries within it the instinct and the blueprint for self-realization.

The Neshamah as a whole is our true desire or deepest state of consciousness—the intuitive power that connects humankind with the divine—it is our superconscious, intuitive mind.[33] According to the ancient Qabalists, this part of the soul remains dormant until the individual is spiritually awakened to its existence. The Neshamah (divine self, higher soul, or higher genius) embraces the elevated aspects of the collective unconscious—it is the divine spark that is common to all of humanity.

Between the Neshamah and the middle part of the soul is a great boundary known as the *abyss*. This is the line of intersection between mortal and eternal, personal and transpersonal, separateness and unity. That which is above the abyss is immortal and common to us all. That which is below the abyss is temporary and individual. The shadowy Sephirah (or rather *non*-Sephirah) of Daath is located within the abyss. Its function is to create a bridge between the higher and middle parts of the soul (Neshamah and Ruach) so that the Neshamah can "descend" and the conscious mind thereby connect with, and perhaps gain some understanding of, the nature of spirit and divinity.

The middle soul or rational self, the *Ruach*, is located in the five Sephiroth from Chesed to Yesod, although it is centered in Tiphareth. It also overlaps, to a lesser extent, Daath and Yesod. This is the conscious mind and reasoning powers—the conscious part of our being which is the abode of the ego. This is the seat of "outer" consciousness, where humanity becomes aware of thought-images and is able to fashion thoughts into actions. It is here that human beings use their powers of discrimination as the mind navigates continuously between both secular and transcendent functions.

Five faculties are to be found in this pentad of spheres: memory (Chesed), will (Geburah), imagination (Tiphareth), emotion (Netzach), and intellect (Hod). The two lowest of these functions, corresponding to the spheres of Netzach and Hod, are quite easy for the average person to understand. The three higher faculties of the Ruach, attributed to the fourth through the sixth Sephiroth, are somewhat more difficult to access. This is because of a demarcation called the Veil of Paroketh that exists on the Tree between Tiphareth and the two lower spheres of Netzach and Hod. Thus the higher Ruach faculties of memory, will, and imagination are obstructed somewhat and are often less accessible to the individual than are the lower functions of thinking and feeling.

The Ruach contains both the *middle unconscious* and the *field of consciousness* of Assagioli's system, as well as his concept of the *conscious self* or ego.

The higher self or lower genius (sometimes called the Augoeides), which mediates between the divine self of the Neshamah and the lower self, is located in the Ruach, primarily in Tiphareth.[34] This is also the seat of the personal ego, which interacts between the divine superconsciousness and the lower self, and constantly attempts to organize and interpret one's personal experience—both inner and outer experience. The persona, a conscious but artificial mask that we present to the outer world, is also to be found in the Ruach.

The *Nephesh*, or lower self, resides in Yesod. Comparable to Assagioli's *lower unconscious*, the Nephesh is a low level of awareness that answers to the primal instincts, fundamental drives, and animal vitality from our prehistoric past. The Nephesh embraces the lowest components of the collective unconscious, those basic aspects which relate to survival, sex, and the reptilian brain. It is also the seat of our personal unconscious. The Nephesh is sometimes equated with the aura and the etheric body, a kind of energy sheath which forms the matrix for physical body. Proper use of the vital raw Nephesh energy is important in many aspects of magic, but it must always remain under the firm control of the Ruach, the conscious mind.

The Nephesh is the most misunderstood part of the soul. Due to its placement and relationship to the Ruach above it and the *G'uph* below it, the Nephesh is also the seat of the shadow, the dark subconscious underside of the conscious ego. The shadow represents those basic desires that run contrary to society and to our own ideals of behavior and personality. During the course of life, personal conflicts and neuroses are created within the psyche which are banished to the Nephesh through the processes of denial and repression. This results in a type of dualism which in turn creates the shadow and its various attributes. This dualism is expressed in the fact that on the one hand the Nephesh contains a vibrant primal energy and raw beauty that is crucial to magical work, but on the other hand, it also contains unconscious impulses which often run contrary to spiritual growth. These impulses can be likened to Freud's id with its demands for instant gratification. Thus the Nephesh and the unconscious mind, together with the shadow, have all been unceremoniously rejected throughout history as scapegoats for problems which originated in the conscious mind (when the neuroses were consciously repressed rather than examined). Thus the Nephesh becomes the abode of many emotionally charged complexes, phobias, obsessions, delusions, and compulsive urges.

Beyond this five-fold division of the human soul, there is one more portion that is sometimes overlooked. The lowest part is called the *G'uph*. Centered in Malkuth, the *G'uph* is closely tied to the physical body and the total range of all psycho-physical functions. It is a low level of subconscious intelligence which communicates the current condition of the human body to the brain.

Transpersonal psychotherapies and reputable systems of magic both work to examine and integrate the shadow of the Nephesh. This integration is a prerequisite for further spiritual/magical work and self-realization. In magical orders such as the Golden Dawn, this is accomplished through initiation rituals which heighten the awareness of the student, combined with intellectual teachings and personal meditations, rituals, visualizations, invocations, and exercises such as the Middle Pillar.[35] Once the shadow is confronted, recognized, and correlated into the psyche, its tremendous energy resources and rich symbology can be harnessed and utilized by the conscious mind which can in turn stimulate the Neshamah. Magical disciplines strive to open a channel for the Neshamah to communicate with the lower portions of soul, bringing to the individual a conscious recognition of the divine self. The higher faculties of the Ruach, including imagination, will, and memory, are also awakened.

In order for this to take place, however, it is essential that the modern reader, who seeks renewed meaning in the purpose of life in addition to an understanding of his or her own inner workings, uniqueness, and place in the greater divine scheme of the universe, have the ability to bridge the ever-shrinking chasm that has divided psychology and magic. Both systems should be examined, and their respective bodies of knowledge culled for the gems of wisdom to be found in each. This process of reconnection between the modern science and the ancient art will be an act of healing, on both a personal and a collective level, which recognizes that all of reality is united under the integrating principle of spirit.

No one should be led to believe that the process of self-realization, whether achieved through the principles of analytical psychology, the techniques of magic, or a combination of the two systems, is an easy matter. But here, even the smallest achievement will be a monumental step in one's personal inner growth. If the mind is kept open to both new and old ways of exploring human development, one will discover that the psychologist's pursuit of a healthy, integrated human psyche, the alchemist's search for the Philosophers' Stone, and the magician's quest to complete the Great Work are all natural complements of each other.

Humanity's spiritual development is a long and arduous journey, an adventure through strange lands full of surprises, difficulties, and even dangers. It involves a drastic transmutation of the "normal" elements of the personality, an awakening of potentialities which had hitherto been dormant, a raising of consciousness to new realms, and a functioning along a new inner dimension.[36]

Endnotes

1. Arnold Toynbee, quoted in Walsh, *Perspectives and Patterns: Discourses on History*, 73.

2. LeShan, *The Dilemma of Psychology*, xiii.

3. One could say that magic and spirituality became the repressed *shadow* of psychology's conscious ego.

4. Hebb, "What Psychology Is About," *American Psychologist 29*, 74.

5. LeShan, *The Dilemma of Psychology*, 88.

6. In addition to *repression*, other defense mechanisms include *displacement*, where dangerous impulses are released in a substitute situation or through camouflaged activities, and *sublimation* or the rerouting of instinctive sexual energy toward other activities. Sublimation may sometimes be a consciously chosen process, in which case it can be constructive without being a defense mechanism.

7. In free association therapy, a person expresses their thoughts immediately after these thoughts arise.

8. Regardie often believed that he witnessed the Oedipus complex in his own patients, along with relaxed complexes of masochism and castration anxiety. He also tended to agree with Freud (over Jung) in his assertion that the sex drive is the primary motivation in humans. However, Regardie disagreed with Freud's idea that repression is a requirement of civilized life. To Regardie, repression was the source of most of humanity's problems. He also disagreed with Freud's rejection of occultism, and in this he sided with Jung.

9. Jung, "The Relations between the Ego and the Unconscious" *The Collected Works of C. G. Jung*, #7, 305.

10. Jacobi quoting Jung, *The Psychology of C. G. Jung*, 8–9.

11. Jung, *The Collected Works of C. G. Jung*, #6, 373.

12. Jung, "On the Nature of the Psyche," *The Collected Works of C. G. Jung*, #8, 412.

13. Jung, "The Meaning of Psychology for Modern Man," *The Collected Works of C. G. Jung*, #10, 289.

14. Jung, "Psychology and Religion," *The Collected Works of C. G. Jung*, #11, 131.

15. If a person's outer personality is self-centered and argumentative, his shadow might well exhibit positive altruistic traits that are repressed by the ego. The fictional character Ebenezer Scrooge would be a good example of a negative personality type who faced his shadow and was able to bring out its positive qualities.

16. Ibid., 131.

17. Ibid., 131.

18. From our book *Self-Initiation into the Golden Dawn Tradition*, 661.

19. Jung, *The Collected Works of C. G. Jung*, #17, 198.

20. Jung, *The Collected Works of C. G. Jung*, #10, 847.

21. *Mana* means "great power." A Polynesian term for the magical force in nature. Comparable to prana or ch'i.

22. Jung, *The Collected Works of C. G. Jung,* #12, 563.

23. See Donald Michael Kraig's article "Do the Gods Exist?" in *The Magical Pantheons,* 260–261.

24. Jacobi quoting Jung, *The Psychology of C. G. Jung,* 131.

25. In Reichian therapy, certain areas massaged approximate the positions of the Sephiroth on the Middle Pillar. It is easy to see why Regardie was so drawn to this type of therapy.

26. Assagioli, *Psychosynthesis,* 6.

27. What Assagioli called the "higher self" is what ceremonial magicians often call the "divine self."

28. Rather than identifying yourself with a weakness, limitation, or obsession ("I am depressed"), disidentify yourself from the source of the problem ("a surge of depression is trying to envelop me").

29. Assagioli thought that this point was an outward projection, but magicians consider it an inward reality, located in the Sephirah of Tiphareth, the seat of the Holy Guardian Angel.

30. In magic, this can be compared to the work of the 27th Path of Peh (known as "The Tower") in which the old outmoded personality is dismantled, and a new personality is rebuilt.

31. *Transconscious* is a term developed by psychologist/magician William Stoltz to describe the psyche's creative and intuitive imagination.

32. Although Hermes is male, he is sometimes seen as an androgyne or hermaphrodite. In fact, the word *hermaphrodite* is a combination of the names Hermes and Aphrodite—the union of the anima and the animus.

33. Sometimes confused with Freud's super-ego, which was an artificial construct composed of external influences in accordance with a process called *introjection*—the incorporation of the characteristics of a person or an object into one's own psyche which occurs unconsciously.

34. The descent of the Neshamah into the individual's field of awareness occurs through the "holy union" of the "king" and the "queen"—the higher and lower self symbolized by Tiphareth and Malkuth.

35. Certain Golden Dawn teachings, such as the symbolism of the Garden of Eden Before and After the Fall, are specifically designed to aid in the integration of the shadow by using myth and metaphor which can be understood on many levels. See our book *Self-Initiation into the Golden Dawn Tradition,* 367–371 and 554–556.

36. Assagioli, *Psychosynthesis,* 39.

CHAPTER SEVEN

THE ART OF RELAXATION

\

I n the Foreword to the second edition of *The Middle Pillar*, Regardie expressed a desire to add more material on the art of relaxation and its importance to the individual's well-being. At that time Regardie wanted to leave his original work intact and unencumbered by afterthoughts. Later, in such books as *The Romance of Metaphysics* (1946), *Twelve Steps to Spiritual Enlightenment*[1] (1969), and *Foundations of Practical Magic* (1979), he went into more detail concerning the psychological and physical benefits to be gained through relaxation. Some of the techniques he suggested to his patients and students alike are given below, along with other methods.

Before the student commences any extended involvement with advanced magical techniques, he or she should first concentrate on gaining proficiency in the art of relaxation. This sounds simple enough, but it is not something to be passed over lightly. Even so, as Regardie noted, few spiritual schools emphasize basic techniques of relaxation, without which, nothing of substance and lasting value can be accomplished. Many esoteric schools seem to focus on the idea that the simple contemplation of a mystical idea alone will naturally result in the required concentration and relaxation. Sometimes this idea is correct, but as Regardie observed, in most cases it is not. More often than not, as soon as the student tries to concentrate on a spiritual affirmation or belief, he or she is beset by a horde of extraneous ideas which lead to distraction. As a result:

> ...(D)istracted, and annoyed by this wandering of his mind, he makes determined efforts to bring the attention back. The total result is added tension of the mind, reflecting neuromuscular hypertonicity in the body, and he becomes a nervous exhausted wreck within the space of a few minutes.

Regardie cites the remedy for this situation:

> It is absolutely imperative that the student should at the outset be taught a method which will enable him to relieve these neuromuscular tensions and this cramp of the mind in such a way as to enable him to continue by the employment of the same method to the contemplation of metaphysical ideas.[2]

The human body is a complex machine which converts food into energy. A great deal of energy is needed to carry out the internal bodily functions alone. But even in a normal state of rest, about one-half of the body's energy can be squandered through tension and anxiety. This is why people often complain of being exhausted even when they've had plenty of sleep. Fatigue and psychic conflicts create tension which eats up precious energy. And unfortunately, the demands of modern life often seem to make relaxation a rare luxury that few can afford.

Like energy from food, the consumption of oxygen is also of primary importance to all somatic operations. Relaxation exercises can regulate the consumption of oxygen through the techniques of rhythmic breathing. To use an automotive metaphor, this helps to keep the human "motor" running smoothly without burning too much oil or fuel. Thus relaxation helps to conserve large amounts of energy that is wasted by neuro-muscular tension. And who would not want to free up this misspent energy and use it for things more meaningful and enjoyable than tense shoulder muscles, a stiff neck, or an upset stomach? Having an abundance of energy will alleviate these tensions and help one live life to its fullest.

Regular performance of the relaxation exercises given here will reward the practitioner with physical and psychological dividends. Among the physical advantages are a decrease in blood pressure, a slowdown in respiration and heartbeat, and a noticeable decrease in muscular tension (along with the "aches and pains" that accompany such tension). The psychological effects are even more profound. Through deep relaxation, the student can achieve a state of pure consciousness in which the physical or somatic element is completely removed. Eventually the body is able to relax so completely (as if all its needs have been fulfilled) that all body consciousness disappears. This has a very healing effect.

Regardie suggested that a new point of view is needed, a scientific approach to metaphysics. This psychological approach will accomplish two things: 1) the complete relaxation of the mind/body mechanism, and 2) the training and education necessary to successfully contemplate spiritual truths.

> ...(T)he mind is able to control the body and its manifold functions — and in fact to affect the entire phenomenal world. ... The methods indicated...will prove to the metaphysical novice that by means of evolving mental pictures he can himself induce a variety of psychological changes in his body. With this acquired ability, a quiet confidence based upon experience will come to him, an assurance that now he will be able to succeed in demonstrating metaphysically his ability to conquer and transcend all physical and mental circumstances of every kind.[3]

When relaxation techniques are successful in bringing about a state of consciousness where awareness of the body vanishes, the mind is no longer restrained by physical sensations, pains, or other corporeal impediments which activate psychological activities that obstruct the higher mental and spiritual functions. It is a feeling of ecstacy—calm and satisfying. Free from physical limitations, the mind is able to focus on profound spiritual truths. This is a real advancement in personal growth which results in increased mental balance and self-confidence. The relaxation of the body, which is so closely connected with the subconscious mind, dissipates those psychic blockages which cause tension, stress, and disease (or *disease*). Beyond these important considerations, relaxation will provide the student with great impetus toward approaching spiritual exercises and magical techniques with a sound psychological basis.

Simply put, you need to relax. Your body requires it. Your spirit will rejoice in it. A few moments each day spent in a state of complete relaxation will be time well spent. And there is no reason two or more people cannot set aside time to perform these methods together and support each other's efforts.

BODY AWARENESS EXERCISE

One of the primary aims of any system of spiritual growth is the procurement of self-awareness or perception. The only way to increase sensitivity is to become aware—aware of that which is within as well as that which is without. Try this Body Awareness Exercise.[4]

Sitting comfortably or lying on the floor, merely attempt to observe what is happening with your own body. (If you have trouble with your lower back, be sure to place a couple of pillows under each knee whenever lying down to meditate.) Simply watch your physical body and its various sensations. Do not do anything special. Breathe normally and don't try to relax or control wandering thoughts. Just try to notice what happens.

After a few moments, find a comfortable position and stay in it, without moving or consciously fidgeting in any way. Remain perfectly still. At first this exercise should be practiced for no more than ten minutes. Gradually increase the time spent in practice so that this exercise is extended to half an hour. Obviously, this exercise will be simple to some, terribly difficult to others. Any urge to wiggle and release tension should resisted.

The powers of concentration should also be developed as this awareness exercise is practiced. If your mind begins to wander, gently bring it back. Your powers of concentration will gradually but steadily become enhanced.

During this practice, you may become aware of itching sensations in various parts of your body. Do not attempt to scratch. Merely observe. Simply be aware of various body sensations without trying to alter or ignore them. Do not make judgments or criticisms about these sensations. Accept them as a part of you.

Sensations will come and go in different areas of the body. Study them. It is sometimes a good idea to verbally express what you are feeling or experiencing.

This exercise will result in a profound relaxation of nervous tension. Daily practice will heighten the function of self-awareness, something that is vital to the work of a magician. All complex ceremonies and rituals actually begin with this heightening of self-awareness.

No special time period needs to be found to practice this. Lying in bed at night or in the morning provides an excellent opportunity to rehearse body awareness. This exercise should be done twice daily for about six months. In addition to this, short periods of temporary pause from activity can be taken throughout the day during bathing, shaving, or dressing, etc., in order to sharpen one's perceptions and observe what is happening within.

~

THE CLEANSING BATH EXERCISE

Take a shower to clean the body. Then fill the bathtub with warm water. Add bath salts or perfumed oil to the water. For an added spiritual effect, white candles and incense may be employed in the room. Some soothing music on the CD or tape player wouldn't hurt either.

Simply soak for a few minutes and let go of any negativity or tension into the cleansing water. Then pull the plug and drain the water while remaining in the tub. Feel your doubts and worries siphon out with the water, leaving you feeling relaxed and energized. Don't rush when getting up.

~

THE PURIFYING BREATH EXERCISE

This simple exercise is an extension of the rhythmic breath and should be employed at the end of all meditations.

Take a deep full breath and hold it in for a few seconds. Then pucker the lips, leaving only a narrow opening in the mouth. Exhale the air strongly through the mouth, gradually and slowly forcing the air out through the small opening in the lips until all the air is gone.

Relax for a moment while maintaining the balance of the air, then repeat. This will impel an automatic rebound of the chest whenever the exhalation of breath is completed in this fashion. Repeat this technique over a long period of time until it can be executed easily and without discomfort.

~

RELAXATION EXERCISE 1

Gravity and Relaxation

Lie face up on a mat or thick blanket placed on the floor and relax. (The floor provides a hard, uncomfortable surface which will immediately let you know about the variety of ways you hold tension within your body. You will either have to get up or relax totally.) A small cushion may be placed under the head. Let the weight of your body sink into the floor. Begin breathing in a rhythmic fashion.

Bring your attention to your torso and head. Inhale and tense the muscles of your stomach, chest, and neck. Exhale and relax totally, feeling the weight of your body sinking into the floor. Do this several times.

Concentrate now on your left arm. Inhale and make a fist, tensing the entire arm, and raise the limb off the floor about six inches. Exhale, and relax your arm. Allow it to drop to the floor. Do this a number of times until the limb feels totally relaxed and falls readily with the force of gravity.

Now center your attention on your right arm from hand to shoulder. As you inhale, make a fist, tensing all the muscles in your arm, and raise your arm off the floor about six inches. Exhale and relax your arm completely, allowing it to fall back to the floor. Repeat several times until the arm is relaxed.

Next, focus your attention on your left leg from hip to foot. As you inhale, lift your leg about eight inches off the floor. Bend your foot so that your toes are pointing toward your head. Tense all the muscles in your leg. Exhale and relax all tension in your leg, letting it drop to the floor. Repeat several times until your leg is fully relaxed.

Focus your attention on your right leg from hip to foot. As you inhale, lift your leg about eight inches off the floor. At the same time, bend your foot so that your toes are pointing toward your head. Tense all the muscles in your leg. Exhale and relax your leg completely, allowing it to fall back to the floor. Do this a number of times until the limb feels totally relaxed and falls readily with the force of gravity.

Tense your whole body several times and then relax totally. Let yourself take a few deep sighs. Do this a number of times until at length you feel as though you were melting into the floor, carrying all the tension out of your body like a stream of water from melting ice. Give yourself up wholly to the support of the floor. Accept the fact that the floor can easily hold up the weight of your body. Relax and let it.

~

RELAXATION EXERCISE 2

For Two People

This exercise is designed for the simple purpose of making one aware of the amount of muscular tension that is held within the body. Two people are needed for this method—one who will receive the benefit of relaxation, and the other who will aid the process. Here we will refer to the first person as the subject and the second as the assistant. For the subject loose-fitting garments, including slacks or sweatpants, are required.

The subject should lie face up on a mat or thick blanket placed on the floor. If lower back pain is a problem, place a number of pillars under the subject's knees. A small cushion may be placed under the head. The subject should lie quietly for a few minutes, becoming aware of the body as in the first exercise. After a short time, the subject will probably come to the realization that he or she cannot totally relax. This is where the assistant comes in.

The assistant should be seated to one side of the subject. He or she should commence by placing one hand under the subject's ankles and raising both legs a few inches off the floor. Next, the assistant should place the other hand under the subject's knees and slowly remove the hand from under the ankles. This will cause the lower part of the legs to drop, unless the subject still holds tension in the muscles.

Now the assistant should hold the ankles together with one hand and remove the hand from under the knees, and gently attempt to separate the knees. If the subject is relaxed, each knee should fall outward. This may take several attempts before the subject relaxes enough to permit the knees to fall.

Next the assistant relaxes the subject's arms one at a time. Each arm should be wiggled as if shaking a rope. Then, holding the elbow to the floor with one hand, the assistant raises the subject's forearm perpendicular to the floor. When the arm is released it should be noted whether it falls easily, hangs in the air, or is lowered by the muscles. Again, many attempts may be required before the forearm is relaxed enough to drop.

Moving on to the shoulders, the assistant elevates the elbow a few inches off the floor and releases it. If the shoulder joint is relaxed the elbow drops effortlessly. Each shoulder can be relaxed further by the assistant placing both hands under it, lifting it slightly, and allowing it to drop to the floor. The body should fall solidly and the head should roll without restraint on the neck.

At this time the assistant should watch for signs of deep relaxation, such as heavy sighs, slow deep breathing, lines on the face softening, and the whole body sinking down onto the floor.

The assistant should then gently push his or her fingers into the abdominal muscles bordering the hips, one side followed by the other. A slight pressure is maintained during which the muscles may give spasms of resistance due to tension. Alternate this application of pressure from one side to the other until the muscles relax.

After this the assistant should apply slight pressure on the chest and sides in the same manner.

For the final part of this exercise the assistant should gently lift the subject's head a couple of inches and allow it to flop back onto the cushion. If this is done several times, the subject should feel deeply relaxed.

After a few moments of restful meditation, the subject and the assistant may switch roles and repeat the exercise.

~

RELAXATION EXERCISE 3

Tension, Relaxation, and Visualization

(Note: If we accept the premise that psychological states can effect immediate responses in the mind/body system, then it follows that mental pictures or visualizations can be used to purposely effect an attitude of total relaxation prior to magical work.)

Lie face up on a mat or thick blanket placed on the floor and relax. Let the weight of your body sink into the floor. Begin breathing in a rhythmic fashion.

Start with the top of the head. Inhale and deliberately tense the muscles of the forehead for a moment. Visualize your brain and the muscles of your brow. Tense the muscles as much as you possibly can. Then exhale, let go of the tension, and relax the forehead totally. *Feel* and *visualize* your muscles as they relax. Do this two or three times.

After a brief period of time, inhale and tense the muscles of your face, squeezing your eyes shut. With your mind's eye, see your face contorted with muscular tension. Then exhale. Release the tension and imagine the muscles of your face slipping back into their natural pose with the eyes gently closed. Repeat two or three times.

Next, inhale and tense the jaw and neck, clenching the teeth and pushing the tongue against the roof of the mouth. Visualize your face with lips pressed firmly shut. Then exhale and release the tension and let your jaw and tongue relax. Repeat as before.

Now turn your attention to the shoulders and upper arms, tensing them as you inhale, using your elbows to press down on the floor. Visualize your shoulders against the floor as you hold them stiffly, slightly off the floor as they seem to shrink inward. Then exhale and release the tension, stop pressing with your elbows and imagine the shoulders expanding slightly outward as they sink back into the floor. Repeat.

Focus on your lower arms and hands. Put your thumbs inside your palms and clench your hands into fists. Press your wrists into the floor to add tension to your forearms as you inhale. Visualize the closed fists and stiff arms. Then exhale. Relax your limbs and see the hands uncurl slightly from their martial pose into a more peaceful one. Repeat.

Center your attention on your back, pushing it into the floor as you inhale. Start with the lower back followed by the upper back. Visualize your spine as it is pressed into the floor. Exhale. Relax your back and imagine it gently springing back to its normal state. Repeat.

Now focus on your chest. Inhale deeply and expand your chest to its absolute fullest capacity. Hold your breath (and the corresponding tension) for a few moments and visualize your chest and ribs extended to their limits. Exhale naturally. With your mind's eye, see your chest gently fall back and assume its normal state. Repeat.

Tense the muscles in your lower abdomen. Inhale and tighten your abdominal muscles as though you were trying to fit into a tight pair of pants, or as if your navel were being pulled toward your spine. Visualize your abdomen being pulled tight against your spine and imagine the organs of your abdomen pressed closer against one another. Then exhale and release the tension. See your muscles and organs spring gently back into place.

Next tense the muscles in your buttocks and thighs, turning your toes in toward each other as you inhale. Visualize that your thighs are as taut as those of a runner who is about to sprint forward. Exhale and allow your legs to drop back into their normal position. See your thigh muscles relaxing. Repeat.

Now observe your knees and lower legs. Inhale, pressing the backs of your knees into the floor and bend your feet so that your toes are pointing toward your head. Visualize your calves and knees pressed firmly against the floor. Then exhale and let your lower legs drop back into their normal position as you see the muscles relax. Repeat.

Focus on your feet and ankles. Inhale and point your feet like a ballerina standing on pointe. Curl your toes. Visualize your feet tensed in this way. Then exhale and allow the feet to bounce back. Visualize your feet and toes totally relaxed. Repeat as before.

Now inhale. Tense your entire body as much as possible. Imagine your body as stiff as a board. Then exhale and relax fully and deeply. Visualize your body becoming almost liquid in its relaxed state. Do this at least three times, then remain totally relaxed. Notice how much more relaxed your body is after the balancing effects of flexing and releasing.

Breathe deeply without strain. Visualize yourself enveloped in a sphere of brilliant white light. Imagine your body bathed in this light and feel its warmth on your skin. As you inhale feel the divine light filling your lungs and spreading throughout your entire body to the ends of your fingers and toes, giving you a sense of ultimate peace and relaxation. As you exhale breathe out a portion of this endless light, giving its tranquil effects back to the divine source in a cycle of flux and reflux. The more light you breathe out, the more light you breathe back in, until your whole being seems as if it is created out of this divine light.

Now visualize a golden sphere of healing light in the center of your body around the area of your heart. Feel its soothing warmth. See this sphere traveling to areas of your body where some tension remains. Whatever part of your body the sphere touches becomes fully relaxed and regenerated. Let the sphere traverse over every part of your body, and when this is done, place it back in its original position, centered on your heart.

Continue to relax in this state for a few moments. Then take a few deep breaths and feel the vitality stirring within as you end the meditation.

(Note: A group of people may elect to perform this exercise together. If this is the case, one person should record the exercise on a tape player, with soothing music in the background. The participants should lie on the floor—in a circle if possible with heads pointing in toward the center—with a fair amount of space between each person. Play the recording and begin the exercise.)

RELAXATION EXERCISE 4

Visualized Circulation

In the previous exercise the student was encouraged to become more aware of the body's physical sensations. In this exercise the student learns how to use the techniques of relaxation to manipulate body sensations in a premeditated fashion in order to cause certain changes that are both physical and psychological.

Relaxation is a crucial step in changing one's conscious awareness from the mundane events of the day to a more spiritual focus. It is also an essential procedure that will always be undertaken prior to more advanced techniques and rituals.

For this technique it would be helpful if the student had a basic understanding of human anatomy.

Before sitting or lying down, spend a minute or two engaged in physical exercise to increase the blood circulation and stimulate deep breathing. (One way to do this is to pretend that you are skipping rope in a stationary position.)

Then stand upright with the legs slightly apart. Take a deep breath and exhale, expelling all of your air as you let yourself fall forward from the waist, completely relaxed, hands hanging near the feet for a moment. Allow yourself to be totally limp from the waist up. Inhale and bring yourself back to the full standing position. Repeat this process about a dozen times. Be aware only of the various body sensations.

The actual relaxation exercise, which lasts approximately one-half hour, can now begin. Take some very deep breaths. Sit or lie down on the floor, and remain aware only of what the body is feeling.

Visualize your brain just as you have seen the human brain in drawings—a large gray-white walnut shaped organ divided into two hemispheres. Imagine it clearly. Concentrate. Do not allow your mind to wander from the visualization. If your mind wanders, gently bring it back. Hold the image of the brain in your mind until you begin to feel a warmth spreading out from the center of your head. Imagine yourself stimulating the flow of blood to the brain, relaxing the blood vessels there. You may be aware of a gentle tingling sensation. Picture the blood vessels within the brain dilating enough to hold larger amounts of blood. This turns the brain pink, resulting in the sensation of warmth that you are experiencing.

Move on to the eyes, visualizing them as two balls held in place by muscles. Imagine the muscles becoming enlarged as you channel more blood to the area. This stimulates the feeling of warmth. Then relax, imagining the eyeballs sinking back gently into their sockets.

Follow this procedure for the rest of the head—visualize the warming blood flowing into the blood vessels of the temples, cheeks, ears, nose, lips, tongue, and chin. In all cases, feel the warmth and the tingling of the blood gradually followed by the feeling of relaxation.

See the heated blood flowing into the muscles of the neck, the shoulder joints, the arms, hands, and fingertips. Imagine the pink muscles saturated with blood. Feel the radiant warmth of the blood tingling within the fibers of your muscles.

You should now be approximately ten minutes into the exercise. The remaining time should be spent visualizing the rest of the body in the same manner—imagine once again the muscles of the neck, the glands, the larynx, the pharynx, and shoulders. Imagine that the blood flows into every artery and capillary. Now concentrate on the abdominal area and the internal organs. Spend a few moments on each organ separately—the heart, the lungs, the bronchi, the liver, pancreas, intestines, kidneys, etc. (The more you relax the abdomen, the more likely it is that the rest of the body will relax also.)

Finally imagine the current of warm blood separating into two mighty arterial rivers of blood which flow from the pelvis into the thighs, knees, legs, feet, and toes. Relax completely.

The increased blood supply caused by the successful performance of this exercise will induce a broad sense of relaxation.

Once you have completed this portion of the exercise, observe how you feel. Let a sense of total repose and fulfillment be permanently recorded in your mind. Feel the pleasure of the moment. Impress the image thoroughly and strongly upon your mind. If you are able to remember this experience clearly, it can be evoked at any time. Whether you are driving a car or riding on an airliner, you can remember the feeling of pleasurable relaxation and evoke the memory which will result in the tension leaving the muscles of your body.

If at any time you wish to relax, simply take a deep breath and imagine the word *relax* as you release the air from your lungs. Inhale deeply, and as you exhale, command yourself to relax. Remember the serenity of complete relaxation and it will be instantly brought back to you. Eventually this will become a conditioned reflex, the effects of which will be complete and automatic.

This exercise should be performed at least once a day. (Twice would be better—once in the morning and once in the evening.) Variations on this technique could also be used to help cure illnesses. One might imagine the stream of blood flowing through and breaking down a cancerous growth for elimination from the body—or the flow of blood may be seen to heal a wound.

~

RELAXATION EXERCISE 5

The Practice of the Divine Essence

For this exercise the student should review and practice all of the relaxation and body awareness exercises prescribed earlier.

To perform this exercise, lie down in a comfortable position. Once relaxed, reflect on the fact that the entire surface of your body is covered by millions of tiny pores. In truth, every muscle and organ in the body is composed of cells which have minute areas of space between them.

Imagine that the pores on the skin of your face (nose, cheeks, and brow) are stretched wide open. (This should only take a matter of seconds if you have performed the previous exercises regularly.) Then proceed to visualize the skin on the scalp and back of the head in the same fashion. Continue on to the skin of the neck, shoulders, arms, chest, abdomen, hips, thighs, legs, and feet. Imagine the surrounding membrane of every part of the body, including the internal organs, permeated by a series of pores loosely weaved together by a net-like substance.

Once you have obtained a feeling of the opening of all the pores in your body, return to reflect upon your head. Imagine that the brain also has become full of open pores and is now somewhat *sponge-like*. Apply this visualization to every part of the body—the bones, muscles, and soft organs—all becoming like sponges.

When this visualization is complete, imagine that the surrounding atmosphere is able to easily penetrate your body, as if the air itself flowed right through the pores and holes of your body. The air saturates you, entering into every pore. Imagine that when you inhale, the air enters your body through the bottoms of your feet; when you exhale, the air leaves your porous body from the top of your head. Experiment with similar visualizations, pushing the inhalations and exhalations of air through your body in various directions.

A relationship exists between the elements of air and spirit. Therefore imagine that the air cascading through your body is the air of the divine spirit—the *Ruach Elohim*. It exists everywhere, surrounding you on all sides—omnipotent and infinite. This spirit is without limitation or opposition. It is eternal truth, wisdom, and love. It is light and life. This is what you should imagine flowing freely through every pore of your body and mind.

Regular practice of this exercise is designed to bring the student to a high level of divine consciousness. Every aspect of mystical experience and knowledge may be brought fully into play during this meditation. Although it is an extension of the aspirant's earlier work, this meditation is designed to bring about a true realization concerning the infinity of the eternal spirit and the complete fulfillment of the divine within.

Many of these exercises require that the student lie on the floor to get the maximum benefit. However, as one relaxes and lets go of all tension, there is always the possibility of falling asleep. This is not a problem and with practice it will pass. Eventually the student will be able to separate mental consciousness from body consciousness. The body will be completely relaxed, while the mind remains active and alert.

~

ADDITIONAL EXERCISES

Finding the Right Position

There may be times when the student will want to be seated for meditation and visualization work. A number of different postures may be used by the student for this purpose.

Eastern Pose

For this pose you will need a pillow, cushion, or folded blanket on the floor. Seat yourself on the front edge of the pillow. (This will help slant the hips forward and support the lower back.) Bend your legs so that you are sitting cross-legged with the left foot under the right thigh and the right foot under the left thigh. Keep your knees level and your spine straight. Rest your hands palms downward on your knees and keep your elbows relaxed. Close your eyes and breathe rhythmically. The main meditation may now commence.

Western Pose

For this pose you will need a chair and a small cushion. Be seated on the front half of the chair with the spine well away from the back of the chair. With the cushion under your feet, be sure that the lower part of your legs forms a ninety-degree angle to your thighs, which may be together or separated slightly. Rest your hands palms downward on your knees and keep the elbows relaxed. The spine should be kept straight. Close your eyes and breathe rhythmically. The main meditation can now begin.

~

MIND AWARENESS EXERCISE

Once the student has gained some experience with the techniques of relaxation, he or she is encouraged to raise the level of awareness from the body to the mind. The exercise employed for this purpose is a form of "free association" used by psychotherapists. It is performed by simply letting the mind wander as it may without obstruction.

Set a predetermined amount of time for the session beforehand and use an alarm clock or timer. (Twenty minutes or half an hour is appropriate.) At the end of the practice, stop immediately so that discipline is maintained.

Sit comfortably in one of the positions mentioned above. A tape recorder should be set up ahead of time to record the entire session.

As you sit, calmly articulate any thought, idea, memory, or feeling that happens to arise, into the microphone. Speak indiscriminately, without planning what to say next. At the end of the session, play back what has been recorded.

This practice will give the student a good idea of the hidden contents within the psyche. Some of it may seem shocking to the student who has not always been mentally "honest" with him or herself. The student may experience the opening of a floodgate of pent-up feelings or thoughts that have been censored for years. However, the simple act of becoming aware of these hidden thoughts is part of the process of being able to come to terms with them. The mental pressure and inner conflicts caused by these repressed thoughts will eventually dissipate along with the number of "breaks" in concentration.

This method of mind awareness should at least be practiced until the shock and anxiety usually encountered by the recognition of one's disturbing thoughts has vanished completely. What is most important about this exercise is that there should be no criticism, judgment or self-loathing concerning anything that might come up during the session. Your thoughts are a part of you, just like your arm or your leg. They are simply childlike parts of yourself that need training. With time and discipline, the energies of these juvenile portions of the psyche can be directed toward higher pursuits.

~

DEVELOPMENT OF THE WILL EXERCISE

The development of the will is one of the most important tasks faced by the student. It is a principal factor in the attainment of spiritual progress.

A practical and most effective method for training the will is to consciously set up specific goals for a predetermined period of time, and if diverted from keeping these goals, to withhold something that gives enjoyment. This method is based on a type of behavior modification therapy. Keep in mind that there is nothing moralistic in this procedure. The student who undertakes this practice is *not* "avoiding (bad) vices in favor of (good) virtues."

The point is to strengthen the will, which in and of itself is neither good nor bad. This exercise is a disciplinary vow that a certain habitual action will be denied by the aspirant. In order to perform this technique properly, the student should deliberately set a goal which is not in any way connected with a "bad" habit, such as smoking, swearing, or drinking. An impersonal and guilt-free attitude of detachment should be maintained. The aspirant should select a personal idiosyncrasy such as tapping the foot to music, saying a certain word, or crossing the legs when sitting. This will help ensure that the student does not make a senseless virtue out of what is merely designed as a discipline exercise.

One of the most effective ways to reinforce the will is to dispense a mild electric shock. (One can usually find a small device which will deliver a slight shock in any store that sells supplies for stage magic.) The shock is very light, but can be quite surprising. If this device is employed immediately following the broken vow, a mental connection is made which will become a fixed and potent reminder that sets up a continual alertness on the part of the will. By doing this the student will reinforce the connection between the unwanted action and the electric shock. It is important to carry the device with you at all times so that the disciplinary action can be delivered immediately after the transgression. It is through this discipline that the will obtains its training and effectiveness. All violations of the oath should be rapidly "punished" in order to make an enduring impression on the student's mind. This can be done either by administering a light shock as described above, or by denying oneself something that is pleasurable.

This technique accomplishes two things. First, a constant vigilance is established which generates a potent will power. Second, the mind itself is placed gradually under the control of the aspirant's will. This in turn helps the student's faculty of concentration immensely.

~

THE RITE OF ELEMENTAL EQUILIBRATION

One of the goals of magical work is to bring to the student an awareness of the inner elemental make-up of his or her psyche. This awareness also includes the ability to *experience* the elements[5] and *balance* them in equal portion within the mind.

It is vitally important that all magical students be able to consciously equilibrate the psychic elements. The simple rite of the Qabalistic Cross is very useful for this purpose, however, we also suggest that the student perform the following Rite of Elemental Equilibration to actively combat any elemental imbalances that may occur during the transformative process of self-development. This is a ritual that should be performed regularly.

Stand facing the east and perform the four-fold breath a number of times until you feel relaxed. Imagine a brilliant light above your head. Reach up with your right hand as if to touch this light and bring the light down to your forehead. Imagine the yellow triangle of air superimposed over the upper part of your body. Vibrate "**SHADDAI EL CHAI**" (Shah-dye El Chai). △

Then picture the black triangle of earth covering the lower portion of your body. Bring your hand down as if pointing to the ground and vibrate "**ADONAI HA-ARETZ**" (Ah-doh-nye ha-Ah-retz). ▽

Visualize the red triangle of fire superimposed over the right side of your body. Touch your right shoulder and intone "**YHVH TZABAOTH**" (Yode-Heh-Vav-Heh Tzah-bah-oth). △

Imagine the blue triangle of water covering the left side of your body. Touch your left shoulder and intone "**ELOHIM TZABAOTH**" (El-oh-heem Tzah-bah-oth). ▽

Bring both hands together, interlocking the fingers with the palms outward, and touch the area of your heart with your knuckles. Imagine the sigil of the spirit wheel in white at the center of your body, uniting the four elemental triangles. Imagine the brilliant light above your head connected with this sigil of spirit. Vibrate "**ETH**." ✪

Continue the four-fold breath with the following visualizations:

Inhale—imagine the fire triangle. △
Full Hold—imagine the water triangle. ▽
Exhale—imagine the air triangle. △
Empty Hold—imagine the earth triangle. ▽

Imagine all of the elemental triangles within your psyche balanced and in harmony under the guidance of spirit. ✪

Endnotes

1. Retitled as *The One Year Manual* (Samuel Weiser, Inc., 1990).
2. Regardie, *The Romance of Metaphysics*, 244–245.
3. Ibid., 246.
4. This exercise, like many in this chapter, is taken from our book *Self-Initiation into the Golden Dawn Tradition*.
5. In magic there are four basic elements (fire, water, air, and earth) which are regarded as realms, kingdoms, or divisions of nature. They are the basic modes of existence and action, and the building blocks of everything in the universe. A fifth element, spirit, is said to bind together and govern the lesser four.

CHAPTER EIGHT

YOGA, CHAKRAS, AND THE WISDOM OF THE EAST

A s Regardie stressed in Chapter Four, the Qabalistic Sephiroth, particularly those of the Middle Pillar, bear some
resemblance to the chakra system of yoga, the Hindu mystical tradition. Many people, including authors, make the common
mistake of calling Tiphareth "the heart chakra" or referring to Yesod
as "the moon chakra." In fact the cover of Llewellyn's second edition of Regardie's *The Middle Pillar* (see Figure 1, p. xi) shows the
chakras superimposed over the Qabalistic Tree of Life with the twin
serpents of the Caduceus of Hermes. As easy as it is for some to
transpose the terms "Sephirah" and "chakra," this habit should be
avoided, since it only adds to confusion between the two systems. It
would be better to refer to the Sephiroth of the Middle Pillar exercise as *galgalim*,[1] which is Hebrew for "whirlings."

There are five Sephiroth on the Middle Pillar in contrast to
seven chakras in the Eastern system. The Sephirah of Kether can be
said to generally correspond to the crown and brow chakras, while
the shadowy sphere of Daath can be compared to the throat
chakra. Tiphareth approximates the heart and solar plexus chakras.
Yesod has certain similarities with the navel chakra. And while
Malkuth can be compared in some ways to the root chakra, the

tenth Sephirah is centered in the feet and ankles, while the root chakra is at the base of the spine.

But differences between the Qabalistic and yoga systems are great. As we have seen, some of the Sephiroth and the chakras are similar, but not exact. Take all of the ten Sephiroth into consideration and this similarity is diminished. The Sephiroth and the chakras have different functions, different correspondences, and a host of other attributes that are specific to the cultural roots of each system. Whereas the chakras are located along the spine and are linked to the endocrine glands and nerve centers, the Sephiroth have little correspondence with the inner organs and are located on the midline of the body. The colors assigned to the Sephiroth are also much different from those of the chakras.[2] Furthermore, the chakras are activated from the lowest to the highest, the exact opposite of the Western system in which the highest is always invoked first.

In many ways, the Middle Pillar exercise is a much safer practice than the eastern technique of activating the chakras through Kundalini yoga, which requires a competent instructor to teach it properly. In Kundalini yoga, it is possible for the student to activate more power than he or she can safely handle, resulting in a shock to the psychic mechanism. This is not true of the Middle Pillar, which never bestows more energy than the student can manage, and which can easily be learned without the benefit of a teacher.

Here we will briefly describe the basics of yoga so that the reader will have a better understanding of the differences and the similarities between the two systems. Both methods provide valid psychological and spiritual tools for the balance, healing, and integration of the human psyche. They relate to different parts of the subtle body, and thus each system requires a different method of working.

Yoga

It is presumed that yoga was developed in India by the inhabitants of the Indus River Valley. The exact methods and philosophy of the practice were gathered into a coherent system by Patanjali, a philosopher of the second century B.C.E. The various disciplines of yoga are not restricted to Hindus, however, for people of all faiths have studied and practiced them. The Sanskrit word *yoga* means "union," and from it is derived the English word "yoke." This implies a "harnessing" of our latent psychic energies. Yoga is a science of physical, mental, and spiritual integration. It is a systematic method of self-development and mystical ascent to universal wholeness on all levels of being. The main objective of yoga is the purification of the soul in order that the incarnated ego may be liberated from the karmic wheel. There are several different types of yoga, such as:

Bhakti Yoga: Union through devotion.

Dharma Yoga: Union through the virtues of religious duties.

Hatha Yoga: Union through physical discipline—breathing and postures.

Karma Yoga: Union through proper action or work in daily life.

Kriya Yoga: Union through the sacred outlook in everyday life, domestic ritual, and purification.

Laya Yoga: Union through developing the "serpent fire" or kundalini force.

Mantra Yoga: Union through spells and incantations.

Raja Yoga: Union though meditation.

Hatha yoga, which emphasizes physical and mental discipline, is by far the most popular type of yoga. The various *asanas* or postures of hatha yoga are the practices that most Westerners associate with Eastern mysticism. *Pranayama* or "the breath way" includes numerous techniques for breath control and vital energy manipulation. The discipline of concentration on a symbol or object is known as *dharana*, "holding." This is the ability to hold one image in the mind to the exclusion of all outside distractions.

Closely affiliated with hatha yoga and sometimes considered a part of it is laya yoga, which is dedicated to the development of the subtle body, including the chakras and that mysterious force known as *prana*.

Prana

According to the system of yoga, vital life force called *prana* courses through the human body by means of a network of minute conduits or canals known as *nadis*. This psycho-physical circuitry is often called the "subtle body."[3] In yoga the physical body is refined not simply for its own sake, but in order that it may serve the subtle body. The main *nadi* or conduit is called the *sushumna*, which runs from the bottom of the spine to the top of the cranium. Along its length the sushumna connects the seven *chakras* or main energy centers. Many more chakras are said to exist within the body, but all are governed by the primary seven.

The two other important nadis are known as the *ida* and the *pingala*. They start at the base of the spine and wind around the sushumna like strands of DNA. The ida ends at the left nostril and is associated with the moon and the left side of the body. The *pingala* terminates at the right nostril and corresponds to the sun and the right side of the body. These two nadis take in prana from the surrounding environment, and they are important to the practice of pranayama or the discipline of breath control. The ability to control breathing is equated with the ability to control the amount of prana retained in the body. In this way the revitalizing prana energy can be fully utilized to the benefit of the practitioner.

The Chakras

The *chakras* ("wheels" or "lotus flowers") are power centers within the aura that correspond to certain glands or organs in the body. They are reservoirs of vibrant energy—psychic sense organs where prana energy is concentrated in the human body. They can be described as spinning whirlpools of energy that exist at certain crossroads where mind and body, or spirit and matter, meet. These centers are listed (in both position and level of consciousness) from the lowest to the highest. They are often visualized as discs or orbs of color running up the center of the body. The mental, psychic, and physical state of any individual can be characterized by analyzing the level of vibrant energy at every chakra. In the average human being, this vital energy is confined to the three lowest centers. As the individual undergoes the process of spiritual growth, the majority of energies are transferred to the higher chakras. These psychic centers must be developed, like any growing flower, so that their petals are allowed to open and bloom.

Like the Western Sephiroth, each chakra has a series of correspondences attributed to it. These include colors, sounds, deities, symbols, planets, exercise positions or *asanas*, and parts of the body, among a host of other associations. All of these correspondences can be called upon for meditation and ritual work with the chakras.

Tattvas

Before describing the individual chakras, we must mention a few words about the tattvas (see Figure 8, p. 164). The word *tattva* means "quality," and it is used to describe a characteristic, essence, truth, or element. There are five primary tattvas which conform to the five basic elements.[4] These tattvas are also used as emblems for some of the chakras (see Figure 9, p. 168).

The first element of earth corresponds to the tattva known as *prithivi* which is represented by a yellow square. Traits of this element include cohesion, materialization, and solidarity. *Apas* is attributed to water, the second element and the principle of liquid, portrayed by a silver crescent. *Tejas* corresponds to fire, the third element, symbolized by a red triangle. Its attributes include transmutation and heat. *Vayu* is assigned to air, the fourth element, represented by a blue circle. Vayu symbolizes motion and the principle of vapor or gas. The fifth and final element of ether or spirit is referred to as *akasha*, symbolized by a black oval. Unity and limitlessness are its characteristics.

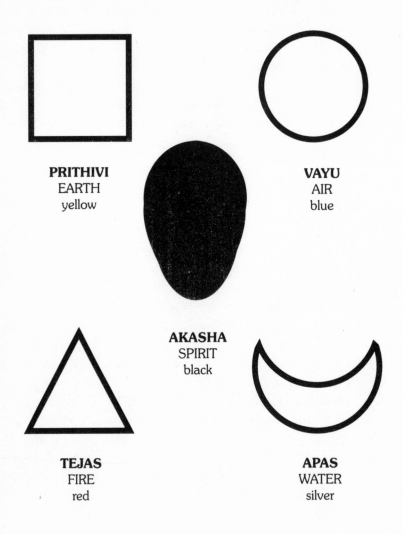

PRITHIVI
EARTH
yellow

VAYU
AIR
blue

AKASHA
SPIRIT
black

TEJAS
FIRE
red

APAS
WATER
silver

Figure 8: The Tattva Symbols.

The Seven Chakras

1. Muladhara, the base or root chakra. The first chakra is located at the sacrum at the base of the spine, near the anus. Associated glands/organs are the ovaries, the testes, and the pelvic plexus.[5] The traditional color of this chakra is yellow.[6] An alternate color given for this center is red.[7] Sometimes called the earth chakra, its symbol is *prithivi*, the yellow square of elemental earth. Basic survival needs are the focus of this center. *Muladhara* means "basic," "fundamental," or simply "root base." This center is associated with the physical self, elimination of waste, and basic needs of movement, sustenance, support, grounding, survival, and protection from danger. It also controls the function of sex, a role it shares with the second chakra. Bowel and sexual disfunctions result from psychic "blocks" at the base center.

2. Svadisthana, the navel chakra, controls sexuality. It is located about three inches below the navel. Associated organs are the kidneys and the adrenal glands. The generative organs and the hypogastric (lower abdominal) plexus are also attributed here. Traditionally this chakra is colored light blue. An alternative color is vermillion (brilliant orange-red).[8] The symbol of this center is *apas*, the silver-white crescent of elemental water. The word *Svadisthana* means "one's own self" or "dwelling place of the self." Sometimes called the "moon chakra," the *Svadisthana* controls the balance and flow of bodily fluids. It functions to preserve the human species through procreation. The issues of family, home, health, and security also correspond here, as well as the raw vitality of "gut-level" emotion, unfettered desire, and the unconscious. Fluid imbalances such as anemia are controlled through this center.

3. Manipura, the solar plexus chakra, is located just below the sternum. Manipura means "diamond," or "city of precious stone." The pancreas, liver, and spleen are also associated here. The traditional color of this chakra is red. An alternative color is gold.[9] Its symbol is *tejas*, the red fire triangle. This chakra is the center of metabolic energy, enthusiasm, ego, identity, and the personal will for power and control. Its foundation is the individual's personal being or essence. (Anyone who has ever experienced the sensation of having a "knot in the stomach" when anxious or tense will appreciate the importance of the solar plexus center. Continuous stress at this center may cause a number of gastro-intestinal disorders.)

4. Anahata, the heart chakra in the middle of the chest, is the center of love, feelings, connection, relationships, associations, cooperation, and compassion. It is also the center of meditation, devotion and prayer. The word *Anahata* means "unstruck sound," implying that its sound is completely inner—a silent sound. The thymus gland and the cardio-pulmonary plexus are associated here. The traditional color of the fourth chakra is green. An alternate color is deep red.[10] Its symbols are *vayu*, the blue circle of elemental air, and the blue hexagram or six-pointed star. This center is the bridge between the more physical energies of the first three chakras, and the transcendent energies of the final three centers. Disorders of the heart and lungs fall under the realm of the fourth chakra.

5. Visuddha, the throat chakra, is located in the hollow of the throat. The thyroid and parathyroid glands are associated here, along with the vocal chords and the pharyngeal plexus. The name *Visuddha* means "purity." The traditional color for this center is purple. An alternate color is gold.[11] Its symbol is the *akasha* or black egg of spirit. The fifth chakra controls respiration, auditory functions, cleansing, sensations, intuition, perception, psychic ability, communication, creativity, and self-expression. It is a center of focus and direction. (When psychic blockage occurs at this center, it is usually described as a feeling of being "all choked up" or having "a lump in the throat.") Malfunctions of the thyroid, as well as speech and hearing disorders, are under the dominion of the fifth chakra. The essence of this center is associated with sound, particularly vibration. In yoga the Visuddha is a very important center of alchemical transmutation. It is also said to produce a secretion of immortality.

6. Ajna, the brow or third eye chakra, is located in the forehead. It is associated with the pituitary gland and the frontal lobes of the brain. The word *Ajna* means "order" or "command," which indicates that activation of this chakra is indicative of true order and mastery. The traditional color here is translucent blue. An alternative color is white.[12] Its symbol is a circle with two wings or petals, which correspond to two pituitary lobes and the two major nadis of *pingala* (right petal) and *ida* (left petal). This center controls all higher intellectual functions, imagination, intuition, insight, consciousness, spiritual wisdom, knowledge, and true sight. Activation of the sixth chakra is thought to be responsible for all experiences of astral vision and astral traveling, as well as all encounters with the higher self. It is attributed to the "element" of light.

7. Sahasrara, the crown chakra located at or above the top of the head, is associated with the pineal gland and the cerebral cortex. Traditionally this center is given the various colors of the rainbow. An alternate color is clear.[13] The word *Sahasrara* means "thousand-petalled lotus," which is the symbol of this chakra, alluding to the thousands of brain cells within the cerebrum. The seventh chakra controls all aspects of mind and body, and it regulates the activities of all the other chakras. Its energy is often described as pure thought, spiritual understanding, bliss, peace, eternal life, super-consciousness, and the divine white light. The seventh chakra is activated at peak instances of oneness with the divine. It is said to be the abode of Shiva (illuminated consciousness), who demolishes ignorance and illusion.[14]

We should add that although the chakras are correlated to certain physical organs, glands, or nerve centers, *they are not solely physical centers*. To think of them in this way is to fall into the trap of Western rationalization. Anyone who believes that the chakra system is a network of purely physical organs and responses will never be able to experience the "raising of the kundalini."

Since they are partially corporeal and partially incorporeal, the chakras can influence and be influenced by both the material and the spiritual worlds. The subtle body of the individual is affected by his or her physical habits (diet, posture, physical tension, etc.) as well as mental and psychological habits (thought processes, emotions, imagination, aptitude, etc.).

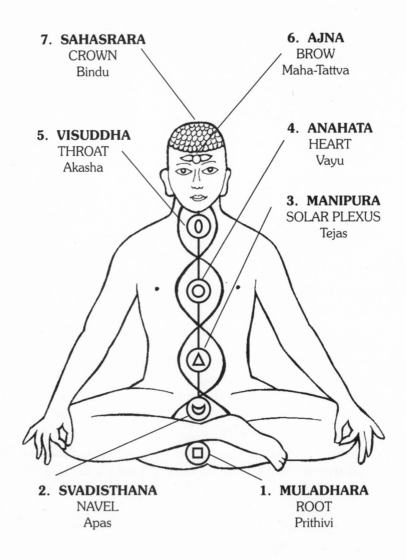

7. SAHASRARA
CROWN
Bindu

6. AJNA
BROW
Maha-Tattva

5. VISUDDHA
THROAT
Akasha

4. ANAHATA
HEART
Vayu

3. MANIPURA
SOLAR PLEXUS
Tejas

2. SVADISTHANA
NAVEL
Apas

1. MULADHARA
ROOT
Prithivi

Figure 9: The Chakras.

Kundalini

The vital energy that is used to activate the chakras is called *kundalini*, a Sanskrit word that means "serpent power." This fiery transformative energy has been described as a sleeping, coiled serpent which rests in the lowest chakra of Muladhara. Through the spiritual disciplines of yoga, exercise, breath control, and meditation, this "serpent power" is stimulated. It rises up the spine, vitalizing, purifying, and equilibrating each chakra it comes into contact with. With each chakra thus attained, the individual reaches new plateaus of spiritual development. "Raising the kundalini" from the lowest to the highest chakra is the Eastern method for attaining higher levels of consciousness that are associated with the experience of union with the divine. It is equivalent to the various stages of the "Great Work" of Western mystics and magicians. Tradition says that when the kundalini unites with the crown chakra, the result is a shock to the nervous system which arouses the pineal gland out of its dormancy to provide the practitioner with various *siddhis* or psychic/sensory powers that have been lost through neglect.

Many yogis[15] warn against practicing kundalini yoga without a teacher and without extensive practice in hatha yoga. This is because the kundalini energy may encounter impurities and psychic blockages in the subtle body as it flows upward. The fiery energy of the kundalini tries to burn its way through such obstacles. If too much obstruction is experienced, the "serpent force" may induce extreme physical and mental repercussions as the blocks are removed.

A far safer method of working with the chakras is to simply visualize them within the aura and contemplate their various attributes.

Chakra Awareness

Many asana positions and breathing exercises are intended to purify and invigorate the chakras, removing any "blocks" from the subtle body. Although such blocks usually have a psychological basis, they often result in physical problems, such as digestive disorders. These psychosomatic tensions can be diffused gradually by focusing the mind on the chakras. The way to do this is to concentrate on the various symbols and correspondences that the chakra system provides. These include geometric symbols, colors, gods and goddesses, Sanskrit letters, animals, and sounds used as mantras.

CHAKRA CORRESPONDENCES

Chakra	Tattva	Element	Symbol	Mantra	God	Goddess
Muladhara	Prithivi	Earth	Square	LaM	Brahma	Dakini
Svadisthana	Apas	Water	Crescent	VaM	Vishnu	Rakini
Manipura	Tejas	Fire	Triangle	RaM	Rudra	Lakini
Anahata	Vayu	Air	Hexagram	YaM	Isa	Kakini
Visuddha	Akasha	Spirit	Egg	HaM	Sadashiva	Shakini
Ajna	Maha-Tattva	Light/Mind	Winged Orb	OM	Sambhu	Hakini
Sahasrara	Bindu	Bliss	Lotus	——	Paramshiva	Maha Shakti

CHAKRA AWARENESS EXERCISE

1. Be seated in a meditative position on the floor or in a chair. Relax but be sure that your spine is straight. Begin to breathe slowly and rhythmically through your nostrils. As you inhale, draw the air into the lower part of your chest, filling the lungs to their fullest capacity without strain. Maintain this relaxed pattern of deep, full breathing throughout the exercise.

2. Imagine a disk or center of light at the base of your spine. Visualize a yellow square within this disk. As you focus on the square, breathe in and begin to notice the weight of your body, its density and mass. Breathe out and visualize the yellow square again.

   Breathe deeply, then intone the mantra "**La-NG**" (Lah-ng). Place special emphasis on the nasal "ng" sound, extending the latter sound out with the remaining breath.[16] On the following inhalation, mentally intone the word "**La-M**" (Lah-m), extending the "m" of the mantra. Repeat this mantra cycle three or four times.

3. Imagine a light blue disk just a few inches below your navel. Visualize a silver-white crescent within this disk. As you focus on the navel center, breathe in and begin to notice that the horns of the crescent are upturned to form a cup. Imagine this

cup filled to the brim with pure, sacred water. Feel this water flowing throughout your body, cleansing and purifying it. Breathe out and again visualize the silver crescent within the light blue disk.

Breathe deeply, then intone the mantra **"Va-NG"** (Vah-ng). Emphasize the "ng" sound, extending it out with the remaining breath. On the following inhalation, *mentally* intone the word **"Va-M"** (Vah-m), extending the "m" of the mantra. Repeat this mantra cycle three or four times.

4. Imagine a disk of light just a few inches below your sternum. Visualize a red triangle within this disk. As you focus on the solar plexus center, breathe in and imagine the red color of the triangle glowing hot. Feel the heat from this center spreading to all parts of your body. As the heat spreads, visualize it burning away all toxins and impurities. Breathe out and visualize the red triangle cooling a bit, returning to its original temperature.

Breathe deeply, then intone the mantra **"Ra-NG"** (Rah-ng). Emphasize the "ng" sound, extending it out with the remaining breath. On the following inhalation, *mentally* intone the word **"Ra-M"** (Rah-m), extending the "m" of the mantra. Repeat this mantra cycle three or four times.

5. Imagine a green disk of light in the area of your heart. Visualize a blue hexagram within this disk. As you focus on the heart center, breathe in and imagine that you are filled with the breath and spirit of God. Feel the cool breeze of the vast sky flowing through you, as if your body were porous. Your heart opens with a feeling of compassion for all things. For a moment you imagine the golden sun with its healing rays in the center of your heart. Breathe out and again visualize the blue hexagram within the green disk.

Breathe deeply, then intone the mantra **"Ya-NG"** (Yah-ng). Emphasize the "ng" sound, extending it out with the remaining breath. On the following inhalation, *mentally* intone the word **"Ya-M"** (Yah-m), extending the "m" of the mantra. Repeat this mantra cycle three or four times.

6. Imagine a violet disk of light in the hollow of your throat. Visualize a black oval or egg shape within this disk. As you focus on the
throat center, breathe in and imagine that you can hear the heartbeat of the universe. You are aware of angelic choirs singing
softly in some far-off heaven, and you have the feeling that if you
opened your mouth to speak, your words would drip honey and
have the aroma of jasmine. Breathe out and again visualize the
black oval within the violet disk.

Breathe deeply, then intone the mantra **"Ha-NG"** (Hah-ng).
Emphasize the "ng" sound, extending it out with the remaining breath. On the following inhalation, *mentally* intone the
word **"Ha-M"** (Hah-m), extending the "m" of the mantra.
Repeat this mantra cycle three or four times.

7. Imagine a disk of clear translucent blue in the middle of your
forehead. Within this disk visualize a white circle with two wings
on either side. As you focus on the brow center, breathe in and
imagine that the wing or petal on the right side is golden like the
sun, while the left-hand wing is silvery like the moon. Inhale and
notice the solar side glowing brightly on the right. Exhale and
visualize the lunar side beginning to shine. Breathe in and again
visualize the white winged circle within the clear blue disk.

Breathe deeply, then intone the mantra **"OM"** (Oh-m), extending the "m" of the mantra. On the following inhalation, *mentally* intone the same word. Repeat this mantra cycle three or
four times.

Continue to breathe rhythmically and visualize an eye in the center of the brow chakra. Now imagine the eye opening. Through it
you are able to perceive the divine light of the higher realms.

8. Imagine a clear disk of light above your head. Within this disk
visualize a lotus flower with a thousand petals—each petal is
colored in one of the hues of the rainbow. All the colors of the
universe are contained within this flower. At the center of the
lotus is the white brilliance and true peace of the divine light.
Inhale and feel a stream of energy extending up your spine, connecting all the chakras you have visualized on your ascent to
the lotus crown. Exhale and imagine the divine light from the

center of the lotus descending, passing through all of the chakra centers, cleansing, maintaining, and balancing each one. Do this several times. There is no sound or mantra that can do the crown center justice—there is only the silence of the divine union. Breathe in and again visualize the lotus flower within the disk of clear light.

9. After all the centers have been meditated on, descend the path of the chakras from the crown to the base. Visualize each center briefly on your journey backwards and be aware of how all the chakras seem more vitalized and equilibrated. When finished with the base chakra, take some time to become conscious of your surroundings before attempting to get up and move about.

Endnotes

1. The singular form is *galgal*.
2. Various yoga traditions also attribute different colors to the chakras.
3. Also called the astral body.
4. In Western alchemy, there are also five elements. However, in samkhya yoga, there are twenty-five tattvas. Compare this with the twenty-five traditional sub-elements of the Western system. In the Golden Dawn system, the Tattvas are used for skrying and astral projection.
5. A plexus is a network, especially of nerves, blood vessels, or lymphatics.
6. The traditional colors listed here are taken from the *Shat-Chakra*, a tantric text.
7. The alternate colors given for the chakras are taken from the tantric text known as the *Shiva Sanhita*. H. P. B.'s (Helena Petrovna Blavatsky) theosophical teachings attributed the color red-orange to this center.
8. Or rose-colored according to H. P. B.
9. H. P. B. has it as green.
10. H. P. B. has it as yellow.
11. H. P. B. has it as light blue.
12. H. P. B. has it as dark blue-violet.
13. H. P. B. has it as violet.
14. Many authorities do not consider the "Thousand-Petalled Lotus" to be one of the chakras because it lies outside the body, just above the crown of the head.

15. Masters of yoga.

16. The "ng" vibrates the sphenoid bone at the base of the skull, causing the sphenoidal sinus to act like a sound chamber, stimulating the pituitary gland.

Suggested Reading

A Chakra & Kundalini Workbook by Dr. Jonn Mumford (Llewellyn Publications, 1994).

Chakras by Harish Johari (Inner Traditions, 1988).

Energy Ecstasy and Your Seven Vital Chakras by Bernard Gunther (Borgo Press, 1983).

Laya Yoga by Shyam Sundar Goswami (Routledge and Kegan Paul, 1980).

Kundalini and the Chakras by Genevieve Paulson (Llewellyn Publications, 1991).

The Kundalini Expereince: Psychosis or Transcendence by Lee Sannella, M.D. (Integral Pub., 1988).

Wheels of Life by Anodea Judith (Llewellyn Publications, 1987).

CHAPTER NINE

THE PENTAGRAM

The Lesser Banishing Ritual of the Pentagram (sometimes called the LBRP) is one of the most important magical tools that the ceremonial magician has at his disposal. The following rendition is only slightly different from the one presented in Chapter Three. It is the version that we prefer to use.

THE QABALISTIC CROSS

Stand and face east. Imagine a brilliant white light touching the top of your head. Reach up with the index finger or blade of a dagger to connect with the light and bring it down to the forehead.

Touch the forehead and vibrate "**Atah**" (Ah-tah—"*Thou art*").[1]

Touch the breast and bring the dagger blade or index finger down till it covers the heart or abdominal area, pointing down to the ground. Imagine the light descending from the forehead to the feet. Vibrate "**Malkuth**" (Mahl-kooth—"*The Kingdom*").

Touch the right shoulder and visualize a point of light there. Vibrate "**ve-Geburah**" (v'ge-boo-rah—"*The Power*").

Touch the left shoulder and visualize a point of light there. See the horizontal shaft of light extending from the opposite shoulder

175

to join this point of light. Vibrate **"ve-Gedulah"** (v'ge-doo-lah—
"The Glory").

Imagine a completed cross of light running from head to feet
and shoulder to shoulder.

Bring the hands outward, away from the body, and finally bring
them together again, clasped on the breast as if praying or interlocking the fingers. Vibrate **"Le-Olahm, Amen"** (lay-oh-lahm, ah-men—
"Forever, unto the ages").

~

THE LESSER BANISHING RITUAL
OF THE PENTAGRAM

Stand and face east.[2] Perform the Qabalistic Cross as described above.

Still facing east, use a dagger or the index finger of the right hand
to trace a large Lesser Banishing Pentagram. Thrust the dagger tip or
index finger through the center of the pentagram and vibrate
"YHVH" (Yode-Heh-Vav-Heh—*the Tetragrammaton* [see Glossary]).

(Keep the right arm extended throughout, never let it drop. The
pentagrams should be visualized in a flaming blue or white light.)

Turn to the south and trace the same pentagram there. Charge
the figure as before, intoning **"Adonai"** (Ah-doh-nye—*"Lord"*).

Turn to the west and trace the pentagram. Charge it with
"Eheieh" (Eh-hey-yay—*"I am"*).

Turn to the north and draw the pentagram, intoning **"AGLA"**
(Ah-gah-lah—*a notariqon* [see Glossary]).

Keep the arm extended. Turn to face the east. Extend both arms
out in the form of a cross and say, **"Before me, RAPHAEL"** (Rah-fay-
el). Visualize before you the great archangel of air rising out of the
clouds in flowing yellow and violet robes, carrying a caduceus wand.

Behind you, visualize another figure and say, **"Behind me,
GABRIEL"** (Gah-bree-el). See the archangel stepping out of the sea
like the goddess Venus, dressed in robes of blue and orange, with
cup in hand.

See to your right another figure in flaming red and green robes carrying a sword. Say, "**On my right hand, MICHAEL**" (Mee-kai-el).

See another great archangel at your left, who rises up from the vegetation of the earth in robes of citrine, olive, russet, and black, holding stems of ripened wheat. Say, "**On my left hand, URIEL**" (Ur-ee-el).

Say, "**For about me flames the pentagram, and in the column shines the Six-rayed Star.**"

Repeat the Qabalistic Cross as in the beginning.

Magical work involves change and creation. And the subject of the magician's work is the *self*. The magician is the focus of his or her own alchemical processes. By adapting one's personal vision to reflect the macrocosm, we can change ourselves to better reflect those divine ideas. We may alter our body, appearance, the chemical composition of our blood, and the configuration of our nervous system. We may tame the feral beasts that dwell within our organic structure. By changing ourselves to resonate with the divine, we may transmute every portion of ourselves and become as purified vessels for the eternal spirit.

Rites such as the Lesser Banishing Ritual of the Pentagram represent this spiritual goal. The LBRP explains this goal in mathematical and Qabalistic terms. It sets a pattern for self-growth which has a powerful influence on the subconscious mind. It symbolically places us in a correct relationship to the one divine source. And when we are in this correct relationship, it becomes much easier for us to fight off any hostile influence from within or from without. By continued practice of rituals such as the LBRP, we can produce the physical and astral conditions which will make it easier for us to realize our true place in the divine universe. The pentagram is a symbol of the logos or the word of creation, which connects the essential divine self in humanity to the one divine self called God.

The Formula of the LBRP

The Lesser Banishing Ritual of the Pentagram is the ceremonial magician's way of casting a circle of protection. Some Wiccan groups will cast a circle around their sacred space by tracing it on the ground with a sword, or by sprinkling salt water around the area. But the ceremonial magician does this by tracing pentagrams around the circle with a specialized dagger or wand.

The ritual begins with a brief moment of meditation to cleanse the mind and begin the process of creating a ritual atmosphere or sacred space. Then the magician performs what is called the Qabalistic Cross. This rite creates a cross of living divine light within the magician's aura.

This cross is based upon the Qabalistic Tree of Life, containing the spheres of Kether, Malkuth, Geburah, Chesed, and Tiphareth. These also represent a balancing of the four elements within the magician's aura: Kether/air, Malkuth/earth, Geburah/fire, and Chesed or Gedulah/water. And although the name of Tiphareth is not vibrated, the balancing element of spirit is indicated by placing the hands over the heart area.

After the Qabalistic Cross, the magician traces the Lesser Banishing Pentagram in all four quarters, beginning in the east and walking clockwise. The symbol of the pentagram refers to the four elements—crowned and completed by the fifth element of spirit. The pentagram is a symbol of protection. When traced, the pentagrams are visualized in flaming astral blue or white light. They are charged by stabbing through the center of the figure when the appropriate Hebrew words are vibrated. The pentagrams are connected to each other by an astral ribbon of the same color. Drawing these banishing pentagrams rids the area of all unwanted energies.

The magician returns to the east, and stands with arms extended in the form of the cross. He identifies himself with the Tau cross of life, a symbol of knowledge gained through sacrifice, but which is also related to the ideas of mercy and justice.

Next comes the invocation of the four archangels. These archangels are associated with the idea of the divine creator governing the four elements and the four directions. Angels and archangels are considered specific aspects of God, each with a particular purpose and jurisdiction. They are humanized symbols of what we believe to be good and holy. Nearly all of the Hebrew angelic names end in the suffixes "el" or "yah." This indicates that they are "of God." Raphael, "the Healer of God," is assigned to air. Gabriel, "the Strong One of God," is assigned to water. Michael, "He who is like God," is assigned to fire. Uriel, "the Light of God," is assigned to earth.[3]

While the pentagrams are drawn for the *purification* of the circle, the archangels are invoked to consecrate the circle with the forces of the divine light.

> *Before me, RAPHAEL, behind me, GABRIEL, on my right hand, MICHAEL, on my left hand, URIEL.*

Then comes the statement, "For about me flame the Pentagrams, and in the column shines the Six-rayed Star." (Refer to Chapter Three, Endnote 20.) The six-rayed star is the hexagram or "Star of David," which is the star of the macrocosm or "greater universe." It is formed from the two triangles of fire and water, and it symbolizes perfection and total balance. While the pentagram is the symbol of man, the hexagram is the symbol of perfected or purified man, balanced within the greater universe.

This is followed once again by the Qabalistic Cross, which further strengthens and seals the cross of light within the magician's aura.

Origins of the Pentagram Ritual

The Lesser Banishing Ritual of the Pentagram was a creation of the Hermetic Order of the Golden Dawn. However, various portions of the ritual are found to have far more ancient sources.

In the New Testament, the Lord's Prayer (Matthew 6:9–13) is obviously based upon Qabalistic principles, showing that Jesus of Nazareth, who was called Rabbi by his followers, knew his Qabalah. This is because the Lord's Prayer is itself based on the Hebrew "Prayer of David" from the Old Testament, found in the first book of Chronicles 29:1. "The Prayer of David at the Foundation of the Temple" reads as follows:

> *Unto Thee, O Tetragrammaton,*
> *are the **Greatness** and the **Power** and the **Beauty***
> *and the **Victory** and the **Glory**,*

for unto Thee is everything in the Heavens and the Earth.
*Unto Thee, O Tetragrammaton, is the **Kingdom**.*

This single verse mentions the names of several Sephiroth, including: Chesed, Geburah, Tiphareth, Netzach, Hod, and Malkuth. The Lord's Prayer from the New Testament states:

*For thine is the **Kingdom** and the **Power** and the **Glory**, forever and ever, Amen.*[4]

This is only slightly different from the Qabalistic Cross, which states (in English):

Thou art the Kingdom and the Power and the Glory,
the World forever, unto the ages. Amen.

The word *Atah* ("Thou art") is linked to the Sephirah of Kether, whose divine name is "I am." *Malkuth* ("the Kingdom") is the tenth sphere on the Tree. *V'geburah* ("and the Power") refers to the fifth Sephirah of power. *V'gedulah*, which means "and the Glory," refers to Chesed since "Glory" (or "Magnificence") is another title of Chesed. *Le-Olahm, Amen* means *"forever unto the ages."*

This is very similar to the Christian Sign of the Cross. One important difference between the Christian Cross and the Qabalistic Cross is that in the Hermetic version, Geburah or "the Power" is attributed to the right shoulder, while in the Christian Cross, it is placed on the left shoulder. This points out a major difference in the way that a ceremonial magician approaches the divine self from the way that the average church-goer and the Christian Rosicrucian approaches God.

Within the Judeo-Christian tradition, the image of God is seen as separate and outside of humanity. The image of God, as projected on the Tree of Life, is usually viewed as something "out there," or something that is too sacred to be approached by sinful earthbound human beings. Thus the Tree of Life as the image of God is sometimes pictured as the *backside* of God by the orthodox religions. In other words, God's face is not turned toward humanity, or as the scriptures tell us, "one cannot look upon the face of God and live." It was safer to "image" the deity from behind. Therefore to the Roman Catholic, Geburah is on the left shoulder—the same as the image of the Tree seen from the back, and outside of the human being.

One Qabalistic diagram often used to illustrate the idea of the divine on the Tree of Life is that of *Adam Kadmon*, the so-called Atziluthic or archetypal man. Adam Kadmon is the "heavenly man" or "body of God." He is the divine prototype of humanity which is circumscribed upon the Tree of Life. The crown of Kether is above his head, Malkuth is at his feet, Geburah is at his left shoulder, and Chesed is at his right shoulder. In his book *Kabbalah: Tradition of Hidden Knowledge*, Z'ev ben Shimon Halevi tells us about the diagram of Adam Kadmon: "…this reflection, however, like that in any mirror, is only a refection and never the reality."[5] Halevi says:

> *The likeness of a man (Ezekiel 1:26) was used by early mystics to describe the Divine Glory. The figure of a primordial, Atziluthic man, God's image is the embodiment of the Sefirot. This, the most perfect image of Divinity, is seen not as God but as His reflection, and therefore a representation of his does not contravene the Second Commandment.*[6]

Adam Kadmon is sometimes called the "Reversed Tree." This is because several glyphs of the Tree of Life are shown with their "roots" in the Supernals. Adam Kadmon is "reversed" from this, with this head in Kether and his feet in Malkuth. We also believe that he is the "Reversed Tree" because his image is reversed not only from top to bottom, but from *side to side*. If you hold the usual *image* of Adam Kadmon (see Figure 10, p. 182) up to a mirror you will see what we believe is the *true non-reversed* appearance of the deity that it is forbidden by the orthodoxy to look upon—Geburah is on the right side, Chesed is on the left. Therefore, the traditional diagram of Adam Kadmon is a *tzelem* or *reflected image* of a spiritual reality—not that reality itself.

Ceremonial magicians are not bound by the admonishments of orthodoxy which state that one cannot view God from the front, or look upon his non-reversed image. Theurgists[7] view the usual diagram of the Tree of Life as the *face or front side* of the divine. This image of the Tree is then *reflected* back into us, as if through a mirror. Thus Geburah, on the deity's right shoulder, is reflected to our right shoulder. This is because the magician seeks to bring the image of God inside the aura. This is a greatly simplified version of a magical operation known as the assumption of godforms, and it points out

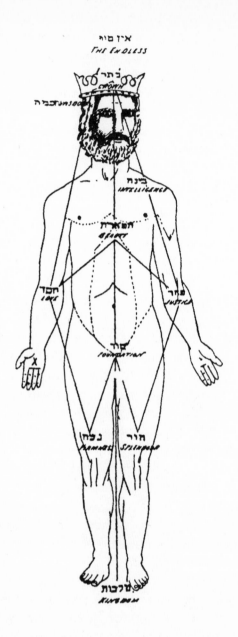

Figure 10: Adam Kadmon, the "Reversed Tree."

the difference between the *exoteric* beliefs of mainstream religion and the *esoteric* practices of ceremonial magicians. (See Figure 11, p. 184.)

Commenting on the Qabalistic Cross in his book *Transcendental Magic*, Eliphas Levi, the man most responsible for the occult revival of the nineteenth century, wrote that: "This Sign, made after this manner, should precede and terminate the Conjuration of the Four."[8]

The Conjuration of the Four refers to the four elements of fire, water, air, and earth. The four archangels in the LBRP are among the best known and most powerful of the Hebrew deities, and they are the governors of the four elements. The invocation of the archangels in the LBRP is very similar to an invocation in a Hebrew Night Prayer printed in an orthodox *Siddur* or Daily Prayer Book translated by Philip Birnbaum.[9] The Siddur reads as follows:

> In the name of the Lord God of Israel, may **Michael** be at my right hand, and **Gabriel** at my left; before me **Uriel**; behind me **Raphael**; and above my head the Divine Presence.

This clearly relates very closely to the calling of the archangels in the LBRP. Although they are in a different order, they are still the same archangels, carrying out the same duties. These orthodox correspondences may reflect an approach that is different from that taken by the Golden Dawn. There are undoubtedly similar versions of the invocation of the archangels still tucked away in Hebrew texts.

What the Pentagram Represents

No one knows the exact magical origins of the pentagram, or *pentalpha*, as it is sometimes called in older texts. For centuries the five-pointed star has been used as a symbol of protection and a talisman for health and well-being. It was popular among the Babylonians, Egyptians, Assyrians, and Hebrews. According to Eliphas Levi, magicians of old used to draw the symbol upon their doorsteps, to keep malevolent spirits out and beneficent spirits in. And as early as the sixth century B.C.E., Pythagoras, the Greek philosopher-mystic, used the pentagram as a holy symbol for his followers.

Five was a number peculiarly associated with the ideas of marriage and union, as it is the first number beyond the monad formed from the union of the first odd and even numbers, male and

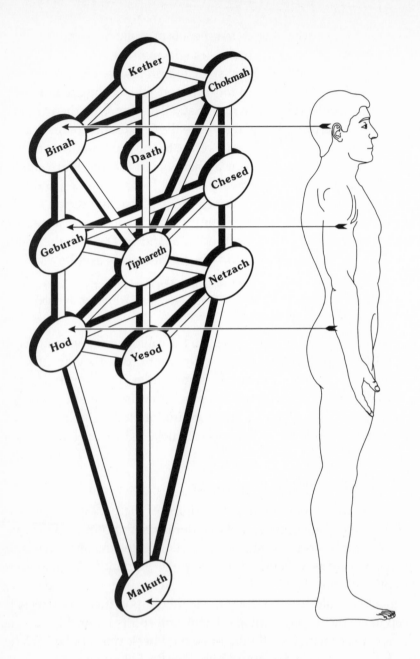

Figure 11: Backing into the Tree.

female. It is also said to represent the human figure, with arms and legs outspread.

The shape of the five-pointed star seems to be one of nature's favorite geometric designs—it can be found in flowers, fruit, and crystalline forms. In magic the pentagram represents the four elements of fire, water, air, and earth—plus one other.

In addition, the number five is attributed to the *Pentagrammaton* or "five-lettered name." This is a natural extension of the *Tetragrammaton*, the holy and hidden "four-lettered name" of God signified by the letters YHVH (יהוה). In the Pentagrammaton the letter Shin is placed in the center of YHVH, resulting in the name of *Yeheshuah*—YHShVH (יהשוה). This is the name of Jesus in Hebrew, but more importantly to magicians, it is the four elements of fire, water, air, and earth, with the addition of the fifth element of spirit.

The element of spirit binds together and governs the other four, which are the metaphysical building blocks of all that exists. The fifth element of spirit, also called the *quintessence,* crowns and connects the other four. It is spirit which transcends the others and makes the whole of the pentagram greater than the sum of its parts. Spirit is the divine and guiding principle. This is one reason magicians stress that it is important to keep the spirit point of the pentagram facing upward. To reverse it would be to subject spirit to the governance of matter. Thus the inverted pentagram signifies chaos and evil.

Levi states that:

> *The Pentagram signifies the domination of the mind over the elements, and the demons of air, the spirits of fire, the phantoms of water and ghosts of earth are enchained by this sign.*[10]

Elsewhere Levi reiterates that "The elementary spirits are subservient to this sign when employed with understanding...."[11] He continues:

> *If it be asked how a sign can exercise so much power over spirits, we inquire in turn why the Christian world bows before the Sign of the Cross. The sign is nothing by itself and has no force apart from the doctrine of which it is the summary and the logos. Now a sign which summarizes, in their expression, all the occult forces of Nature, a sign which has ever exhibited to elementary spirits and others a power greater than their own, fills them naturally with respect and fear, enforcing their obedience by the*

empire of science and of will over ignorance and weakness. By the Penta-
gram is also measured the exact proportions of the great and unique
Athanor necessary to the confection of Philosophical Stone and of the
Great Work. The most perfect alembic in which the Quintessence can be
elaborated is conformable to this figure, and the Quintessence itself is
represented by the Sign of the Pentagram.[12]

Here Levi gives us clues about the numerical dimensions of
the pentagram, for by it is "measured the exact proportions" of
the athanor, the alchemical oven which is used to obtain the
Philosopher's Stone—a symbol for spiritual illumination and
expanded consciousness. What is so important about the proportions of the pentagram?

Through the number five, the number of points on this figure,
the pentagram is connected to the sphere of Geburah on the Tree of
Life, and to its corresponding planet, Mars. The pentagram represents that fiery, purifying power of the divine that takes the name
of *Pachad* or "fear," one of the titles of Geburah, whose other primary title is "strength." Another higher function of Geburah is that
of *Din* meaning "justice," "judgment," or "severity." The divine
name of Geburah is *Elohim Gibor* or "God of Battles." According to
Iamblichus, a Neoplatonic philosopher-magician of the fourth century C.E., "The pentad is highly expressive of justice, and justice
comprehends all the other virtues."[13] In his book *Numbers, Their
Occult Power and Mystic Virtues*, W. Wynn Westcott states that the
pentad is called "the Unconquered." Westcott also states:

Proclus on Hesiod gives two reasons for its semblance to Justice,
"because it punishes wrong, and takes away inequality of possession,
and also equalizes what is less, to benefit."[14]

Thus the number five provides us with the ideas of fear, strength,
severity, power, and justice. The awesome energy of Geburah can
strike fear into the minds of negative powers and those who do not
understand its harsh, purifying, and equilibrating power. Eliphas
Levi tells us that the pentagram is a potent sign that extends its power
over the elementary intelligences that inhabit the astral realms:

The Pentagram...exercises a great influence upon spirits and terrifies
phantoms.[15]

However, to the magician who uses it with a divine intent, the pentagram is a potent symbol of strength and justice.

The pentagram has always been misunderstood and feared by those who do not comprehend its sacred meaning:

> We proceed to the explanation and consecration of the Sacred and Mysterious Pentagram. At this point, let the ignorant and superstitious close the book; they will either see nothing but darkness, or they will be scandalized. The Pentagram, which in the Gnostic schools is called the Blazing Star, is the sign of intellectual omnipotence and autocracy. It is the Star of the Magi; it is the Word made flesh...The Sign of the Pentagram is also the sign of the Microcosm, and it represents what the Kabalists of the book Zohar term the Microprosopus. The complete comprehension of the Pentagram is the key of the two worlds. It is absolute philosophy and natural science.[16]

> As will be seen, all Mysteries of Magic, all symbols of the Gnosis, all figures of occultism, all kabalistic keys of prophesy are summed up in the Sign of the Pentagram, which Paracelsus proclaims to be the greatest and most potent of all signs.[17]

Gematria of the Pentagram

One way to study the pentagram is through the use of *gematria* or Hebrew numerology that is concerned with the numerical value of the letters of the Hebrew alphabet.[18] Words and images that have the same value are thought to be related. By its number, five, the pentagram is connected to Geburah and to the Hebrew letter Heh (ה), a symbol of creative power. Through the letter Heh, the pentagram becomes a symbol of intuition and understanding. But it is also a symbol of sight, which is the sense attributed to Heh. Therefore it is the magical symbol of true vision. The letter Heh is also connected with the sign of Aries, the warrior-protector, and the tarot card of "The Emperor," who is the ruler and executor of the divine law. In human physiology, Aries is especially referred to the head (symbolized by the uppermost point of spirit in the pentagram). Aries is ruled by Mars and its exaltation is the Sun, the symbolic source of all light. This again leads us to ideas of strength and protection through the warrior energy of Mars-Aries, as well as solar light and health.

Another word associated through gematria with the number five is *bahbah* (בבא), meaning "gate."

The Fifth Key of the tarot is the card of "The Hierophant," who is the teacher, the expounder of the mysteries, and the channel for spiritual instruction.

There are other numbers associated with this figure as well. Refer to the diagram of the pentagram and its enclosing pentagon (see Figure 12, p. 189). The pentagon is a figure that is implied, if not actually traced, when drawing a pentagram. In length every line of the pentagon is composed of thirteen units. The number thirteen is associated with a multitude of occult references: twelve spheres are needed to surround a central (thirteenth) sphere; Moses and the twelve tribes of Israel; Jesus and the twelve apostles; the sun and the twelve signs of the zodiac. In addition, many important Qabalistic words have the numerical value of thirteen, including *achad* (אחד), "unity" and *ahavah* (אהבה), "love." Other words tied to this number include *gahah* (גהה), "healing" or "health"; *ziv* (זו), "glory"; and *hegeh* (הגה), "to separate," or "to imagine."

The Thirteenth Key of the tarot is titled "Death," and it is attributed to Scorpio, transformation, and change. The Thirteenth Path of the *Sepher Yetzirah*, an important Qabalistic text, corresponds to the tarot card of "The High Priestess" and is attributed to the Moon. This path is the primary conduit by which the higher, divine consciousness flows down to lower levels. It is also a path of change.

Interestingly, thirteen multiplied by two is twenty-six, the value of *YHVH* (יהוה) and *kabedh* (כבד) "to honor." The Twenty-sixth Path of the *Sepher Yetzirah* is attributed to the tarot card of "The Devil," to which is assigned the powers of material force and generation.

Thirteen multiplied by three is thirty-nine, the value of *YHVH Achad* (יהוה אחד) or "YHVH is One." Thirteen multiplied by four is fifty-two, the number of YHVH spelled out.[19] It is also the value of *Aima* (אימא), the Supernal Mother and *Ben* (בן), the Reconciling Son.

Finally, thirteen multiplied by five (the number of lines that comprise the pentagon) is sixty-five, the number associated with *Adonai* (אדני). It is also the number formed by the Latin letters for "light"—LVX (L = 50, V = 5, X = 10). The whole of the figure can be described as a sigil of the name of Adonai or the light of LVX.

Sixty-five is also the number associated with the Hebrew words *hekel* (היכל), meaning "temple or palace" (the Zohar tells us that Adonai is the palace of YHVH); *has* (הס), "to be silent," *dumiah* (דומיה), "silence"; and *gam yechad* (גמ יחד), "together in unity."

The long segment of each line of the pentagram is eight units in length. The number eight corresponds to the Sephirah of Hod, the sphere of intellect, communication, words of power, and magic. It also corresponds to the Hebrew letter Cheth (ח) which means "fence or enclosure," pointing to further protective qualities. The Eighth Key of the tarot is titled "Strength,"—it is a fiery path which leads to the sphere of Geburah. Through gematria, the number eight is associated with the word *agad* (אגד) "to bind."

The shorter segment of each line of the pentagram is five units in length, affirming once again the same ideas stated above.

The actual pentagram is composed of five lines which are each twenty-one units in length. The Twenty-first Key of the tarot is called "The Universe," and it is the completion of cosmic manifestation. Twenty-one is the value of *Eheieh* (אהיה), the divine name of Kether. Eheieh is one of the highest names that is associated with the act of creation.

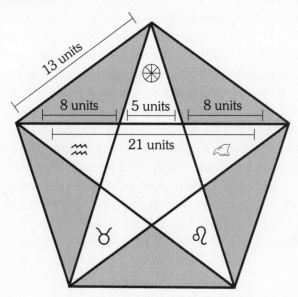

Figure 12: The Pentagram and Pentagon.

Other words that correspond to the number twenty-one are *hagig* (הגיג), "meditation" and *khezev* (חזו), "vision." The Twenty-first Path of the *Sepher Yetzirah* is called "The Wheel of Fortune" and it is attributed to the planet Jupiter. In addition, the mystic number of Tiphareth is twenty-one.

The total length of all lines on the pentagram (twenty-one multiplied by five) is 105, which is formed by adding all the numbers from one to fourteen. The Fourteenth Key of the tarot is "Temperance," the card of the HGA or higher self. The Fourteenth Path of the *Sepher Yetzirah* is attributed to Daleth (ד), the "door" of initiation. Fourteen is also a number associated with the Hebrew words *atad* (אטד), "thorn, the piercer"; *debach* (דבח), "sacrifice"; *gaye* (גיא), "rising earth"; *dai* (די), "abundance"; *david* (דוד), "beloved"; *habhab* (הבהב), "sacrificial offering"; *hadah* (הדה), "to direct with the hand"; *yod* (יד), "hand"; and *zahav* (זהב), "gold."

Other words associated with the number 105 are *hepek* (הפכ), "to change or transform"; *pekeh* (פכה), "to flow or pour forth"; and *tziyah*[20] (ציה), "to glow, to burn or to glitter."

So what does all this mean? In tracing a pentagram, the magician invokes the power of Eheieh. This is a glittering, glorious power that pours forth abundantly; pierces and binds all negativity; encloses and separates the pure from the impure; opens and closes gates or doors between different worlds; gives rise to meditation, visions, love, unity, and healing; and to the magician who silences the chatter of his mind, sacrifices his lower desires, and aligns himself with the divine will, it can be employed with justice as a potent force for transformation, generation, and change (particularly on the material or earth plane) which can be directed by the hand and used to obtain spiritual "gold." Through the number five (the creative *Heh*, and the five elements), Eheieh, as asserted through the tracing of a pentagram, is an expression of the five-fold existence of the power of the divine self and the light (LVX) of Adonai, who is the palace of YHVH. It is that which created the cosmos and which rules over it with justice and strength, permeating every aspect of creation. Everything in the universe is composed of the one true *self* which is both the power that transforms and the object of the transformation.[21]

Divine Hebrew Names Associated with the LBRP

The Lesser Banishing Ritual of the Pentagram is said to be most effective in the Qabalistic realm of Assiah—the physical, active world that is associated with the tenth Sephirah of Malkuth. This is the realm in which we live and function. Malkuth is said to contain the four elements of the manifest universe. This is why in many drawings, Malkuth is shown divided into four sections. The sub-elements are: air of Malkuth, water of Malkuth, fire of Malkuth, and earth of Malkuth. But for our purposes it would be better to refer to them simply as air, fire, water, and earth—the elements of our physical plane.

With respect to the entire Tree of Life, Malkuth is the only Sephirah to which is assigned the element of earth. This is why the *banishing earth pentagram*[22] in particular is used throughout the LBRP. However, in this instance it would be better to refer to the pentagram used in this ritual as the *lesser banishing pentagram* to avoid confusion.[23]

All of the divine Hebrew names intoned in the Lesser Banishing Ritual of the Pentagram are composed of four letters. And the specific names used are attributed to the four sub-elements of Malkuth. The name of *YHVH*, the Tetragrammaton, is vibrated after the pentagram is drawn in the east, the direction attributed to elemental air. Tradition tells us that YHVH is a symbol for the highest, most divine name of God. Therefore it is appropriate that this name is vibrated in the east, the place of the dawning of the light. YHVH is our sunrise, our source of life.

The east symbolizes elemental air which has further correspondences with Mercury, the highest of the three alchemical principles. Alchemists often refer to Mercury as spirit. All of this is in keeping with the idea of the "highest name of God."

Adonai, meaning "lord," is the name vibrated after the figure is traced in the south. This name is particularly associated with Malkuth, whose complete divine name is Adonai ha-Aretz. The name "lord" carries with it connotations of high rank, especially power, rulership, and dominion.[24] Here the name is associated with fire and the south, the direction of the sun's greatest strength. This is a reminder that here on Malkuth, our immediate symbolic link with the lord of light and strength is through the life-giving rays of the sun.

The name of *Eheieh* is vibrated after the western pentagram is drawn. *Eheieh*, meaning "I am," is the divine name of Kether. The west is the place of sunset, the completion of the sun's journey across the sky. It represents rest and peace. To the ancient Egyptians, Ra, the Sun god died each night when he entered Amentet (the west). The west is a symbol of the completion of the soul's journey and the goal of spiritual growth. Therefore the west is an emblem of Kether, the goal which we seek throughout our incarnation on earth and which we hope to reach at the end of life, when we (like Ra) journey to Amentet. The name *Eheieh* vibrated in the west suggests that the goal of all esoteric work is the magician's complete identification with the true and eternal self of Kether.

After the northern pentagram is drawn, the word *Agla* is vibrated. This is not really a word but rather a notariqon which uses the first letter of each word in a sentence to form a single word. In this case the sentence from which Agla is formed is *Atah Gebur Le-Olam Adonai*. This means, "Thou art great forever, my Lord," which is a powerful invocation—clearly calling upon all the might of Adonai to aid and guide us through the darkness of things unknown. Agla is vibrated in the north because that is the direction of the greatest symbolic cold, darkness, shadow, illusion, and the unfamiliar. It is "the place of Forgetfulness, Dumbness (silence), and Necessity, and of the greatest symbolical Darkness."[25] It represents all the dormant and unmanifested forces of the universe, as well as those which are hidden or veiled to us. These are forces which we are largely ignorant of. However, all things, manifest or unmanifest (light or dark), exist then, now, and always under the rulership of Adonai. This we affirm by the phrase "Thou art great forever, my Lord!"

How to Draw a Perfect Pentagram

Refer to Figure 13, p. 194, the diagram of the pentagram.[26]

1. With pencil and straight edge, draw a straight horizontal line on a piece of paper.

2. Place two points on this line that will be known as A and B. (AB will be the length of the line between the earth and fire points of the pentagram.)

3. Find the center of line AB and mark it with another point. We will call this point O.

4. From O, draw a line perpendicular to AB. We will call this new line OH.

5. Starting with point O, mark off a section of line OH that is equal in length to AB. The new point will be called C.

6. Draw a straight line from B to C, and continue the line well past point C.

7. From C, measure off a portion of the new line that is equal in length to OA and mark it with another point. This will be point F.

8. The next part will require a compass. Starting at point B as the center, with line BF as the radius, draw circle FKD, bisecting line OH at point D. (This is the spirit point of the pentagram.)

9. Draw a line connecting A to D. Draw a line to connect B to D.

10. Adjust the compass so that the radius is equal to the length of line AB.

11. With B as the center, draw a semicircle toward the upper right-hand corner of the paper.

12. With D as the center, draw a semicircle toward the lower right-hand corner of the paper. This semicircle will intersect the previous one at point E. (This is the water point of the pentagram.)

13. With A as the center, draw a semicircle toward the upper left-hand corner of the paper.

14. With D as the center, draw a semicircle toward the lower left-hand corner of the paper. This semicircle will intersect the previous one at point G. (This is the air point of the pentagram.)

15. Draw lines to connect A to E, B to G, and G to E.

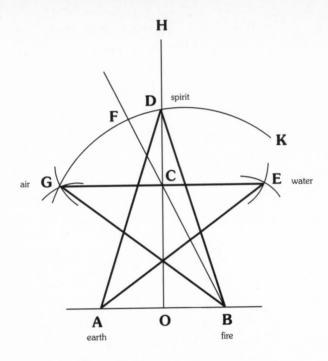

Figure 13: Drawing a Pentagram.

Uses of the Lesser Banishing Ritual of the Pentagram

In addition to its psychotherapeutic uses, this simple yet powerful cleansing ritual can be used as a protection against the impure magnetism of others. It is also a method for getting rid of negative thoughts or emotional distress.

As a magician, you can make a mental image of a particular thought or disturbance and visualize it before you. One way of doing this is to project it out of your aura with the Projection Sign of a Neophyte (also called the the *Attacking Sign*; see Figure 14, p. 198). When the unwanted energy is away from you, you can prevent its return with the Sign of Silence (or the *Sign of Protection*). Then imagine the negative form in the east and perform the Lesser Banishing Ritual of the Pentagram. See the form dissolving on the outside of your ring of flaming pentagrams.

The LBRP can also be used to aid your powers of focus and concentration. While lying down, formulate yourself standing up in robes and holding a dagger. Place your consciousness in this astral form and go to the east. Make yourself "feel" that you are there by touching the wall, opening your eyes, and stomping on the floor. Then let your astral form perform the ritual, circumambulating the room, and mentally vibrating the words. When you are finished, try to see your results astrally. Then walk back and stand behind your physical body and let your astral body be reabsorbed.

In the beginning of one's magical training, the LBRP is to be performed daily for no less than a period of six months. In fact, it should be practiced daily by any magician no matter how long one has been doing the work. Some Golden Dawn and Stella Matutina manuscripts suggested doing the *invoking form* of this Ritual in the morning and the banishing form at night. However, we feel that the beginner needs to concentrate only on the *banishing form*.[27] Beginners have a tendency to have their auras light up on the astral—they unknowingly attract all kinds of elementals at this early stage of the work.

It's far more important for the beginner to know how to banish rather than to invoke. Anyone can attract an elemental or energy form. Getting rid of it can be more difficult.

The following section describes a number of different versions of the LBRP, including Egyptian, Greek, Gaelic, and Shamanic renditions.

AN EGYPTIAN PENTAGRAM RITUAL

The Egyptian Qabalistic Cross

Stand and face east. Imagine a brilliant white light touching the top of your head. Reach up with the index finger or blade of a dagger to connect with the light and bring it to the forehead.

Touch the forehead and say: **"Entek Pau"** (pronounced "en-tek pow," meaning "Thou art He who Is").

Touch the breast and say: **"ta Sutenit"** (pronounced "tah su-ten-it," meaning "the Kingdom").

Touch the right shoulder and say: **"ta Sakhem"** (pronounced "tah sahk-hem," meaning "the Divine Power").

Touch the left shoulder and say: **"ta Djeser"** (pronounced "tah d-jes-er," meaning "and the Glory").

Clasp the fingers over the breast and say: **"ta Taui en Hah"** (pronounced "tah tow-ee en hah," meaning "the World, Forever").

Say: **"Nedj Her"** (pronounced "ned-j her," meaning "Homage to Thee").

The Pentagrams

Face east. Use dagger or the index finger of the right hand to trace a large lesser banishing pentagram. As you do so, vibrate **"Nudjeru Yebeta"** (pronounced "nud-jeh-ru yeh-beh-tah," meaning "Gods of the East"). Thrust the dagger tip or index finger through the center of the pentagram and vibrate **"NEF"** ("Air"). Keep the right arm extended throughout, never let it drop. The pentagrams should be visualized in a flaming blue or white light.

Go to the south and draw the same pentagram while vibrating: **"Nudjeru Resu"** (pronounced "nud-jeh-ru reh-su," meaning "Gods of the South"). Thrust through the center of the pentagram and intone **"ASH"** ("Fire").

Go to the west and draw the same pentagram while vibrating: **"Nudjeru Amenta"** (pronounced "nud-jeh-ru ah-men-tah," meaning "Gods of the West"). Thrust through the center intoning **"MU"** ("Water").

Go to the north and trace the pentagram while vibrating: **"Nudjeru Mehta"** (pronounced "nud-jeh-ru meh-tah," meaning "Gods of the North"). Charge the figure with **"TA"** ("Earth").

Invocation

Return to the east and form the Tau Cross. Say: **"Before me, HATHOOR, the Mother of Light. Behind me, TOUM of the setting sun. On my right hand, SAKHMET, mighty lady of Flame. On my left hand, HAPI-WER, the Bull of the Earth. For about me** flames **SEHEDJ**" ("a heaven of stars"). **And above me shines TAU NUDJER**" ("the star of God").[28]

Repeat the Egyptian Qabalistic Cross as in the beginning.

〜

EGYPTIAN BANISHING RITUALS

Alternative Versions

The student may choose to replace the pentagram in the above ritual with symbols that retain a more Egyptian character. Rather than tracing the pentagram in the four quarters, the magician could draw the sign of the *ankh* or the *wedjat* (the Eye of Horus). Both were considered powerful amulets for protection. The ankh is the symbol of eternal life, while the wedjat is the symbol for health, wholeness, protection, and general well-being. (See Figure 14, p. 198.)

To trace the ankh in the air before you, start on the left side at the point where the circle meets the crossbar and, drawing in a clockwise motion, trace the circular "head" of the ankh. Next, trace the shaft of the ankh, leading from the middle of the crossbar to the lowest point of the shaft. Finally, start at the left point of the crossbar and move straight across to the right point of the crossbar.

To trace the Eye of Horus in the air before you, start at the left point of the eyebrow line and trace clockwise. Next, trace the outline of the eye itself, starting from the left and proceeding clockwise, around the pupil, and back around the bottom of the eyelid, ending at the left side of the eye near the starting point. Then trace the lowermost line of the figure starting from the right-hand point and tracing toward the left.

〜

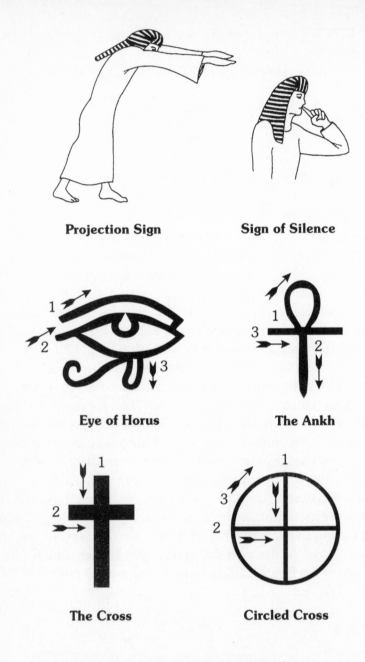

Projection Sign   **Sign of Silence**

Eye of Horus   **The Ankh**

The Cross   **Circled Cross**

Figure 14: Ritual Signs and Symbols of Protection.

A GREEK BANISHING PENTAGRAM RITUAL

The Greek Qabalistic Cross (Stauros Kabalistikos)

Stand and face east. Imagine a brilliant white light touching the top of your head. Reach up with the index finger or blade of a dagger to connect with the light and bring it to the forehead.

Touch the forehead and say: "**Sou estin**" (pronounced "soo-es-tin," meaning "Thine is"—σου εστιν).

Touch the breast and say: "**he Basileia**" (pronounced "hay bah-sih-lay-uh," meaning "the Kingdom"—η Βασιλεια).

Touch the right shoulder and say: "**kai he Dynamis**" (pronounced "kigh hay din-ah-mees," meaning "and the Power"—και η δυναμις).

Touch the left shoulder and say: "**kai he Doxa**" (pronounced "kigh hay dox-ah," meaning "and the Glory"—και η δοξα).

Clasp the fingers over the breast and say: "**eis tous Aionas ton Aionon**" (pronounced "ace tooce eye-oh-nas tone eye-own-own," meaning " to the Aeon of Aeons"—εις τους Αιωνας των Αιωνων). Say: "**Amen**" (pronounced "Ah-may-n"—Αμην).

The Pentagrams

Face east. Use dagger or the index finger of the right hand to trace a large lesser banishing pentagram. As you do so, vibrate "**Theios Aer**" (pronounced "Thay-os Ah-ay-r," "Divine Air"—Θειος Αηρ). Thrust the dagger tip or index finger through the center of the pentagram and vibrate "**Pneuma**" (pronounced "P'ne-oo-mah," "Spirit"—Πνευμα).

Go to the south and draw the same pentagram while vibrating: "**Theion Pyr**" (pronounced "Thay-on Peer," "Divine Fire"—Θειον Πυρ). Thrust through the center of the pentagram and intone "**Psyche**" (pronounced "P'sy-kay," "Soul"—Ψυχη).

Go to the west and draw the same pentagram while vibrating: "**Theion Hydor**" (pronounced "Thay-on Hy-dor," "Divine Water"—Θειον Υδωρ). Thrust through the center of the pentagram and intone "**Nous**" (pronounced "Noos," "Mind"—Νους).

Go to the north and draw the same pentagram while vibrating: **"Theia Ge"** (pronounced "Thay-ah Gay," "Divine Earth"—Θεια Γη). Thrust through the center intoning **"Soma"** (pronounced "Soh-mah," "Body"—Σωμα).

Invocation

Return to the east and stand in the position of the Tau Cross. Say: **"Before me, AIOLOS** (pronounced "Ai-oh-los"—Αιολος), **Guardian of the Winds. Behind me, TETHYS** (pronounced "Tay-thys"— Τηθυς), **Queen of the Seas. On my right hand, HESTIA** (pronounced "Heh-stee-ah"—Εστια), **Lady of the Flame. On my left hand, DEMETER** (pronounced "Day-may-tayr"—Δημητηρ), **the Great Mother of Earth. For about me flames STEPHANOS ASTERON"** (pronounced "Stef-ah-nohs ah-ster-ohn," "a crown of stars"—Στεφανος Αστερων). **"And above me shines the DUO TRIGONA"** (pronounced "Doo-oh Tri-gon-ah," "two triangles"[29]— Δυο Τριγωνοα).

"**Ah, eh, ee, ii, oo, uu, aw.**" (α ε η ι ο υ ω—the seven vowels of the Greek alphabet, said by some to be the true name of God.)

Closing

Repeat the Greek Qabalistic Cross.

~

ALTERNATIVE GREEK VERSION

A Christian Banishing Ritual

The pentagram was used by Pythagoras and his followers as a sacred symbol. Thus it fits well into a Greek framework such as that outlined in the ritual above. However, Christian magicians can easily employ a version that expresses their particular faith and also takes advantage of a Greek foundation. The cross, a sacred symbol of protection, can be readily substituted for the pentagram as in the following ritual.

To trace the cross in the air before you, begin at the shaft of the cross starting at the top and drawing downward. Then start at the left point of the crossbar and move straight across to the right point of the crossbar. (See Figure 14, p. 198.)

The Stauros Kabalistikos

Perform the Greek Qabalistic Cross as given in the preceding ritual.

The Flaming Crosses

Face east. Use dagger or the index finger of the right hand to trace a large cross. Thrust the dagger tip or index finger through the center of the cross and intone **"Pater hamon ho en tois Ouranois"** (pronounced "Pah-ter hay-mon ho en toh-ees Oo-ran-oh-ees," "Our Father in Heaven who art in the Heaven"—Πατερ ημων ο εν τοις Ουρανοις).

Go to the south and draw the cross again. Thrust through the center of the figure and vibrate: **"Ho Kyrios Meta Sou"** (pronounced "Hoh-Kree-os meh-tah soo," "The Lord is with thee"—ο Κυριος μετα σου).

Go to the west and draw the cross. Charge the figure with: **"Oudeis erchetai pros ton Patera ei me di emou"** (pronounced "Oo-days er-che-tai pros ton pah-ter-ah eh may dee em-oo," "No one cometh unto the Father, but by me"—Ουδεις ερχεται προς τον Πατερα ει μη δι εμου).

Go to the north and draw the cross. Charge the figure with: **"To Phos en te Skotia Phainei"** (pronounced "Toh fohs en tay sko-ti-ah fai-nay," "The Light shineth in Darkness"—Το Φως εν τη Σκοτια Φαινει).

Invocation

Return to the east and stand in the position of the Tau Cross. Say: **"Before me, RAPHAEL. Behind me, GABRIEL. On my right hand,**

MICHAEL. On my left hand, URIEL. For about me flames HE STAUROS TOU KLEOS" (pronounced "Heh Stow-ros too Klee-os," "the Cross of Glory"—η Σταυρος του Κλεος). "And above me shines HE CHARITI TOU THEOS" (pronounced "Heh Chah-ree-tee too Thay-os," "the Grace of God"—η χαριτι του Θειος).

Closing
Repeat the Greek Qabalistic Cross.

~

A GAELIC BANISHING PENTAGRAM RITUAL

The Gaelic Qabalistic Cross
Stand and face east. Imagine a brilliant white light touching the top of your head. Reach up with the index finger or blade of a dagger to connect with the light and bring it to the forehead.

Touch the forehead and say: **"Bhuait, a Cruithear"** (pronounced "voo-uhch, uh Xroo-uhr," meaning "From you, Creator").

Touch the breast and say: **"na Rìoghachd"** (pronounced "nah ree-uhchk," meaning "the Kingdom").

Touch the right shoulder and say: **"na Neart"** (pronounced "nah nyarst," meaning "the Power").

Touch the left shoulder and say: **" 's na Miadh"** (pronounced "snah mee-uhgh,"[30] meaning "and the Honor").

Clasp the fingers over the breast and say: **"An Talamh, gu sìor"** (pronounced "an tal-uhv, goo shee-or," meaning "the World, everlasting").

Say: **"Fàilte"** (pronounced "faal-chuh,"[31] meaning "Hail!").

The Pentagrams
Face east. Use dagger or the index finger of the right hand to trace a large lesser banishing pentagram. As you do so, vibrate "**Gaoth an**

Ear" (pronounced "goo-uh a nyar," meaning "east wind"). Thrust the dagger tip or index finger through the center of the pentagram and vibrate **"Adhar"** (pronounced "aar," meaning "air"). Keep the right arm extended throughout, never let it drop. The pentagrams should be visualized in a flaming blue or white light.

Go to the south and draw the same pentagram while vibrating: **"Gaoth a Deas"** (pronounced "goo-uh a jays," meaning "south wind"). Thrust through the center of the pentagram and intone **"Teine"** (pronounced "chay-nuh," meaning "fire").

Go to the west and draw the same pentagram while vibrating: **"Gaoth an Iar"** (pronounced "goo-uh a neeuhr," meaning "west wind"). Thrust through the center intoning **"Uisge"** (pronounced "oosh-guh," meaning "water").

Go to the north and trace the pentagram while vibrating: **"Gaoth a Tuath"** (pronounced "goo-uh a too-uh," meaning "north wind"). Charge the figure with **"Talamh"** (pronounced "tal-uhv," meaning "earth").

Invocation

Return to the east and stand in the position of the Tau Cross. Say: **"Before me, DON, Queen of the Heavens. Behind me, LLYR, King of the Sea. On my right hand, BRIGID, Lady of the ever-burning Fire. On my left hand, CERNUNNOS, Lord of the Forest. For about me are NA DÈATHAN"** (pronounced "nah jee-aahn," meaning "the Gods"). **"And in the center is CO-COTHROM"** (pronounced "co-cho-ruhm," meaning "Equilibrium").

Repeat the Gaelic Qabalistic Cross as in the beginning.

~

ALTERNATIVE GAELIC BANISHING RITUAL

A circled cross may be substituted for the pentagram in the ritual above. This symbol has several meanings, one of which is the circle of the heavens containing the four elements or four cardinal points.

To draw the circled cross in the air before you, trace the shaft of the cross starting at the top and drawing downward. Next, start at the left point of the crossbar and move straight across to the right point of the crossbar. Finally, start at a point on the left side of the circle and trace clockwise. (See Figure 14, p. 198.)

~

A SHAMANIC BANISHING RITUAL

(NOTE: This ritual employs the names of deities from several different Native American tribes.)

The Shamanic Cross

Stand and face east. Imagine a brilliant white light touching the top of your head. Reach up with the index finger or blade of a dagger to connect with the light and bring it to the forehead.

Touch the forehead and say: "**To WAKANDA.**"[32] Touch the breast and say: "**To MICHABO.**"[33] Touch the right shoulder and say: "**To IOSKEHA.**"[34] Touch the left shoulder and say: "**To WHOPE.**"[35]

Clasp the fingers over the breast and say: "**And to all the Ancestors, I give thanks.**"

The Pentagrams

Face east. Use dagger or the index finger of the right hand to trace a large lesser banishing pentagram. As you do so, vibrate "**WABUN.**"[36] Go to the south and draw the same pentagram while vibrating: "**MANITOU.**"[37] Go to the west and draw the same pentagram while vibrating: "**KABUN.**"[38] Go to the north and trace the pentagram while vibrating: "**INNUA.**"[39]

Invocation

Return to the east and stand in the position of the Tau Cross. Say:
"Before me, SILA,[40] of the air. Behind me, AULANERK,[41] ruler of waves. On my right hand, ABABINILI,[42] of the flames. On my left hand, NOKOMIS,[43] the Grandmother. For about me are the Four Winds, and upon me shines UTEA."[44]
Repeat the Shamanic Cross as in the beginning.

Endnotes

1. *Atah* is the more correct Hebrew pronunciation of this word than the traditional pronunciation of *Atoh* used by magicians in the past.

2. For the Qabalistic Cross the magician may choose to stand either in the eastern part of the room or in the center of the room, facing east. For the drawing of the first pentagram, however, the magician should walk to the eastern part of the room and move to the southern, western, and northern portion of the temple as required for the tracing of the pentagrams. For the Invocation of the Archangels and the final Qabalistic Cross, the magician can again move to the center of the room. If the temple space is very small, the magician can simply stand in the center of the room throughout the entire ritual and turn toward the quarters to trace the pentagrams.

3. Michael, Gabriel, and Raphael are the three archangels that are most often cited in the Bible. The *Bahir*, an important Qabalistic text, lists the three major angels as Michael, Gabriel, and Uriel (see *The Bahir* translated by Aryeh Kaplan, page 41). Uriel also figures prominently in non-canonical lore, but in some texts, Uriel is confused or replaced with Phanuel.

   One of the most important magical texts used by magicians, Agrippa's *Three Books of Occult Philosophy*, published in 1531, lists Michael, Raphael, Gabriel, and Uriel as the "the four princes of the angels, which are set over the four winds, and over the four parts of the world." (Refer to page 533 of the Llewellyn edition, edited by Donald Tyson.)

4. Compare to 2 Timothy 4:18, "The Lord will deliver me from every evil work, and will save me to his celestial *Kingdom; to whom be glory to the Aeon of Aeons. Amen.*

5. Halevi, *Kabbalah: Tradition of Hidden Knowledge*, 12.

6. Ibid., 68.

7. Ceremonial magicians. Literally "god-workers."

8. Levi, *Transcendental Magic*, 234.

9. From a 1977 paper titled *A Possible Source for the Lesser Pentagram Ritual in a Hebrew Night Prayer* by Bill Heidrick.

10. Levi, *Transcendental Magic*, 63.

11. Ibid., 67–68.

12. Ibid., 70.

13. Waterfield, *The Theology of Arithmetic, attributed to Iamblichus*, 68.

14. Renamed *The Occult Power of Numbers*, 59.

15. Levi, *Transcendental Magic*, 239.

16. Ibid., 237.

17. Ibid., 241.

18. Some of the material cited in this section comes from an anonymous paper from the late 1970s or 1980s entitled simply *Pentagram Ritual*.

19. Yod is spelled out as *Yod Vav Daleth*, Heh is spelled *Heh Heh*, Vav is spelled *Vav Vav*, and Heh is *Heh Heh*. The total value is fifty-two.

20. From which is derived the word *Zion*.

21. It's interesting to note that many of the numbers associated with the pentagram, 5, 8, 13, and 26, are also associated with the Vault of the Adepti—the ritual chamber of the Golden Dawn's Inner Order. Each wall of the Vault is 5 feet wide and 8 feet high. Every one of the seven triangles formed from the intersecting lines of the Vault's heptagram has a base of 8 units and a height of 5 units. If the heptagon of the Vault were circumscribed by a circle, the radius of the circle would be 13 units, and its diameter would be 26 units.

22. The *banishing earth pentagram* is drawn starting from the earth point and moving toward the spirit point. The *invoking earth pentagram* is drawn starting from the spirit point and moving toward the earth point.

23. The invoking form would be the *lesser invoking pentagram*.

24. Used in this context, *Adonai* or "lord" is a term of sovereignty, not of gender. It should be thought of like the Egyptian title of *Pharaoh*, which applied to both male and female rulers.

25. From the Neophyte Ritual. See Regardie, *The Golden Dawn*, 124.

26. Based on the Golden Dawn's Flying Roll No. VIII, published by Francis King in *Astral Projection, Ritual Magic, and Alchemy by S. L. MacGregor Mathers and Others*.

27. This has been affirmed by an A. O. version of the same manuscript.

28. This Invocation contains the names of Egyptian Gods rather than Hebrew Archangels. (The Greek and Gaelic rituals that follow also use deities from their respective traditions.) Angels may correctly be called *Gods*, just as they were in ancient times. (See "This Holy Invisible Companionship" by Adam P. Forrest, published in *The Golden Dawn Journal, Book II, Qabalah: Theory and Magic*, 189–190.)

29. A hexagram.

30. "Gh" is difficult for those who do not speak Gaelic. It should sound something like "gy."

31. "aa" as in "awl."

32. The "Great Spirit" of the Lakota tribes, who was also known as Wakan Tanka. "The power above" who was the source of all.

33. The "Great Hare" of the Algonquin tribe, said to be the creator of the earth.

34. Creator god of the Iroquois and Huron tribes, who was known for defeating demons, and giving magic.

35. The "Peace Goddess" of the Dakota (Sioux) tribes.

36. Algonquin god of the east wind.

37. The "Great Spirit" known to many tribes.

38. Algonquin god of the west wind. The son of the twilight.

39. The Great Spirit of the Innuit (Eskimo) peoples of the north.

40. Eskimo god of the air, and the energy of the universe.

41. Innuit sea god.

42. Chickasaw god of fire.

43. Algonquin earth goddess.

44. Yaqui god of "Power." Power as given by the ancient people.

CHAPTER TEN

THE MIDDLE PILLAR EXERCISE

A n abbreviated form of the Middle Pillar exercise can be found in a manuscript that was given to initiates of the Stella Matutina who had attained to the Portal grade.[1] Long before this exercise became well known to many people, Regardie insisted that the Middle Pillar exercise was a valuable and potent technique for self-growth. It may well be the finest method created for such a purpose. The basic introductory formula of the Middle Pillar can be easily adapted into a variety of exercises with varying levels of complexity and spiritual development. This simple yet potent exercise is the foundation of a diverse number of magical techniques, and it can be layered with a virtually endless number of correspondences, leading to ever more complex ceremonies. A number of such rites are given in this chapter. There are also Egyptian, Greek, Gaelic, and Shamanic renditions, as well as several exercises for healing. Additional Middle Pillar-style rituals can be found in "This Holy Invisible Companionship"[2] by Adam P. Forrest and in our book *Experiencing the Kabbalah*.

THE EXERCISE OF THE MIDDLE PILLAR

Establishing the Pillar

(This exercise can be performed either standing, sitting, or lying down.) After a few minutes of relaxation, imagine a sphere of white light just above your head. Vibrate the name "**Eheieh**" (pronounced "Eh-hey-yay," meaning "I am"). Keep vibrating this word until it is the only thought in your conscious mind. Then imagine a shaft of light descending from your Kether center to your Daath center at the nape of the neck.

Form a sphere of light at the Daath center. Vibrate the name "**Yhvh Elohim**" (pronounced "Yode-heh-vav-heh El-oh-heem," meaning "the Lord God"). Intone the name until it is the only thing in your conscious mind.

Bring a shaft of light down from the Daath center to the Tiphareth center around your heart. Form a sphere of light there. Vibrate the name "**Yhvh Eloah ve-Daath**" (pronounced "Yode-heh-vav-heh El-oh-ah v'-Dah-ath," meaning "Lord God of Knowledge") several times until it fills your consciousness.

See the shaft of light descending from Tiphareth into the Yesod center in the genital region. Imagine a sphere of light formed there. Intone the name "**Shaddai El Chai**" (pronounced "Shah-dye El-Chai,"[3] meaning "Almighty Living God") several times as before.

Visualize the shaft of light descending from Yesod into your Malkuth center at the feet and ankles. Vibrate the name "**Adonai ha-Aretz**" (pronounced "Ah-doe-nye ha-Ah-retz," meaning "Lord of Earth") a number of times as before.

Imagine the Middle Pillar complete. Then circulate the light you have brought down through the Middle Pillar around the outside of your body to strengthen your aura. (Perform each circulation a number of times.)

Circulation One: Side to Side

Using the cycles of rhythmic breathing, bring the light down one side of the body and up the other, from Kether to Malkuth and back to Kether. Exhale and visualize the light descending the left side of the body. Inhale and imagine the light ascending the right side of the body back to Kether.[4]

Circulation Two: Front to Back

After performing this for a short space of time, imagine the ribbon of light descending from Kether down the front of your body to Malkuth and rising up your back, returning again to Kether.[5]

Circulation Three: The Shower of Light

Still employing rhythmic breathing, visualize the sphere of Malkuth, then see the shaft of light rising up the Middle Pillar in the center of your body. When it reaches Kether, imagine a shower of light cascading down the outside of your body as it descends to Malkuth again. Circulate the light in this manner for some time.

Circulation Four: The Ascending Spiral

Then see the light rise again in a ribbon that spirals around the outside of your body from Malkuth to Kether.

Closing

Finally focus some of the energy back into your Tiphareth center, the seat of equilibrium and balance.

You may decide to end the exercise with the Qabalistic Cross to indicate that you have called down the light of your Kether and balanced it in your aura. Then let your imagination dwell on the aura and see it oval and clear, pulsating with the glow from Tiphareth.[6]

This simple exercise of Middle Pillar is the basis for many complex formulas of magic.

If you are called to see anyone who is ill, depressed, or who has a depressing effect on you, you should perform this exercise beforehand. You may also imagine that your aura is hardened at the edge, so that a person is unable to penetrate it and deplete you of vitality.

When you have practiced the exercise of the Middle Pillar for some time and can visualize the spheres easily, you can establish the other Sephiroth within your aura by vibrating the deity names.

The exercise of the Middle Pillar can be done as an alternative to the Pentagram Ritual as a preparation for meditation.

THE MIDDLE PILLAR RITUAL

(Revised Version for ⑤=⑥)

by Israel Regardie

Copyright © 1996 by Darcy Küntz

Part I: Spirit ⊛

1. Relax soul, mind, and body.

2. Perform the Lesser Banishing Ritual of the Pentagram.

3. Formulate a flaming sphere of white brilliance above the head. Concentrate on this sphere.

4. Vibrate the divine names: **"AHIH"** (Eh-hey-yay) and **"AGLA"** (Ah-ga-lah).

5. Continue to concentrate on the white brilliance, and when you feel it is aroused say:

> I am the Resurrection and the Life.
> He that believeth on Me, though he were dead,
> yet shall he live.
> And whatsoever liveth and believeth on Me,
> the same shall have everlasting life.
> I am the First and I am the Last.
> I am He that liveth and was dead,
> and behold I am alive for evermore,
> and hold the keys of Hell and of Death.
> For I know that my Redeemer liveth
> and He shall stand at the latter day upon the Earth.
> I am the Way, the Truth, and the Life.

No man cometh unto the Father but by Me.
I am the purified.
I have passed through the Gates of Darkness unto Light.
I have fought upon the Earth for good.
I have finished my work,
I have entered into the Invisible.
I am the Sun in His rising.
I have passed through the hour of cloud and of night.
I am AMOUN the Concealed One, the Opener of the Day.
I am OSIRIS ONNOPHRIS, the Justified One.
I am Lord of Life Triumphant over death.
There is no part of me that is not of the Gods.
I am the Preparer of the Pathway,
the Rescuer unto the Light.
Out of the darkness, let the Light arise.
I am the Reconciler with the Ineffable.
I am the Dweller of the Invisible.
LET THE WHITE BRILLIANCE OF THE SPIRIT DESCEND!

(Visualize the brilliance descending into the body.)

6. Vibrate: **"EXARP, BITOM, NANTA,"** and **"HCOMA"** (Ex-ar-pay, Bay-ee-toh-em, En-ah-en-tah, and Hay-koh-mah).

Part II: Air △

1. See a shaft of light come down, in the skull, to the neck.

2. Formulate a flaming sphere of brilliant yellow and see the ball extend all the way through the neck, and see it extend up into the head.

3. Superimpose on the yellow sphere the sign of Aquarius ♒ in the complementary color of purple.

4. Vibrate: **"YOD-HEH-VAV-HEH,"** and the angelic names: **"RAPHAEL"** and **"CHASSAN."**

5. When you feel the ball is alive and real, and spiritual power is pouring through you, and when you feel the power of the names,

6. Say the Prayer of the Sylphs:

    Holy art Thou, Lord of the Air,
    Who has created the Firmament.
    SHADDAI EL CHAI.

> Almighty and everlasting, ever-living be Thy Name
> Ever-magnified in the Life of all.
> We praise and we bless Thee in the
> changeless empire of created Light;
> And we aspire without cessation unto
> Thy Imperishable and Immutable Brilliance. AMEN.

Part III: Fire △

1. See a shaft of light descend once more to the heart center or solar plexus.

2. Formulate a flaming sphere of brilliant red. See the ball extending from front to back.

3. Superimpose on the red sphere the sign of Leo ♌ in the complementary color of emerald green.

4. Vibrate: "**ELOHIM**," and the angelic names: "**MICHAEL**" and "**ARAL**."

5. When you feel the ball is alive and real, and spiritual power is pouring through you, and when you feel the power of the names,

6. Say the Prayer of the Salamanders:

> Holy art Thou, Lord of the Fire,
> Wherein Thou hast shown forth the Throne of Thy Glory.
> YOD-HEH-VAV-HEH TZABAOTH.
> Leader of Armies is Thy Holy Name.
> O, Thou Flashing Fire, Thou illuminatest all things.
> With Thy insupportable Refulgence
> Whence flow the ceaseless streams of Splendor
> Which nourisheth Thine Infinite Spirit.
> Help us, Thy children, whom Thou hast loved.
> Since the birth of the Ages of Time. AMEN.

Part IV: Water ▽

1. See a shaft of light descend once more to the region of the hips, the generative region.

2. See a flaming sphere of brilliant ultramarine blue.

3. Superimpose on the blue sphere the sign of Scorpio ♏ in the complementary color of orange.

4. Vibrate: "**EL**," and the angelic names: "**GABRIEL**" and "**TALIHAD**."

5. When you feel the ball is alive and real, and spiritual power is pouring through you, and when you feel the power of the names,

6. Say the Prayer of the Undines:

> **Holy art Thou, Lord of the Mighty Waters,**
> **Whereon Thy Spirit moved in the Beginning.**
> **ELOHIM TZABAOTH.**
> **Glory be unto Thee RUACH ELOHIM.**
> **Whose Spirit hovered over the Great Waters of Creation.**
> **O Depth, O inscrutable Depth,**
> **which exhalest unto the height:**
> **Lead Thou us into the True Life,**
> **through Liberty, through Love,**
> **So that one day we may be found worthy to know Thee,**
> **To unite with Thy Spirit, in the silence,**
> **for the attainment of Thy Understanding. AMEN.**

Part V: Earth ▽

1. See a shaft of light descend once more to the feet, from about the ankles.

2. Formulate a flaming sphere of brilliant indigo.

3. Superimpose on the indigo sphere the sign of Taurus ♉ in the complementary color of pale yellow.

4. Vibrate: "**ADONAI**," and the angelic names: "**AURIEL**" and "**PHORLAKH**."

5. When you feel the ball is alive and real, and spiritual power is pouring through you, and when you feel the power of the names,

6. Say the Prayer of the Gnomes:

> **Holy art Thou, Lord of the Earth,**
> **Which Thou hast made for Thy footstool.**
> **ADONAI HA-ARETZ, ADONAI MELEKH.**
> **Unto Thee be the Kingdom, the Power and the Glory.**
> **MALKUTH, GEBURAH, GEDULAH. AMEN.**
> **The Rose of Sharon, and the Lily of the Valley.**

> O Thou Who hidest beneath the Earth,
> in the Valley of Gems,
> The marvellous seed of the Stars.
> Live, reign, and be Thou the eternal Dispenser
> of Thy treasures,
> Whereof Thou hast made us the wardens. AMEN.

Part VI: Circumambulation

1. Circumambulate[7] the light. See all the power in the feet center. See it rush up like water powerfully pushed up as in a fountain.

2. As it rushes up, it takes all the power from each of the spheres on its ascent. So imagine as it goes from ball to ball, it takes all the power out of each sphere in turn until it gets to the white light. So this power will be a combination of all the colors, but "see" the sense of power rather than the color. The power remains a white power.

3. Make sure the power is circulating away from the centers and the result will be that you have formed around you an aura by the power issuing up the shaft.

4. In the circulation of the fountain, the power goes up the centers. Then with the exhalation down the left side, and the inhalation up the right side, exhale down the front of the body, inhale up the back of the body. This will cause the aura to be in a subtle state of great activity, the light pouring through and making it a great and dynamic power.

5. Close with the OSIRIS Godform. Keep that as long as you like.

6. Perform the Lesser Banishing Ritual of the Pentagram.

Regardie's Notes on the Revised Middle Pillar Ritual

Part I: Spirit ✹

The top center is above the head. Its color is white, and its divine name will be AHIH [or EHEIEH] (אהיה), and AGLA (אגלא). You will vibrate these names in the usual way and concentrate on the white light. After a few minutes when you feel the white light has been aroused and you feel it vibrating, then recite the Invocation, and in the last sentence which says, "Let the white brilliance of the spirit descend!" you will vibrate the four Enochian names: EXARP, BITOM, NANTA, and HCOMA. These names should equilibrate the white light.

Part II: Air △

Then see the shaft come down in the skull in the usual way into the neck, and in the neck you form another ball that extends all the way through the throat and neck, and this time you will see it colored yellow, which is the color of Air. See in this ball the Kerubic Sign of Aquarius. Then you say the Prayer of the Sylphs. You visualize the light in yellow. Superimposed on that sphere in its absolute complement of purple you see the two lines of the symbol of Aquarius (♒). You are to see these lines inside the yellow in purple color, and you vibrate: YOD-HEH-VAV-HEH (יהוה). Follow it with the archangel: RAPHAEL (רפאל) and the angel CHASSAN (חשן). When you feel the ball is alive and real, and you can feel spiritual power pouring through it, then say the Prayer of the Sylphs.

Part III: Fire △

See your shaft descend once more to the solar plexus, or just above the end of the sternum, the little breast bone. See the ball extending from front to back—a big ball of red fire, a brilliant flaming red. See the shaft in white and the balls in different colors. The color of this center is red. This is the sphere of Fire. I want you to see inside the center of this ball the symbol of Leo (♌) in emerald green, and vibrate the name: ELOHIM (אלהים). Then your archangel: MICHAEL (מיכאל) and the angelic name: ARAL (אראל). Vibrate the names, and when you feel their power start on the Prayer of the Salamanders.

Part IV: Water ▽

The shaft descends once more to the region of the hips, the generative region, and there you will see another ball formed. This time it will be in a very lovely ultramarine blue. When you have this sphere formed in blue, visualize inside this sphere the symbol of Scorpio (♏) in orange. This is the sphere of Water. Then you vibrate the name of EL (אל). Then vibrate your archangelic name:

GABRIEL (גבריאל) and your angelic name: TALIHAD (תליהד). Then the Prayer of the Undines.

Part V: Earth ▽

Then your shaft goes down again to the feet, and forms again in the feet another ball. The usual color of the element of Earth is black. But since it is difficult to get a complement color of black, I am going to give you indigo. Superimposed on this will be the symbol of Taurus (♉) in a very light yellow, the complement of indigo. The divine name is ADONAI (אדני) which you vibrate. Then vibrate the archangelic name: AURIEL (אוריאל) and the angelic name: PHORLAKH (פורלאך). That will be followed by the Prayer of the Gnomes.

Part VI: Circumambulation

Here you have five balls on the central sphere. When you get down to the feet, stop and see this shaft with the five balls all glowing, then start what I call the *Formula of Circumambulation;* but the first method is to be the *Fountain.* See all the power in the feet center and then see it rush up from the feet center like the water in a fountain. As this power rushes up see it take away all the power from all the other spheres on its ascent to the top, so that you can imagine as it goes from ball to ball, it takes all the power out from each sphere in turn until it gets to the white light; then visualize it drawing up the power of the different centers so it will be a combination of all the colors from indigo up.

See the sense of power rather than the literal sense of color. See it. You circulate power from the different balls until it is a fountain. Make sure the power is circulating away from the centers. The result will be that you will have formed around you an aura by the circulation of power issuing up through the shaft. Then follow with the other two methods. The circulation down the left side and up the right, and the circulation from the head down the front of the body, under the feet and up the back. Use the inhalation and exhalation. The aura will be in a state of great activity. The light is pouring through and making it a great power. In order to close assume the godform of OSIRIS and keep that as long as you feel like it. I want you to make the Banishing Ritual a habit. Begin and end every ritual with it. This Middle Pillar Ritual can be done either sitting or lying flat.

~

THE TREE OF LIFE EXERCISE

(The Rite of Three Pillars)

(See Figure 15, p. 220.) This exercise can be performed either standing, sitting, or lying down. After a few minutes of relaxation, imagine a sphere of white light just above your head. Vibrate the name **"Eheieh"** ("Eh-hey-yay"). Keep vibrating this word until it is the only thought in your conscious mind. Maintain a strong visualization of the white sphere.

Then imagine a shaft of white light descending from your Kether center to your Chokmah center at the left temple of your forehead. Visualize a sphere of white light there. Intone the name of **"Yah"** (meaning "Lord"). Keep vibrating the name until it is the complete focus of all your attention.

Bring a shaft of white light horizontally across from your Chokmah center to your Binah center at the right temple of your forehead. Form a sphere of white light there. Vibrate the name **"Yhvh Elohim"** ("Yode-heh-vav-heh El-oh-heem") a number of times until it occupies all of your mind.

Now bring a shaft of white light down diagonally from your Binah center to your Daath center at the nape of your neck. Visualize a sphere of white light there. Vibrate the name **"Yhvh Elohim."** Intone the name until it is the only thing in your conscious mind.

Next, visualize a shaft of white light down diagonally from the Daath center to your Chesed center at your left shoulder. Form a sphere of light there. Vibrate the name **"EL"** (meaning "God") a number of times until it fills your mind.

Bring a shaft of white light horizontally from Chesed to your Geburah center at your right shoulder. Visualize a sphere of light

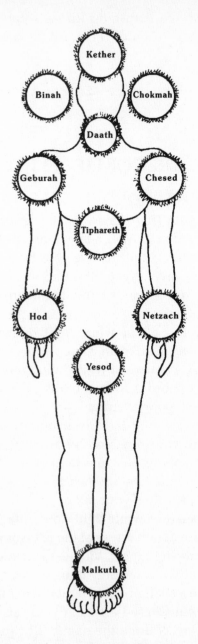

Figure 15: The Tree of Life in the Human Body.

there. Vibrate the name **"Elohim Gibor"** ("El-oh-heem Ge-boor," meaning "God of Battles"). Intone the name until it is the only thing in your conscious mind.

Now bring a shaft of light diagonally across from Geburah to your Tiphareth center around the area of your heart. Form a sphere of light there. Vibrate the name **"YHVH Eloah ve-Daath"** ("Yode-heh-vav-heh El-oh-ah v'-Dah-ath") several times until it fills your consciousness.

Next, visualize a shaft of white light down diagonally from the Tiphareth center to your Netzach center at your left hip. Form a sphere of white light there. Vibrate the name **"YHVH Tzabaoth"** ("Yode-heh-vav-heh Tzah-bah-oth," meaning "Lord of Hosts") a number of times until it occupies all of your mind.

Bring a shaft of white light horizontally from Netzach to your Hod center at your right hip. Form a sphere of light there. Vibrate the name **"Elohim Tzabaoth"** ("El-oh-heem Tzah-bah-oth," meaning "God of Hosts"). Intone the name until it is the only thing in your conscious mind.

Now see the shaft of white light descending diagonally from Hod into the Yesod center in the genital region. Imagine a sphere of light formed there. Intone the name **"Shaddai El Chai"** ("Shah-dye El-Chai," meaning "Almighty Living God") several times as before.

Next, visualize the shaft of light descending straight down from Yesod into your Malkuth center at the feet and ankles. Imagine a sphere of light formed there. Vibrate the name **"Adonai ha-Aretz"** ("Ah-doe-nye Ha-Ah-retz," meaning "Lord of Earth") a number of times as before.

Imagine the Tree complete. Then circulate the light you have brought down throughout all the spheres of the Tree. Move the energy around your aura using the four Circulations of Light described earlier.

Finally focus some of the energy back into your Tiphareth center, the seat of equilibrium and balance.

~

THE RITE OF FIVE PILLARS

The following exercise is a very simplified method for exploring the idea of a three-dimensional Tree of Life.[8] Using this method, a total of five pillars are formed within the student's sphere of sensation—the two outer pillars of Mercy and Severity are duplicated, while the Middle Pillar maintains the pivotal balance. The image of the Tree of Life is reflected into the human body (see Chapter Nine, pages 180–184) so that the practitioner faces the archetypal image of the Tree, which is in turn reflected behind him (see Figure 16 below).[9] Many more complex variations of the Five Pillar exercise are possible.

This exercise is best performed either standing or sitting. After a few minutes of relaxation, vibrate the divine names of the Middle Pillar Sephiroth, one time each, establishing the central column within your Sphere of Sensation. Then use the four Circulations of Light mentioned earlier to visualize and strengthen your aura, which extends several feet out from your physical body—a sphere of oval-shaped light.

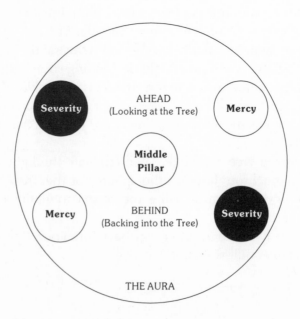

Figure 16: The Five Pillars.

Once you have visualized the Sphere of Sensation, establish the four outer pillars which curve around the outer edges of your aura as follows.

Return to your topmost center, Kether. Imagine a sphere of white light just above your head. Vibrate the name "**Eheieh**." Keep vibrating this word until it is the only thought in your conscious mind.

Imagine a ball of white light several feet in front of and to the right of your head. When this is fixed in your mind's eye, visualize a corresponding ball of white light several feet behind and to the left of your head. Intone the name of "**Yah**." Keep vibrating the name until both Chokmah spheres are glowing intensely with light.

Now imagine a ball of white light several feet in front of and to the left of your head. When this image is fixed in your mind, visualize a corresponding ball of white light several feet behind and to the right of your forehead. Intone the name of "**Yhvh Elohim**." Keep vibrating the name until both Binah spheres are radiating with light.

Next, imagine a sphere of white light at your Daath center at the nape of your neck. Vibrate the name "**Yhvh Elohim**." Intone the name until it is the only thing in your conscious mind.

Visualize a ball of white light several feet in front of and to the right of your right shoulder. When this image is firm in your mind, visualize a corresponding ball of white light several feet behind and to the left of your left shoulder. Intone the name of "**El**." Keep vibrating the name until both Chesed spheres glow brightly with light.

Next imagine a ball of white light several feet in front of and to the left of your left shoulder. When this image is fixed in your mind, visualize a corresponding ball of white light several feet behind and to the right of your right shoulder. Intone the name of "**Elohim Gibor**." Keep vibrating the name until both Geburah spheres are radiating with light.

Now, imagine a sphere of white light at your Tiphareth center around the area of your heart. Vibrate the name "**Yhvh Eloah ve-Daath**." Intone the name until it is the only thing in your conscious mind.

Visualize a ball of white light several feet in front of and to the right of your right hip. When this image is firm in your mind, visualize a corresponding ball of white light several feet behind and to the left of your left hip. Intone the name of "**Yhvh Tzabaoth**." Keep vibrating the name until both Netzach spheres glow brightly with light.

Next imagine a ball of white light several feet in front of and to the left of your left hip. When this image is fixed in your mind, visualize a corresponding ball of white light several feet behind and to the right of your right hip. Intone the name of "**Elohim Tzabaoth**." Keep vibrating the name until both Hod spheres are radiating with light.

Now, imagine a sphere of white light at your Yesod center in the genital region. Intone the name "**Shaddai El Chai**" several times as before.

Visualize a sphere of light at your Malkuth center at the feet and ankles. Vibrate the name "**Adonai ha-Aretz**" a number of times as before.

Imagine that the Five Pillars have now been fully established in your aura. Then circulate the light you have brought down throughout all the spheres of the Tree. Circulate the light and energy using the same breathing/visualization techniques of the standard Middle Pillar exercise.

Finally focus some of the energy back into your Tiphareth center, the sphere of harmony and equipoise.

AN EGYPTIAN MIDDLE PILLAR EXERCISE

Imagine a sphere of white light just above your head at your Kether point. Vibrate: "**Nudjer ao**" (pronounced "nud-jeh-r ah-oh," meaning "The Great God, self-produced"). Keep vibrating until it is the only thought in your conscious mind. Then imagine a shaft of light descending from your Kether center to your Daath center at the nape of the neck.

Form a sphere of light at the Daath center. Vibrate: **"Neb Iri Khet"** (pronounced "neb ee-ree khet," meaning "The Lord Creator"). Intone the name until it is the only thing in your conscious mind.

Bring a shaft of light down from the Daath center to the Tiphareth center around your heart. Form a sphere of light there. Vibrate: **"Sia"** (pronounced "see-ah," meaning "God of Knowledge, and Wisdom"). Intone the name several times until it fills your consciousness.

See the shaft of light descending from Tiphareth into the Yesod center in the genital region. Imagine a sphere of light formed there. Intone the phrase: **"Neb Ankh"** (pronounced "neb ah-nk," meaning "Lord of Life"). Do this several times.

Visualize the shaft of light descending from Yesod into your Malkuth center at the feet and ankles. Vibrate the phrase: **"Nudjer ta"** (pronounced "nud-jeh-r tah," meaning "God of Earth"). Intone a number of times as before.

Imagine the Middle Pillar complete. Move the energy around your aura using the four Circulations of Light described earlier. Using the cycles of breathing, bring the light down one side of the body and up the other, from Kether to Malkuth and back again. After performing this for a short period of time, imagine the ribbon of light descending down the front of your body and rising up your back.

Still employing rhythmic breathing, visualize the shaft of light rising up the Middle Pillar in the center of your body. When it reaches Kether, imagine a shower of light surrounding the outside of your body as it descends to Malkuth again. Circulate the light in this manner for some time. Then see the light rise again in a ribbon that spirals around the outside of your body.

Finally focus some of the energy back into your Tiphareth center.

~

THE EGYPTIAN RITE OF THREE PILLARS

After a few minutes of relaxation, imagine a sphere of white light just above your head. Vibrate the phrase **"Nudjer ao"** (pronounced "nud-jeh-r ah-oh," meaning "The Great God, self-produced").

Keep vibrating this word until it is the only thought in your conscious mind. Maintain a strong visualization of the white sphere.

Then imagine a shaft of light descending from your Kether center to your Chokmah center at the left temple of your forehead. Visualize a sphere of white light there. Intone the phrase of "**Atef Nudjer**" (pronounced "ah-tef nud-jeh-r," meaning "Divine Father"). Keep vibrating the name until it is the complete focus of all your attention.

Bring a shaft of white light horizontally across from your Chokmah center to your Binah center at the right temple of your forehead. Form a sphere of white light there. Vibrate the phrase "**At**" (pronounced "ah-t," meaning "Great Lady") a number of times until it occupies all of your mind.

Now bring a shaft of light down diagonally from your Binah center to your Daath center at the nape of your neck. Visualize a sphere of white light there. Vibrate the phrase "**Neb Iri Khet**" (pronounced "neb ee-ree khet," meaning "The Lord Creator"). Intone the name until it is the only thing in your conscious mind.

Next, visualize a shaft of white light down diagonally from the Daath center to your Chesed center at your left shoulder. Form a sphere of light there. Vibrate the phrase "**On-Nofer**" (pronounced "ohn-noh-fer," meaning "The Good Being") a number of times until it occupies all of your mind.

Bring a shaft of white light horizontally from Chesed to your Geburah center at your right shoulder. Visualize a sphere of light there. Vibrate the phrase "**Smaa kheru**" (pronounced "smah ker-ru," meaning "the Justifier"). Intone the name until it is the only thing in your conscious mind.

Now bring a shaft of light diagonally across from Geburah to your Tiphareth center around the area of your heart. Form a sphere of light there. Vibrate "**Sia**" (pronounced "see-ah," meaning "God of Knowledge and Wisdom") several times until it fills your consciousness.

Next, visualize a shaft of white light down diagonally from the Tiphareth center to your Netzach center at your left hip. Form a sphere of light there. Vibrate the phrase "**Wer Nefuti**" (pronounced "wehr neh-fu-tee," meaning "Great of Victories") a number of times until it occupies all of your mind.

Bring a shaft of white light horizontally from Netzach to your Hod center at your right hip. Form a sphere of light there. Vibrate the phrase **"Wer Heka"** (pronounced "wehr heh-kah," meaning "Great of Magic"). Intone the name until it is the only thing in your conscious mind.

Now see the shaft of light descending diagonally from Hod into the Yesod center in the genital region. Imagine a sphere of white light formed there. Intone the phrase **"Neb Ankh"** (pronounced "neb ah-nk," meaning "Lord of Life") several times as before.

Next, visualize the shaft of light descending straight down from Yesod into your Malkuth center at the feet and ankles. Imagine a sphere of white light formed there. Vibrate the phrase **"Nudjer ta"** (pronounced "nud-jeh-ru tah," meaning "God of Earth") a number of times as before.

Imagine the Tree complete. Then circulate the light you have brought down throughout all the spheres of the Tree. Circulate the energy using the same breathing/visualization techniques of the standard Middle Pillar exercise.

Finally focus some of the energy back into your Tiphareth center.

~

A GREEK MIDDLE PILLAR EXERCISE

Imagine a sphere of white light just above your head at your Kether point. Vibrate: **"Ego Eimi"** (Εγω ειμι pronounced "eh-gaw eh-mee," meaning "I am"). Keep vibrating until it is the only thought in your conscious mind. Then imagine a shaft of light descending from your Kether center to your Daath center at the nape of the neck.

Form a sphere of light at the Daath center. Vibrate: **"Sophia"** (Σοφια pronounced "soh-fee-ah," meaning "Wisdom"). Intone the name until it is the only thing in your conscious mind.

Bring a shaft of light down from the Daath center to the Tiphareth center around your heart. Form a sphere of light there. Vibrate the word: **"Gnosis"** (Γνωσις pronounced "g'naw-sis,"[10] meaning "Knowledge"). Intone the name several times until it fills your consciousness.

See the shaft of light descending from Tiphareth into the Yesod center in the genital region. Imagine a sphere of light formed there. Intone the word "**Zoe**" (Ζωη pronounced "zaw-ay," meaning "Life"). [11] Do this several times.

Visualize the shaft of light descending from Yesod into your Malkuth center at the feet and ankles. Vibrate the word: "**Naos**" (Ναος pronounced "na-os," meaning "Temple"). Intone a number of times as before.

Imagine the Middle Pillar complete. Move the energy around your aura using the four Circulations of Light described earlier. Using the cycles of breathing, bring the light down one side of the body and up the other, from Kether to Malkuth and back again. After performing this for a short period of time, imagine the ribbon of light descending down the front of your body and rising up your back.

Still employing rhythmic breathing, visualize the shaft of light rising up the Middle Pillar in the center of your body. When it reaches Kether, imagine a shower of light surrounding the outside of your body as it descends to Malkuth again. Circulate the light in this manner for some time. Then see the light rise again in a ribbon that spirals around the outside of your body.

Finally focus some of the energy back into your Tiphareth center.

~

THE GREEK RITE OF THREE PILLARS

After a few minutes of relaxation, imagine a sphere of white light just above your head. Vibrate the phrase "**Ego Eimi**" (Εγω ειμι pronounced "eh-gaw eh-mee," meaning "I am").

Keep vibrating this word until it is the only thought in your conscious mind. Maintain a strong visualization of the white sphere.

Then imagine a shaft of light descending from your Kether center to your Chokmah center at the left temple of your forehead. Visualize a sphere of white light there. Intone the word "**Theos**"

(Θεος pronounced "theh-os," meaning "God"). Keep vibrating the name until it is the complete focus of all your attention.

Bring a shaft of white light horizontally across from your Chokmah center to your Binah center at the right temple of your forehead. Form a sphere of white light there. Vibrate the word "**Thea**" (Θεα pronounced "theh-ah," meaning "Goddess") a number of times until it occupies all of your mind.

Now bring a shaft of white light down diagonally from your Binah center to your Daath center at the nape of your neck. Visualize a sphere of white light there. Vibrate the word "**Sophia**" (Σοφια pronounced "soh-fee-ah," meaning "Wisdom"). Intone the name until it is the only thing in your conscious mind.

Next, visualize a shaft of white light down diagonally from the Daath center to your Chesed center at your left shoulder. Form a sphere of light there. Vibrate the name "**Agathos**" (Αγαθος pronounced "ah-gath-os," meaning "the Good") a number of times until it fills your mind.

Bring a shaft of white light horizontally from Chesed to your Geburah center at your right shoulder. Visualize a sphere of light there. Vibrate the word "**Krisis**" (Κρισις pronounced "kree-sis," meaning "Judgment"). Intone the name until it is the only thing in your conscious mind.

Now bring a shaft of light diagonally across from Geburah to your Tiphareth center around the area of your heart. Form a sphere of light there. Vibrate "**Gnosis**" (Γνωσις pronounced "g'naw-sis," meaning "Knowledge") several times until it fills your consciousness.

Next, visualize a shaft of white light down diagonally from the Tiphareth center to your Netzach center at your left hip. Form a sphere of light there. Vibrate the word "**Daimon**" (Δαιμων pronounced "dye-mawn," meaning "Spirit") a number of times until it occupies all of your mind.

Bring a shaft of white light horizontally from Netzach to your Hod center at your right hip. Form a sphere of light there. Vibrate the word "**Nous**" (Νους pronounced "noose," meaning "Mind"). Intone the name until it is the only thing in your conscious mind.

Now see the shaft of light descending diagonally from Hod into the Yesod center in the genital region. Imagine a sphere of white light formed there. Intone the word "**Zoe**" (Ζωη pronounced "zaw-ay," meaning "Life") several times as before.

Next, visualize the shaft of light descending straight down from Yesod into your Malkuth center at the feet and ankles. Imagine a sphere of white light formed there. Vibrate the word "**Naos**" (Ναος pronounced "na-os," meaning "Temple") a number of times as before.

Imagine the Tree complete. Then circulate the light you have brought down throughout all the spheres of the Tree. Circulate the energy using the same breathing/visualization techniques of the standard Middle Pillar exercise.

Finally focus some of the energy back into your Tiphareth center.

~

A GAELIC MIDDLE PILLAR EXERCISE

Imagine a sphere of white light just above your head at your Kether point. Vibrate: "**Crún**" (pronounced "croon," meaning "Crown"). Keep vibrating until it is the only thought in your conscious mind. Then imagine a shaft of light descending from your Kether center to your Daath center at the nape of the neck.

Form a sphere of light at the Daath center. Vibrate: "**Fios**" (pronounced "fee-uhs," meaning "Knowledge"). Intone the name until it is the only thing in your conscious mind.

Bring a shaft of light down from the Daath center to the Tiphareth center around your heart. Form a sphere of light there. Vibrate: "**Grinneas**" (pronounced "green-nyuhs," meaning "Beauty"). Intone the name several times until it fills your consciousness.

See the shaft of light descending from Tiphareth into the Yesod center in the genital region. Imagine a sphere of light formed there. Intone the name: "**Bunait**" (pronounced "boo-nuhch," meaning "Foundation"). Do this several times.

Visualize the shaft of light descending from Yesod into your Malkuth center at the feet and ankles. Vibrate the name:

"**Rìoghachd**" (pronounced "ree-uhch-k," meaning "Kingdom"). Intone a number of times as before.

Imagine the Middle Pillar complete. Move the energy around your aura using the four Circulations of Light described earlier. Using the cycles of breathing, bring the light down one side of the body and up the other, from Kether to Malkuth and back again. After performing this for a short period of time, imagine the ribbon of light descending down the front of your body and rising up your back.

Still employing rhythmic breathing, visualize the shaft of light rising up the Middle Pillar in the center of your body. When it reaches Kether, imagine a shower of light surrounding the outside of your body as it descends to Malkuth again. Circulate the light in this manner for some time. Then see the light rise again in a ribbon that spirals round the outside of your body.

Finally focus some of the energy back into your Tiphareth center.

~

THE GAELIC RITE OF THREE PILLARS

After a few minutes of relaxation, imagine a sphere of white light just above your head. Vibrate the name "**Crún**" (pronounced "kroon," meaning "Crown"). Keep vibrating this word until it is the only thought in your conscious mind. Maintain a strong visualization of the white sphere.

Then imagine a shaft of white light descending from your Kether center to your Chokmah center at the left temple of your forehead. Visualize a sphere of white light there. Intone the name "**Gliocas**" (pronounced "glee-uh-cas," meaning "Wisdom"). Keep vibrating the name until it is the complete focus of all your attention.

Bring a shaft of light horizontally across from your Chokmah center to your Binah center at the right temple of your forehead. Form a sphere of white light there. Vibrate the name "**Ciall**" (pronounced "kee-uhl," meaning "Understanding") a number of times until it occupies all of your mind.

Now bring a shaft of white light down diagonally from your Binah center to your Daath center at the nape of your neck. Visualize a sphere of white light there. Vibrate the name **"Fios"** (pronounced "fee-uhs," meaning "Knowledge"). Intone the name until it is the only thing in your conscious mind.

Next, visualize a shaft of white light down diagonally from the Daath center to your Chesed center at your left shoulder. Form a sphere of light there. Vibrate the name **"Iochd"** (pronounced "yoke," meaning "Mercy") a number of times until it fills your mind.

Bring a shaft of white light horizontally from Chesed to your Geburah center at your right shoulder. Visualize a sphere of light there. Vibrate the name **"Neart"** (pronounced "ny-arst," meaning "Power"). Intone the name until it is the only thing in your conscious mind.

Now bring a shaft of light diagonally across from Geburah to your Tiphareth center around the area of your heart. Form a sphere of light there. Vibrate the name **"Grinneas"** (pronounced "green-nyuhs," meaning "Beauty") several times until it fills your consciousness.

Next, visualize a shaft of light down diagonally from the Tiphareth center to your Netzach center at your left hip. Form a sphere of white light there. Vibrate the name **"Buaidh"** (pronounced "boo-eye," meaning "Victory") a number of times until it occupies all of your mind.

Bring a shaft of white light horizontally from Netzach to your Hod center at your right hip. Form a sphere of light there. Vibrate the name **"Mòralachd"** (pronounced "mor-uh-luhchk," meaning "Majesty"). Intone the name until it is the only thing in your mind.

Now see the shaft of light descending diagonally from Hod into the Yesod center in the genital region. Imagine a sphere of white light formed there. Intone the name **"Bunait"** (pronounced "boo-nuhch," meaning "Foundation") several times as before.

Next, visualize the shaft of light descending straight down from Yesod into your Malkuth center at the feet and ankles. Imagine a sphere of white light formed there. Vibrate the name **"Rìoghachd"** (pronounced "ree-uhch-k," meaning "Kingdom") a number of times as before.

Imagine the Tree complete. Then circulate the light you have brought down throughout all the spheres of the Tree. Circulate the energy using the same breathing/visualization techniques of the standard Middle Pillar exercise.

Finally focus some of the energy back into your Tiphareth center.

~

A SHAMANIC MIDDLE PILLAR EXERCISE

(NOTE: The two rituals that follow employ the names of deities from several different Native American tribes.)

Imagine a sphere of white light just above your head at your Kether point. Vibrate: **"Wakanda"** ("Great Spirit").[12] Keep vibrating until it is the only thought in your conscious mind. Then imagine a shaft of light descending from your Kether center to your Daath center at the nape of the neck.

Form a sphere of light at the Daath center. Vibrate: **"Baaxpee"** ("Spiritual Transformative Power").[13] Intone the name until it is the only thing in your conscious mind.

Bring a shaft of light down from the Daath center to the Tiphareth center around your heart. Form a sphere of light there. Vibrate: **"Wakinyan"** ("Light Spirit").[14] Intone the name several times until it fills your consciousness.

See the shaft of light descending from Tiphareth into the Yesod center in the genital region. Imagine a sphere of light formed there. Intone the name: **"Amala"** ("One who supports the world").[15] Do this several times.

Visualize the shaft of light descending from Yesod into your Malkuth center at the feet and ankles. Vibrate the name: **"Nokomis."**[16] Intone a number of times as before.

Imagine the Middle Pillar complete. Move the energy around your aura using the four Circulations of Light described earlier. Using the cycles of breathing, bring the light down one side of the body and up the other, from Kether to Malkuth and back again. After performing this for a short period of time, imagine the ribbon of light descending down the front of your body and rising up your back.

Still employing rhythmic breathing, visualize the shaft of light rising up the Middle Pillar in the center of your body. When it reaches Kether, imagine a shower of light surrounding the outside of your body as it descends to Malkuth again. Circulate the light in this manner for some time. Then see the light rise again in a ribbon that spirals around the outside of your body.

Finally focus some of the energy back into your Tiphareth center.

~

THE SHAMANIC RITE OF THREE PILLARS

After a few minutes of relaxation, imagine a sphere of white light just above your head. Vibrate the name ""**Wakanda**" ("Great Spirit").[17] Keep vibrating this word until it is the only thought in your conscious mind. Maintain a strong visualization of the white sphere.

Then imagine a shaft of white light descending from your Kether center to your Chokmah center at the left temple of your forehead. Visualize a sphere of white light there. Intone the name "**Skan**" ("Creator God").[18] Keep vibrating the name until it is the complete focus of all your attention.

Bring a shaft of light horizontally across from your Chokmah center to your Binah center at the right temple of your forehead. Form a sphere of white light there. Vibrate the name "**Ataentsic**"[19] a number of times until it occupies all of your mind.

Now bring a shaft of white light down diagonally from your Binah center to your Daath center at the nape of your neck. Visualize a sphere of white light there. Vibrate the name "**Baaxpee**" ("Spiritual Transformative Power").[20] Intone the name until it is the only thing in your conscious mind.

Next, visualize a shaft of white light down diagonally from the Daath center to your Chesed center at your left shoulder. Form a sphere of light there. Vibrate the name "**Aulanerk**"[21] a number of times until it occupies all of your mind.

Bring a shaft of white light horizontally from Chesed to your Geburah center at your right shoulder. Visualize a sphere of light there. Vibrate the name "**Ioskeha**."[22] Intone the name until it is the only thing in your conscious mind.

Now bring a shaft of light diagonally across from Geburah to your Tiphareth center around the area of your heart. Form a sphere of light there. Vibrate the name "**Wakinyan**" ("Light Spirit")[23] several times until it fills your consciousness.

Next, visualize a shaft of light down diagonally from the Tiphareth center to your Netzach center at your left hip. Form a sphere of white light there. Vibrate the name "**Pinga**" ("the one on high")[24] a number of times until it occupies all of your mind.

Bring a shaft of white light horizontally from the Netzach to your Hod center at your right hip. Form a sphere of light there. Vibrate the name "**Tirawa**."[25] Intone the name until it is the only thing in your conscious mind.

Now see the shaft of light descending diagonally from Hod into the Yesod center in the genital region. Imagine a sphere of white light formed there. Intone the name "**Amala**" ("One who supports the world")[26] several times as before.

Next, visualize the shaft of light descending straight down from Yesod into your Malkuth center at the feet and ankles. Imagine a sphere of white light formed there. Vibrate the name "**Nokomis**"[27] a number of times as before.

Imagine the Tree complete. Then circulate the light you have brought down throughout all the spheres of the Tree. Circulate the energy using the same breathing/visualization techniques of the standard Middle Pillar exercise.

Finally focus some of the energy back into your Tiphareth center.

～

Deities on the Tree of Life

The Tree of Life is a magnificent map—a template of the divine universe. We encourage readers to experiment with the Tree and apply their own layers of symbolism to its framework. New rituals based on the Middle Pillar Exercise can easily be developed along these lines. The following list shows how the various gods and goddesses of several pantheons can be attributed to the Tree. Bear in mind, however, that finding correspondences between one culture's spiritual system and another is an inexact science at best. The associations given here are only one of several that are possible.

A LIST OF DEITY CORRESPONDENCES

Sephirah	Egyptian	Greek	Roman	Celtic	Norse	Hindu
Kether	Nudjer	Aither	Aether	Dagda	Ymir	Brahman
	Ptah	—	—	—	—	—
Chokmah	Thoth	Uranus	Coelus	Lugh	Odin	Vishnu
Binah	Isis	Rhea	Juno	Danu	Frigga	Mahasakti
	—	Hera	—	—	—	—
Chesed	Amoun	Zeus	Jupiter	Llyr	Frey	Indra
Geburah	Horus	Ares	Mars	Morrigan	Thor	Shiva
	—	—	—	—	Tyr	—
Tiphareth	Osiris	Apollo	Sol	Angus	Balder	Krishna
	Ra	—	—	mac Og	—	Surya
Netzach	Hathor	Aphrodite	Venus	Brigit	Freya	Lakshmi
	—	—	—	—	—	Parvati
Hod	Anubis	Hermes	Mercury	Ogma	Loki	Hunuman
	Khnum	—	—	—	Bragi	—
Yesod	Shu	Artemis	Diana	Cerridwen	Nanna	Chandra
	Khonsu	—	—	—	—	Soma
Malkuth	Geb	Demeter	Ceres	Cernunnos	Nerthus	Ganesha
Daath	Nephthys	Hypnos	Janus	Arianrhod	Heimdall	Aditi
	—	—	—	—	—	Pushan

Color and Visualization

As Regardie stated in Chapter Five, once students are familiar with the basic exercise of the Middle Pillar (and the Three Pillars), they can expand their practices by visualizing the Sephiroth in their appropriate colors: Kether is white, Chokmah is gray, Binah is black, Daath is lavender,[28] Chesed is blue, Geburah is red, Tiphareth is Yellow, Netzach is green, Hod is orange, Yesod is violet, Malkuth contains earth tones of citrine, russet, olive, and black.

Formulating the spheres in these colors will not only help to strengthen the reader's integration of their specific energies, it is an important element of certain Middle Pillar healing techniques.[29]

Symbols and other images visualized within the spheres often result in potent variations of the Middle Pillar exercise. Flower buds, either roses or lotuses, can be imagined to open into full blossom as the divine name of a particular Sephirah is vibrated. For example, Tiphareth could be imagined as a sphere containing a yellow rosebud. As the divine name of the sphere is intoned, the bud unfolds into a magnificent yellow rose. Flames, chalices, tools, gemstones, geometric shapes, and a host of other images could be visualized as well. The only limit on the number and variety of this exercise is the boundary of one's imagination.

Consecration of Talismans

One of the most unique methods of using the Middle Pillar exercise that was developed by Regardie was as a tool for consecrating talismans. This method requires that the magician first activate the spheres within his or her body. Then, employing mental focus and rhythmic breathing, the magician can charge the talisman by transferring the invoked energy into the talisman. Talismans dedicated to a specific purpose can be "fine-tuned" by projecting energy from the corresponding Sephirah (and its appropriate color) within the body.

Healing Rituals

It can be said that the Middle Pillar exercise is by its very nature a ritual for self-healing. Regular performance of this ritual, like the practice of the Relaxation Rites previously mentioned, can help alleviate the neuro-muscular tensions that lead to more serious illnesses. This exercise can also be used to heal others as well. Regardie discovered that he could project healing energy to his patients by performing the Middle Pillar exercise beforehand. Keep in mind, however, that this should only be attempted by experienced practitioners. Don't rush into becoming "a healer" without first becoming proficient in the various preliminary techniques of relaxation, the LBRP, and the Middle Pillar.

Magical methods of healing, like other forms of theurgy, involve a type of auto-hypnosis, wherein the magician is totally focused on the goal of the operation. It also employs the manipulation and movement of energies. Usually, the healer extends energy to the recipient, where it works to remove psychic blockages, energy imbalances, or physical injuries/illnesses. The healer must be able to manipulate the subtle bodies of two people—his or her own and that of the recipient. Therefore it is crucial that the practitioner be psychically sound and balanced. If not, there is a danger that 1) the healer will absorb the psychic "ailment" of the recipient, or 2) the healer's own imbalanced energies will be absorbed by the recipient, making matters worse.

In the Golden Dawn, magicians were warned:

> It is better at first to keep your aura to yourself, rather than to try to flow out towards others. Unless you are particularly vital and well-balanced, you will only waste energy. So-called modes of healing and of 'doing good to others' should be eschewed for a time. Such methods have a technique of their own and require trained and balanced minds and bodies to carry them out. Get yourself right before you attempt to interfere with others....[30]

This advice is as sound today as it was a century ago.

A MIDDLE PILLAR HEALING RITUAL

Place two chairs in the middle of the room, one for you and one for the recipient. (This can be done with or without the recipient being in the room with you.) Perform the LBRP. Instruct the recipient to sit facing you, holding both of your hands in a relaxed and receptive manner, with eyes closed.

You (the healer) then perform the basic Middle Pillar exercise. The names may be intoned verbally or silently. The recipient may also vibrate the names if he or she wants, but you are in control of guiding all visualizations and vibrations. The main point is that you are awakening the spheres *within yourself*, in order that you may then use this energy to heal the recipient.

When the energies of the Middle Pillar have been fully activated within you, visualize within yourself the red sphere of Geburah in the area of your right shoulder. Silently vibrate the divine name of Geburah, **"Elohim Gibor."** (At this point the recipient should merely be receptive and should not vibrate or attempt to activate his or her Geburah center.) Once you have established the sphere of Geburah within your sphere of sensation, project a red ray of light from Geburah to your Tiphareth center. Then project the red ray from Tiphareth to the source of the ailment or infection. Visualize this ray purging the illness, purifying it with the fiery ray of Geburah.[31] Visualize the source of the problem gradually being eliminated. When this is accomplished, project a ray of healing yellow light from your Tiphareth center to mend the affected area and begin the process of healing. As you do so, mentally vibrate the divine name of Tiphareth **"YHVH Eloah ve-Daath."** Visualize health and vigor returning to the recipient.

Close by vibrating (both you and the recipient) the divine names of the Middle Pillar Exercise for equilibrium.

Variations of the Healing Ritual

Version 1

Sit facing the recipient, but do not hold the recipient's hands. After establishing the Middle Pillar within yourself, hold your hand (whichever hand you favor)[32] just in front of the affected area on the recipient. (Your other hand may be placed on your Tiphareth center.) If needed, you may touch the affected area as you direct the red ray at it. Visualize the red ray being issued directly from Tiphareth toward the affliction or see it travel from Tiphareth down your arm to the source of the problem.

Version 2

Have the recipient sit with his or her back to you. After establishing the Middle Pillar within yourself, establish it in the recipient by placing your hand(s) just in front of their corresponding spheres.

Version 3

Rather than using a red ray from Geburah, try using a blue ray from the watery sphere of Chesed to wash away the source of infection and cleanse the area.

Version 4

Visualize your own inner Sephiroth in their King Scale colors.[33] Your Geburah will be orange, and your Tiphareth will be rose pink. Their corresponding rays of light will also be projected in these colors. The recipient's Sephiroth can be visualized in the Queen Scale colors (their usual colors) or simply white.

Version 5

Incorporate massage therapy into the exercise. Have the recipient lie down (face up or face down) on a massage table or on a blanket on the floor. Walk the recipient through one of the relaxation techniques given earlier but combine it with healing massage techniques. Then, after establishing the Middle Pillar within yourself, establish it in the recipient by placing your hands on the sphere centers of the person and applying a slight pressure.[34] Charge the recipient's Sephiroth by silent vibration of the divine names. Project a white ray of light from your Tiphareth center (directly or through your hands) into each sphere to charge them. See these spheres in their usual Queen Scale colors or simply white. Then bring a ray of light from Geburah, in one of the appropriate colors mentioned above, into your Tiphareth center and project it into the afflicted area with the usual visualizations. Visualize the source of the problem being eliminated. When this is accomplished, project a ray of healing light from your Tiphareth center to mend the affected area and begin the process of healing. Close by gently massaging the entire body and silently vibrating the divine names of the Middle Pillar for equilibrium.

∼

Endnotes

1. See Regardie, *The Golden Dawn*, 90.

2. Published in *The Golden Dawn Journal, Book II: Qalabah: Theory and Magic*.

3. The "ch" in *Chai* is to be pronounced like the "ch" in the Scottish word *loch*.

4. The direction of this circulation (down the left and up the right) has a tendency to energize power in the Middle Pillar, resulting in a feeling of energy increase and a swelling in the Body of Light. The other direction (down the right and up the left) tends to relax the energy body, possibly resulting in a trance-state.

5. This direction of circulated energy tends to cleanse the Subtle Body.

6. We personally like to end the exercise by vibrating the divine names *Yeheshuah* and *Yehovashah* while concentrating on the Tiphareth center.

7. Circulation of the Light would be a better description.

8. "The Tree of Life as Projected in a Solid Sphere" (Regardie, *The Golden Dawn*, 594), describes a three-dimensional Tree which is similar but not identical to the one that we describe here. (The Tree in the Five Pillar Exercise uses the pillars in the cross-quarters rather than the cardinal quarters.)

9. It is this reflected image that the magician "backs into" (see Chapter Nine, pages 192–196).

10. This is the classical Greek pronunciation. It is acceptable to treat the "g" as silent. The letter omega is pronounced as "aw" like in the word "saw." Thus, the first vowel in the word *gnosis* sounds like the first vowel in the word *gnostic*.

11. An alternative vibration would be Θεμελιος—"Themelios" or "foundation," pronounced "theh-mel-lee-ohs."

12. The "Great Spirit" of the Lakota tribes.

13. A god of the Crow tribe of the plains.

14. A healing spirit of the Dakota (Sioux) tribes.

15. An Atlas-like god of the Tsimishian tribe of the Pacific Northwest.

16. Algonquin earth goddess.

17. The "Great Spirit" of the Lakota tribes. (Alternative deities for Kether would be *Manitou*, the Great Spirit known to many tribes, the Iroquois' *Orenda*, the Oglala's *Wakan Tanka*, and the Eskimo's *Innua*.)

18. Creator God of the Dakota (Sioux) tribes.

19. Iroquois/Huron great mother goddess. (An alternative deity for Binah would be *Eagentic*, the Seneca's "ancient woman" or first mother.)

20. A god of the Crow tribe of the plains. (An alternative deity for Daath would be *Estsanatlehi*, the Navajo "woman who changes." A shape-shifter who signified transformation and immortality.)

21. Eskimo sea god who rules the waves and the tides. He also brings joy.

22. Creator god of the Iroquois and Huron tribes who was known for defeating demons and giving magic. Giver of the herb tobacco.

23. A healing spirit of the Dakota (Sioux) tribes. (An alternative deity for Tiphareth would be *Shakuru*, the Pawnee Sun god.)

24. Eskimo goddess of game and hunting.

25. Pawnee sky god who taught the skills of speech, fire-making, hunting, clothing, agriculture, and religious ceremonies. (Alternative deity for Hod would be *Coyote*, known to many tribes, *Yanauluha*, the great medicine man of the Zuni tribe, and *Waukheon*, the "thunderbird" known to many tribes as a rain and messenger god.)

26. An alternative deity for Yesod would be *Igaluk*, the Eskimo Moon god.

27. Alternative deities for Malkuth include: *Onatha*, Iroquois goddess of harvest and *Iyatiku*; Pueblo goddess of corn, agriculture, and the underworld; *Tekkeit-sertok*, Eskimo god of the earth and the hunt; and *Yolkai Estasan*, the Navajo "white shell woman"—an earth goddess who rules the land and the seasons.

28. Daath's King Scale color is lavender; its Queen Scale color is gray-white.

29. See our book, *Experiencing the Kabbalah*, for more on color magic.

30. Regardie, *The Golden Dawn*, 91.

31. This method of healing, using the red ray of Geburah, was taught to us by Israel Regardie. It has proven to be highly effective.

32. We are not of the opinion that the right hand must always be used to project, no matter what traditional correspondences have to say about the matter. If you are left-handed, that is obviously the hand that projects energy for you. Both hands may also be used.

33. See Regardie's *The Golden Dawn*, 99. Also refer to the final chapter of *Experiencing the Kabbalah*, 228.

34. For Yesod, the pressure may be applied to the area just above the groin and below the navel.

APPENDIX

THE MUSICAL QABALAH
Musical Notes For Hebrew Letters

Copyright © 1996 by Thom Parrott

T he musical correspondences for the Hebrew letters in "The Musical Qabalah" come from the Golden Dawn notebooks of Allan Bennett. Among Bennett's students were Dion Fortune and Aleister Crowley. Paul Foster Case applied these correspondences to form a system of invocation and healing which is still being taught by the Builders of the Adytum (BOTA).

In the Golden Dawn system, four scales of color are used, each one assigned to the twelve astrological signs, the seven ancient planets, and the three most ancient elements. In Western music, the scale is divided into twelve semi-tones. Bennett assigned the twelve semi-tones of the chromatic scale (*chroma* is Greek for "color") to the twelve signs, beginning with the note C and the sign Aries. As each of the signs had a color associated to it, Bennett had, by this process, derived colors for each of the musical notes as well. Since all the colors allotted to the planets and elements were included in the twelve colors of the rainbow associated with the signs, they were assigned notes based on color (in the King Scale of the Golden Dawn), thus:

Color	Note	Sign	Planet	Element
Red	C	Aries	Mars	Fire
Red-Orange	C#	Taurus		
Orange	D	Gemini	Sun	
Yellow-Orange	D#	Cancer		
Yellow	E	Leo	Mercury	Air
Yellow-Green	F	Virgo		
Green	F#	Libra	Venus	
Blue-Green	G	Scorpio		
Blue	G#	Sagittarius	Moon	Water
Blue-Violet	A	Capricorn	Saturn	
Violet	A#	Aquarius	Jupiter	
Red-Violet	B	Pisces		

In the Golden Dawn system, the twenty-two letters of the Hebrew alphabet are each associated with a sign, planet, or element. By extending the correspondences in the preceding chart to the associated Hebrew letters, we get the following:

Hebrew Letter		Note	Astrology	Color
א	Aleph	E	Air	Yellow
ב	Beth	E	Mercury	Yellow
ג	Gimel	G#	Moon	Blue
ד	Daleth	F#	Venus	Green
ה	Heh	C	Aries	Red
ו	Vav	C#	Taurus	Red-orange
ז	Zayin	D	Gemini	Orange
ח	Cheth	D#	Cancer	Yellow-orange
ט	Teth	E	Leo	Yellow
י	Yod	F	Virgo	Yellow-green
ך,כ	Kaph	A#	Jupiter	Violet
ל	Lamed	F#	Libra	Green
ם,מ	Mem	G#	Water	Blue
ן,נ	Nun	G	Scorpio	Blue-green
ס	Samekh	G#	Sagittarius	Blue
ע	Ayin	A	Capricorn	Blue-violet
ף,פ	Peh	C	Mars	Red
ץ,צ	Tzaddi	A#	Aquarius	Violet

ק	Qoph	B	Pisces	Red-violet
ר	Resh	D	Sun	Orange
ש	Shin	C	Fire	Red
ת	Tav	A	Saturn	Blue-violet

In assigning the notes, no octave is specified. (See Figures 17–20 on the following pages.) I have chosen to set the music between middle C and the B above it, dropping below middle C occasionally, for melodic convenience. While I chose this particular range arbitrarily and purely for the sake of convenience, I also enjoy the melodies it produces, and I have experienced their power both alone and in a formal ceremonial hall with a dozen experienced ceremonial Qabalists.

It would be equally valid to use the twelve tones from G to the F# above it, for instance, or any other octave. If singing (chanting) the names as written here is too high or too low for your voice, *don't transpose*—reset the same notes beginning your octave at the comfortable bottom of your range. You will get a somewhat different but equally valid melody.

In chanting the various words and names, sing one note for each Hebrew letter, regardless of the normal pronunciation of the word. The syllable you produce for each note is derived from the pure sound of the letter and the sound it has in context. For example: אלהים is usually spelled and pronounced "Elohim"—five letters are reduced to three syllables—in chanting this name, five letters get five syllables: "Eh-lo-hay-ee-em."

Hebrew is written right to left. Because music and English are both written left to right and need to be written parallel with the Hebrew letters, the Hebrew words are spelled backward—left to right—for example, Elohim: אלהים becomes מיהלא.

A single bar denotes the end of a word within a name containing two or more words, while a double bar denotes the end of a name, for example: Elohim / Gibor //. Take a short inhalation at a single bar and a deep inhalation at a double bar.

All notes are written as whole notes. In practice, the notes should have equal or similar length and emphasis. Sing slowly and reverently. Smiling while you sing gives a sweeter tone to your voice and greater clarity and power to the words. "Make a joyful noise unto יהוה all ye hosts!"

Musical Setting for the
QABALISTIC CROSS

Atah

א ת ה

Ah ta ah

Malkuth

ת כ ל ם

Mm al ku oo ooth

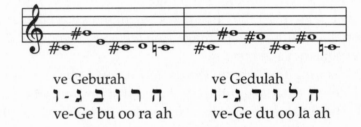

ve Geburah

ה ר ו ב ג - ו

ve-Ge bu oo ra ah

ve Gedulah

ה ל ו ד ג - ו

ve-Ge du oo la ah

le Olahm

ם ל ו ע ל

Le aa oh la am

Amen

ן ם א

Ah mm en

Figure 17: The Musical Qabalah: The Qabalistic Cross.

LESSER RITUAL OF THE PENTAGRAM
Divine and Archangelic Names

Figure 18: The Musical Qabalah: The LBRP.

THE MIDDLE PILLAR
Divine Names in Atziluth

Eheieh   YHVH Elohim

א י ה י ה   ה ו ה י   ם י ה ל א

Eh he ee eh   Yod He Vav He Eh lo he ee em

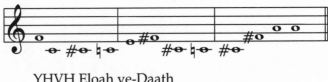

YHVH Eloah ve-Daath

י ה ו ה   א ל ו ה   ו ד ע ת

Yod He Vav He Eh lo oh ah   ve- D aa ath

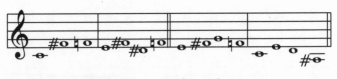

Shaddai El Chai   Adonai ha Aretz

ש י ד א ל י ה נ ד א ה א ר ץ

Sha da ee Eh ll cha ee Ah do na ee ha Ah re etz

Figure 19: The Musical Qabalah: The Middle Pillar.

DIVINE NAMES
Attributed to The Sephiroth

Figure 20: The Musical Qabalah: Divine Names.

GLOSSARY

Abyss: A chasm or gulf which separates the three Supernal Sephiroth from the rest of the spheres on the Tree of Life. Considered a division between the noumenal and the phenomenal.

Adonai: Hebrew word for "lord," associated with the south in the LBRP.

Adonai ha-Aretz: Hebrew phrase for "lord of earth." Divine name associated with Malkuth in the exercise of the Middle Pillar.

Adonai Melekh: Hebrew phrase for "lord and king." Associated with earth and Malkuth.

Agla: Hebrew notariqon for the phrase *Atah Gebur Le-Olahm Adonai* or "Thou art Great forever, my Lord." Associated with the north in the LBRP.

Augoeides: Greek word meaning "higher genius." Usually refers to the HGA or Higher Self.

AHIH: See *Eheieh*

Ajna: Sanskrit word meaning "order" or "command." Refers to the brow or third eye chakra.

Akasha: Derived from a Sanskrit word meaning "to shine." The Tattva associated with the element of spirit. Its symbol is the black egg.

Amen: A notariqon or acronym for the Hebrew phrase *Adonai Melekh Na'amon*, meaning "Lord, faithful King." Its implied meaning is "so be it," or "so mote it be."

Anahata: Sanskrit word meaning "unstruck sound." Refers to the heart chakra.

Analysand: A person who is undergoing psychotherapy.

Analytical Psychology: A term used by C. G. Jung to describe his particular method of psychotherapy.

Anima: An archetypal "soul image" which is the embodiment of the reflective feminine nature of man's subconscious.

Anima Mundi: "The Soul of the World."

Animus: An archetypal "soul image" which is the embodiment of the creative masculine nature of woman's subconscious.

Apas: Derived from a Sanskrit word meaning "water." The Tattva associated with the element of water. Its symbol is the silver crescent.

Aral: A ruling spirit traditionally associated with fire, though in modern times associated with air.

Archetype: Often referred to in Jungian psychology to mean a pre-existent idea, mode of thought, or godform that manifests through the collective unconscious of humanity.

Asanas: Various positions used in hatha yoga.

Assiah: The Qabalistic world of action and matter attributed to Malkuth and the element of earth.

Atah: See *Atoh*. Hebrew word meaning "Thou art." Used in the Qabalistic Cross.

Atoh: See *Atah*.

Atziluth: The Qabalistic world of archetypes attributed to Kether and the element of fire.

Aura: A shell or layer of astral substance which surrounds and permeates the physical body. Also called the Sphere of Sensation. See *Subtle Body*.

Auriel: See *Uriel*.

Binah: Hebrew word for "understanding" referring to the third Sephirah on the Tree of Life.

Bitom: Enochian word associated with the element of fire.

Briah: The Qabalistic world of creation consisting of Chokmah and Binah and attributed to the element of water.

Chakra: Sanskrit word meaning "wheels" or "lotus flowers." Refers to energy centers within the aura that correspond to certain glands or organs within the body.

Chassan: Hebrew angel associated with the element of air.

Chesed: Hebrew word for "mercy," referring to the fourth Sephirah on the Tree of Life. Also called *Gedulah* which means "greatness, magnificence."

Chiah: In Qabalah the part of the soul located in Chokmah which is described as the life force, divine will, and source of action.

Circulation: Movement in a circle or circuit. In the Middle Pillar exercise, light or energy is circulated around and through the body.

Circumambulate: To "walk around," especially as part of a ritual.

Chokmah: Hebrew word for "wisdom," referring to the second Sephirah on the Tree of Life.

Collective Unconscious: In Jungian psychology, those mental patterns and primordial images that are shared by all of humanity.

Comananu: The name of an Enochian governor.

Complex: A group of related, often repressed ideas and impulses that compel characteristic or habitual patterns of thought, feelings, and behavior. An exaggerated or obsessive concern or fear.

Conscious: The component of waking awareness. The state of being awake and perceptive.

Consciousness: One's personal or collective identity consisting of many levels of conscious and unconscious realities. To expand one's consciousness implies gaining access and/or awareness of these various levels.

Conscious Self: The ego or point of self-awareness.

Daath: Hebrew word for "knowledge." The so-called "Invisible Sephirah" on the Tree of Life, Daath is not really a Sephirah, but rather a conjunction of the energies of Chokmah and Binah. It can be likened to a passageway across the abyss.

Divine Self: Our true, pure, transcendent self which contains a spark of divinity.

Dharana: Sanskrit word meaning "holding." Refers to the yogic discipline of concentration on an object or symbol.

Ego: That portion of the psyche which is conscious, most directly governs thought and behavior, and is most concerned with outer reality. Also called the conscious self.

Eheieh: Hebrew word meaning "I am." Divine name associated with Kether and employed in the exercise of the Middle Pillar.

El: (or **Al**) Hebrew word meaning "god." Divine name associated with Chesed.

Elexarpeh: Name of an Enochian governor.

Elohim: Hebrew word meaning "god(s)."

Elohim Gibor: Hebrew phrase meaning "Almighty God." Divine name associated with Geburah.

Elohim Tzabaoth: Hebrew phrase meaning "God of Armies." Divine name associated with Hod.

Ens: "The One" or "the Essense."

Exarp: Enochian word associated with the element of air.

Field of Consciousness: The incessant flow of observable images, feeling, thoughts, sensations, and impulses.

Free association: A spontaneous, logically unconstrained and undirected association of ideas, emotions, and feelings. A psycho-analytic technique in which a patient's articulation of free associations is encouraged in order to reveal unconscious thoughts and emotions, such as traumatic experiences that have been repressed.

Gabriel: Hebrew archangel of elemental water.

Galgal: Hebrew word meaning "whirling." The plural form is *galgalim*, referring to the Sephiroth as they exist within the human aura or sphere of sensation.

Geburah: Hebrew word for "power" or "severity," referring to the fifth Sephirah on the Tree of Life. The phrase *ve-Geburah*, meaning "and the power" is used in the Qabalistic Cross.

Gedulah: Hebrew word for "greatness, magnificence." A title of Chesed. The phrase *ve-Gedulah*, meaning "and the glory," is used in the Qabalistic Cross.

Gematria: A form of Hebrew numerology that uses the numerical values of the letters of the Hebrew alphabet.

Gevurah: See *Geburah*.

Gnomes: Elemental spirits of earth.

Great Work: A term borrowed from alchemy's *magnum opus*. Refers to the path of human spiritual evolution, growth, and illumination.

G'uph: The lowest part of the soul, centered in Malkuth. A low level of subconscious intelligence which is closely tied to the physical body.

Hcoma: Enochian word associated with the element of water.

Heilsweg: A German word which means "sacred way." It was a term used by Jung to describe a method for psychological healing and individuation.

Hermetic: Of or relating to Hermes Trismegistus or the works ascribed to him. Having to do with the occult sciences, especially alchemy, astrology, and magic deriving from Western sources (Hebrew, Egyptian, and Greek).

HGA: Holy Guardian Angel. See *Higher Self*.

Higher Self: A personification of the transcendent spiritual self that is said to reside in Tiphareth and mediate between the divine self and the lower personality. Sometimes referred to as the Holy Guardian Angel, the Lower Genius, and the Augoeides.

Higher Unconscious: See *Superconscious*.

Hod: Hebrew word for "splendor," referring to the eighth Sephirah on the Tree of Life.

Hypnosis: A sleeplike state usually induced by another person in which the subject may experience forgotten or suppressed memories, hallucinations, and heightened suggestibility.

Id: According to Freud, an unconscious division of the psyche which functions as the origin of instinctual impulses and demands for instant gratification of primal needs. See *Nephesh*.

Ida: A primary *nadi* which starts at left nostril, goes to the crown of the head, crosses back and forth through the chakras, and terminates at the base of the spine on the left side.

Individuation: The process by which a person becomes self-realized or differentiated as a separate indivisible unity or "whole" which contains all aspects of the self.

Jagrata: The fourth and lowest world of consciousness according to Hindu tradition. The physical world.

Kether: Hebrew word for "crown," referring to the first Sephirah on the Tree of Life.

Kundalini: Sanskrit word meaning "serpent power." A fiery transformative power that resides in the base chakra. The yogic practice known as "Raising the Kundalini" to connect with all the chakras is said to unleash a great amount of energy.

LBRP: Lesser Banishing Ritual of the Pentagram.

Le-Olahm, Amen: Hebrew phrase meaning roughly "the World forever, unto the Ages." See *Amen*.

Libido: According to Freud, it is the sexual urge, but according to Jung it is total of all psychic energy and vitality, and its expression is through instinct, desire, and function.

Logos: A Greek word meaning "word." To the Gnostics this was the term for deity manifest in the universe. The creative principle and underlying law of the universe.

Lower Unconscious: An unconscious part of the psyche which contains fundamental drives, primitive urges and complexes. See *Id, Nephesh.*

Magic: The art of causing change to occur in one's environment and one's consciousness. Willpower, imagination, intention, and the use of symbols and correspondences play a major role in this art. See *Theurgy.*

Mana: "Great power." A polynesian term for the magical force in nature. Comparable to *prana* or *ch'i.*

Mana Personality: A term Jung used to describe an archetypal figure of a person's psyche.

Manipura: Sanskrit word meaning "diamond" or "city of precious stone." Refers to the solar plexus chakra.

Malkuth: Hebrew word for "kingdom," referring to the tenth Sephirah on the Tree of Life.

Metaphysics: The branch of philosophy that examines the nature of reality, including the relationship between mind and matter, substance and attribute, fact and value. Speculation upon questions that are unanswerable to scientific observation, analysis, or experiment.

Michael: Hebrew archangel of elemental fire.

Middle Unconscious: An inner region similar and accessible to that of the waking consciousness. The unconscious blueprint of the conscious mind.

Monad: From Greek *monos,* meaning "alone, single, sole." One indivisible. Sometimes used to describe Kether.

Muladhara: Sanskrit word meaning "basic." In Hindu mysticism it refers to the root chakra.

Nadis: (singular *nadi*) Sanskrit word meaning "motion." In Hindu mysticism it refers to a series of minute conduits which carry the vital life force known as *prana*.

Nanta: Enochian word associated with the element of earth.

Nephesh: In Qabalah, the part of the soul located in Yesod which is described as the lower self or lower unconscious. Contains primal instincts, fundamental drives and animal vitality. See *Id*.

Neshamah: In Qabalah, the highest part of the soul. The Greater Neshamah encompasses Kether, Chokmah, and Binah (to which are attributed the *Yechidah*, *Chiah*, and *Neshamah* [proper]). The highest aspirations of the soul (see *Superconscious*). The Neshamah proper, or intuitive soul, is found in Binah.

Netzach: Hebrew word for "victory," referring to the seventh Sephirah on the Tree of Life.

Neurosis: Any of various mental or emotional disorders arising from no apparent organic lesion or change and involving symptoms such as insecurity, anxiety, depression, and irrational fears. Not as detrimental as psychosis, a person with a particular neurosis can otherwise function normally.

Notariqon: A Qabalistic method for obtaining the hidden meanings of Hebrew words by viewing them as acronyms of phrases, or vice versa.

Oedipus complex: An unconscious sexual desire in a child, especially a boy, for the parent of the opposite sex, that is usually combined with hostility to the parent of the same sex. This complex, if unresolved, may result in neurosis and an inability to form normal sexual relationships in adulthood.

Orgone: According to Reich, a vital life force which permeates all living things.

Pentagram: A geometric figure based upon the pentangle, which has five lines and five "points." Figures based on the pentangle include the pentagram and the pentagon. The pentagram, or five-pointed star, is also called the figure of the microcosm, the pentalpha, and the wizard's foot.

Pentagrammaton: A Greek word which means "five-lettered name." Refers to the Hebrew name of Yeheshuah (יהשוה).

Pentalpha: Another name for the pentagram.

Persona: A mask of the personality created by the conscious mind and presented to others as the "real" self.

Phorlakh: Angel associated with elemental earth.

Pingala: A primary *nadi* which starts at right nostril, goes to the crown of the head, crosses back and forth through the chakras, and terminates at the base of the spine on the right side.

Prana: In yoga, the vital life force which courses through the nadis of the human body.

Pranayama: Sanskrit word for "the breath way." Yogic techniques for breath control and vital energy manipulation.

Prithivi: The Tattva associated with the element of earth. Its symbol is the yellow square.

Projecting Sign: Also called the "Attacking Sign," and the "Sign of Horus." One of the Neophtye Signs of the Golden Dawn.

Protecting Sign: Also called the "Sign of Silence" and the "Sign of Harpocrates." One of the Neophtye Signs of the Golden Dawn.

Psyche: The Greek word for "soul." The mind functioning as the center of thought, emotion, and behavior and consciously or unconsciously adjusting or mediating the body's responses to the social and physical environment.

Psychiatry: The branch of medicine that deals with the diagnosis, treatment, and prevention of mental and emotional disorders.

Psychoanalysis: A term coined by Freud to describe his method of psychotherapy.

Psychology: The study of the mind, mental processes, and human behavior.

Psychopomp: Greek word meaning "guide of souls."

Psychosis: A severe mental disorder, with or without organic damage, characterized by derangement of personality and loss of contact with reality and causing deterioration of normal social functioning.

Psychosomatic: From the Greek words *psyche* or "soul" and *soma* or "body." Of or relating to a disorder having physical symptoms but originating from mental or emotional causes.

Psychosynthesis: A term used by Assagioli to describe his method of psychotherapy which includes the use of symbolism and allegory, and which accepts the idea of the soul, the libido, and the imagination as essential aspects of the human being.

Psychotherapy: The healing of the psyche. The treatment of mental disorders with methods that revolve around the interpersonal relationship between therapist and client. Freud's *psychoanalysis* and Jung's *analytical psychology* are two forms of psychotherapy.

Qabalah: Hebrew word meaning "tradition."

Quintessence: The "fifth essence." Refers to spirit.

Raphael: Hebrew archangel of elemental air.

Repression: The unconscious exclusion of painful impulses, desires, or fears from the conscious mind.

Ruach: Hebrew word for "breath," "air," and "spirit." The Middle part of the Qabalistic soul, representing the mind and reasoning powers.

Ruach Elohim: Hebrew for "Spirit of God."

Sahasrara: Sanskrit word for "thousand-petalled lotus." In yoga it refers to the crown chakra. Some authorities do not consider it to be an actual chakra, although most modern practitioners do.

Salamanders: Elemental spirits of Fire.

Sammasati: A form of Buddhist meditation that examines and cultivates the memory.

Self-realization: Complete development or fulfillment of one's own spiritual and psychological potential.

Sephiroth: Hebrew word meaning "numbers, spheres, emanations." Refers to ten divine states or god-energies depicted on the Qabalistic Tree of Life. The singular form is *Sephirah*.

Shaddai El Chai: Hebrew phrase meaning "Almighty Living God." Divine name of Yesod used in the exercise of the Middle Pillar.

Shadow: The sum of all personal and collective elements which are rejected or refused expression in life and consequently unite into a somewhat independent splinter personality.

Siddhis: From a Sanskrit word which means "to succeed, accomplish." Psychic powers and abilities that most people are unaware of having, but which develop as the student advances on the path of Yoga.

Solve et Coagula: Latin phrase meaning "dissolve and coagulate." Alchemical axiom which points to the practice of reducing a solid to a liquid and back to a solid again. Used as a metaphor for the practice of psychotherapy and self-integration, or the magical processes of initiation and spiritual growth.

Sphere of Sensation: The aura.

Subtle Body: The psycho-physical circuitry of a human being through which the life force flows. Energy blue print for the physical body. Sometimes called the astral body, etheric double, or body of light.

Superconscious: According to Assagioli, the *higher unconscious* or transpersonal level of consciousness which contains higher intuitions, inspirations, latent psychic functions, and spiritual energies.

Super-ego: According to Freud, an unconscious part of the psyche which is created by the internalization of moral standards taken from parents and society.

Supernal: Celestial or heavenly. In Qabalah it refers to the three highest Sephiroth on the Tree of Life which are often called the Supernal Triad.

Sushumna: The primary nadi which starts at the base of the spine and runs to the top of the cranium.

Sushupti: The second world of consciousness according to Hindu tradition. The causal world.

Sutra: The Sanskrit word for "thread." Buddhist or Hindu scriptures.

Svadisthana: Sanskrit word for "dwelling-place of the self." Refers to the navel chakra.

Swapna: The third world of consciousness according to Hindu tradition. The astral world.

Sylphs: Elemental spirits of air.

Tabitom: Name of an Enochian governor.

Talihad: Angel associated with elemental water.

Talisman: An object which is charged or consecrated toward the achieving of a specific end. Usually intended to draw something to the magician.

Tao: Chinese for the "way." The Absolute or noumenal reality.

Tattva (or **Tattwa**): Sanskrit word meaning "quality." The five main tattvas, *Tejas, Apas, Vayu, Prithivi,* and *Akasha,* correspond to the five elements of fire, water, air, earth, and spirit.

Tejas: Sanskrit word meaning "sharp." The Tattva associated with the element of fire. Its symbol is a red triangle.

Telesmatic: From the Greek word *telesmata* meaning "talismans." Usually refers to a created or visualized image of a deity or angel, particularly images that have been built using Hebrew letter correspondences.

Tetragrammaton: A Greek word meaning "four-lettered name." Refers to the highest divine Hebrew name of God, YHVH (יהוה).

Thaumaturgy: Greek word meaning "miracle-working." Magic used to create changes in the material world.

Theurgy: Greek word meaning "God-working." Magic used for personal growth, spiritual evolution, and for becoming closer to the divine.

Theurgist: "God-worker." A ceremonial magician.

Tiphareth: Hebrew word for "beauty," referring to the sixth Sephirah on the Tree of Life.

Turya: The first and highest world of consciousness according to Hindu tradition. Described as conscious, meditative sleep.

Transconscious: A term used by William Stoltz to describe the psyche's creative and intuitive imagination.

Transference: In psychoanalysis, the process by which emotions and desires originally associated with one person, such as a parent or sibling, are unconsciously shifted to another person, especially to the analyst.

Transpersonal: Transcending or reaching beyond the personal or individual.

Unconscious: In psychoanalytic theory, the division of the mind containing elements of psychic makeup, such as memories or repressed desires, that are not subject to conscious perception or control but that often affect conscious thoughts and behavior.

Undines: Elemental spirits of water.

Uniting Symbol: According to Jung, a symbol which portrays the union or successful integration of all parts of the psyche.

Uriel or **Auriel:** Hebrew archangel of elemental earth.

Vayu: Sanskrit word meaning "to blow." The Tattva associated with the element of air. Its symbol is the blue circle.

Vegetotherapy: A Reichian method of therapy which uses deep massage to unlock muscular tension and release repressed material.

Vibratory Formula: A method by which divine names and words are intoned forcefully and with authority in a "vibration."

Visuddha: Sanskrit word meaning "purity." Refers to the throat chakra.

Yah: Divine Hebrew name associated with Chokmah.

Yang: In Chinese Taoism the positive, active, male principle.

Yechidah: In Qabalah, the highest part of the soul located in Kether and is described as the true divine self. The purest form of consciousness.

Yeheshuah: Hebrew name for Jesus. A divine name associated with the five elements of fire, water, air, earth, and spirit. Referred to as the *Pentagrammaton*.

Yesod: Hebrew word for "foundation," referring to the ninth Sephirah on the Tree of Life.

Yetzirah: The Qabalistic world of formation, consisting of Chesed, Geburah, Tiphareth, Netzach, Hod, and Yesod. Attributed to the element of air.

YHVH: (יהוה) Four letters which stand for the highest Hebrew name for God, which is considered unknown and unpronounceable. Often referred to the *Tetragrammaton*.

YHVH Elohim: Divine Hebrew name of Binah, meaning "the Lord God." Associated with Daath in the exercise of the Middle Pillar.

YHVH Eloah ve-Daath: Divine Hebrew name of Tiphareth meaning "Lord God of Knowledge." Used in the exercise of the Middle Pillar.

YHVH Tzabaoth: Divine Hebrew name of Netzach, meaning "Lord of Armies."

Yin: In Chinese Taoism the negative, passive, female principle.

Yoga: Sanskrit word meaning "union." The Eastern science of physical, mental, and spiritual integration.

BIBLIOGRAPHY

Agrippa. *Three Books of Occult Philosophy*. Edited and annotated by Donald Tyson. St. Paul, MN: Llewellyn Publications, 1993.

Assagioli, Roberto. *Psychosynthesis*. New York: Penguin Books, 1976.

Blank, William. *Torah, Tarot, & Tantra*. Boston, MA: Coventure Ltd., 1991.

Blavatsky, H. P. *The Voice of the Silence*. Theosophical Publishing House. Wheaton, IL: 1992.

Brown, Francis, S. R. Driver, and Charles A. Briggs, *A Hebrew and English Lexicon of the Old Testament*. Oxford, Clarendon Press, 1972.

Budge, E. A. Wallis. *An Egyptian Hieroglyphic Dictionary*. Vol. 1 & 2. New York: Dover Publications, Inc., 1969.

Cicero, Chic and Sandra Tabatha. *Experiencing the Kabbalah*. St. Paul, MN: Llewellyn Publications, 1997.

Cicero, Chic and Sandra Tabatha. *The Golden Dawn Journal, Book II, Qababah: Theory and Magic*. St. Paul, MN: Llewellyn Publications, 1994.

Cicero, Chic and Sandra Tabatha. *The Magical Pantheons: A Golden Dawn Journal*. St. Paul, MN: Llewellyn Publications, 1998.

Cicero, Chic and Sandra Tabatha. *Secrets of a Golden Dawn Temple.* St. Paul, MN: Llewellyn Publications, 1992.

Cicero, Chic and Sandra Tabatha. *Self-Initiation into the Golden Dawn Tradition.* St. Paul, MN: Llewellyn Publications, 1995.

Crowley, Aleister. *The Book of the Law.* York Beach, ME: Samuel Weiser, Inc., 1976.

Davidson, Gustav. *A Dictionary of Angels.* New York: The Free Press, a division of Macmillan, Inc., 1992.

de Laslo, Violet S. *The Basic Writings of C. G. Jung.* New York: The Modern Library, 1959.

Godwin, David. *Godwin's Cabalistic Encyclopedia.* 3rd ed. St. Paul, MN: Llewellyn Publications, 1994.

Godwin, David. *Light in Extension.* St. Paul, MN: Llewellyn Publications, 1992.

Greer, John Michael, *Pathways of Wisdom*. St. Paul, MN: Llewellyn Publications, 1996.

Halevi, Z'ev ben Shimon. *Kabbalah: Tradition of Hidden Knowledge.* New York: Thames and Hudson, 1988.

Halevi, Z'ev ben Shimon. *Psychology & Kabbalah.* York Beach, ME: Samuel Weiser, Inc., 1991.

Hebb, D. O. "What Psychology Is About," *American Psychologist 29.* 1973.

Heidrick, Bill, *A Possible Source for the Lesser Pentagram Ritual in a Hebrew Night Prayer.* Unpublished paper, 1977.

Hulse, David Allen. *The Key of It All, Book One, The Eastern Mysteries.* St. Paul, MN: Llewellyn Publications, 1995.

Jacobi, Jolande. *The Psychology of C. G. Jung.* New Haven: Yale University Press, 1973.

Jung, C. G. *The Collected Works of C. G. Jung, #6, Psychological Types.* Princeton, NJ: Bollingen Series, Princeton University Press, 1971.

Jung, C. G. *The Collected Works of C. G. Jung, #7, Two Essays on Analytical Psychology.* Princeton, NJ: Bollingen Series, Princeton University Press, 1966.

Jung, C. G. *The Collected Works of C. G. Jung, #8, The Structure and Dynamics of the Psyche.* Princeton, NJ: Bollingen Series, Princeton University Press, 1969.

Jung, C. G. *The Collected Works of C. G. Jung, #10, Civilization in Transition.* Princeton, NJ: Bollingen Series, Princeton University Press, 1970.

Jung, C. G. *The Collected Works of C. G. Jung, #11, Psychology and Religion.* Princeton, NJ: Bollingen Series, Princeton University Press, 1969.

Jung, C. G. *The Collected Works of C. G. Jung, #12, Psychology and Alchemy.* Princeton, NJ: Princeton University Press, 1980.

Jung, C. G. *The Collected Works of C. G. Jung, #17, The Development of Personality.* Princeton, NJ: Bollingen Series, Princeton University Press, 1981.

Kaplan, Aryeh. *The Bahir.* York Beach, ME: Samuel Weiser, Inc., 1989.

King, Francis. *Astral Projection, Ritual Magic, and Alchemy By S. L. MacGregor Mathers and Others.* Rochester, VT: Destiny Books, 1987.

King, Francis. *Ritual Magic in England.* London: Neville Spearman Limited, 1970.

King, Francis, and Isabel Sutherland. *The Rebirth of Magic: The Fascinating story of Western Occultism from the Middle Ages to the Present Day.* London: Corgi Books, 1982.

Küntz, Darcy. "The Middle Pillar, Revised Version for ⑤=⑥ by Israel Regardie."

Larousse *World Mythology.* New York: G. P. Putnam's Sons, 1965.

LeShan, Lawrence. *The Dilemma of Psychology.* New York: Dutton, 1990.

Levi, Eliphas. *Transcendental Magic.* York Beach, ME: Samuel Weiser, Inc., 1972.

Liddell and Scott's Greek-English Lexicon. London: Oxford University Press, 1961.

Mumford, Dr. Jonn. *A Chakra & Kundalini Workbook.* St. Paul, MN: Llewellyn Publications, 1995.

Pentagram Ritual. A paper by an anonymous author, probably written in the late 1970s or early 1980s.

Regardie, Israel. *The Complete Golden Dawn System of Magic*. Phoenix, AZ: Falcon Press, 1984.

Regardie, Israel. *The Eye in The Triangle*. Phoenix, AZ: Falcon Press, 1982.

Regardie, Israel. *The Golden Dawn*, 6th Edition. St. Paul, MN: Llewellyn Publications, 1994.

Regardie, Israel. *The Lazy Man's Guide to Relaxation*. Phoenix, AZ: Falcon Press, 1983.

Regardie, Israel. *The Middle Pillar*, 2nd Edition. St. Paul, MN: Llewellyn Publications, 1985.

Regardie, Israel. *My Rosicrucian Adverture* (1936). Later retitled with additional material from various authors as *What You should Know about the Golden Dawn*. Phoenix, AZ: Falcon Press, 1988.

Regardie, Israel. *The Romance of Metaphysics*. Chicago, IL: Aries Press, 1946.

Regardie, Israel. *The Tree of Life*. York Beach, ME: Samuel Weiser, Inc., 1972.

Scott, Walter. *Hermetica*. Great Britain: Solos Press, 1993.

Stoltz, William. *The Psychology of the Soul: A Transpersonal Perspective on the Functions of the Imagination*. Unpublished: 1993.

Suster, Gerald, *Crowley's Apprentice*. York Beach, ME: Samuel Weiser, Inc., 1990.

Thomas, William, and Kate Pavitt. *The Book of Talismans, Amulets & Zodiacal Gems*. North Hollywood, CA: Wilshire Book Company, 1970.

Walsh, W. B. *Perspectives and Patterns: Discourses on History*. Syracuse, NY: University Press of Syracuse, 1962.

Waterfield, Robin. *The Theology of Arithmetic, Attributed to Iamblichus*. Grand Rapids, MI: Phanes Press, 1988.

Westcott, W. Wynn. *The Occult Power of Numbers*. North Hollywood, CA: Newcastle Publishing Co., Inc., 1984.

INDEX

A

Adonai, 66, 82, 90, 157, 176, 188-192, 206, 210, 215, 218, 221, 224

Adonai ha-Aretz, 90, 157, 191, 210, 215, 221, 224

Adonai Melekh, 215

Agla, 56, 66, 176, 192, 212, 216,

AHIH, 56, 72, 82, 90, 212, 216 (see Eheieh)

Ajna, 166, 170

Akasha, 163, 166, 170

Al, 67, 72, 90, 100 (see El)

Anahata, 166, 170

Analysand, 7, 113, 115

Analytical Psychology, xiv, xxi, xxii, 1, 3-5, 20-21, 35, 40, 49, 98, 103, 108, 136

Anima, 26, 30-32, 36, 38, 96, 107, 109, 116-117, 130, 133-134, 138, 170

Anima Mundi, 26

Animus, 30-32, 38, 43, 109, 116-117, 130-131, 138

Apas, 163, 165, 170

Aral, 214, 217

Archetype, xiv, 26, 31, 37, 41, 43, 46, 60, 109, 116, 118-120, 124-125, 127, 130

Asanas, 161, 163

Assiah, 46, 65, 191

Atah, 66, 175, 180, 192, 205 (see Atoh)

Atoh, 47-49, 53, 205 (see Atah)

Atziluth, 46, 65, 99, 181

Augoeides, 134

Aura, xxi, 42, 46, 66, 82, 87, 134, 162, 169, 178-179, 181, 194-195, 210-212, 216, 218, 221-225, 228, 231, 233, 238

Auriel, 57, 61-62, 215, 218 (see Uriel)

B

Binah, 23, 45-46, 82, 90, 99-100, 131, 133, 219, 223, 226, 229, 231-232, 234, 236, 241

Bitom, 213, 217

Briah, 46, 65, 99

C

Chakra, xxiii, 46, 77-78, 83, 159-163, 165-174

Chassan, 213, 217

Chesed, 9, 23, 45-46, 64, 90, 131, 133-134, 178, 180-181, 219, 223, 226, 229, 232, 234-236, 240

Chiah, 30-32, 36, 46, 131, 253, 258

Chokmah, 23, 45-46, 82, 90, 98, 131, 219, 223, 226, 228-229, 231, 234, 236

Circulation, 3, 36, 46, 87-88, 91, 95, 98, 150, 210-211, 216, 218, 221-222, 225, 228, 231, 233, 241

Circumambulate, 216

Collective Unconscious, 26, 29-30, 32, 43, 60, 77, 91-92, 108, 110, 118, 124, 133-134

Comananu, 91

Complex, xxviii, 3-5, 15, 19, 26, 40, 58, 61-62, 69, 87, 107, 127, 135, 137, 140, 142, 209, 211, 222,

Conscious, xxvii, xxviii, xxix, 9-11, 13, 18-21, 23, 25, 30-36, 41, 43, 46, 50, 55, 74-75, 91-92, 106, 108, 110-111, 113, 117-122, 124-125, 127, 129, 133-137, 150, 173, 210, 219, 221, 223-235

Conscious Self, xxvii, 74, 124, 134

D

Daath, xxii, 71-72, 74, 82, 89-91, 99, 133, 159, 210, 219, 223-227, 229-230, 232-234, 236, 241-242

Dharana, 161

Divine Self, 103, 128, 131, 133-134, 136, 138, 177, 180, 190

E

Ego, xxvi, xxvii, xxviii, 11-12, 21, 23, 26, 32-33, 38-39, 41-42, 49, 57, 71, 74-75, 91-92, 94, 106-108, 110-111, 113-114, 118-119, 121, 123-125, 128, 133-135, 137, 161, 165, 227-228

Eheieh, 66, 74, 82, 176, 189-190, 192, 210, 216, 219, 223, , 254

El, 157, 179, 210, 213, 215, 217, 219, 221, 223-224 (see Al)

Elexarpeh, 91

Elohim, 82, 99, 153, 158, 186, 210, 214-215, 217, 219, 221, 223-224, 239, 245

Elohim Gibor, 99, 186, 221, 223, 239, 245

Elohim Tzabaoth, 99, 158, 215, 221, 224

Ens, 27

Exarp, 213, 217

F

Field of Consciousness, 51, 87, 125, 134

Free Association, 17, 79, 106-107, 129, 137, 155

G

G'uph, 46, 135
Gabriel, 57, 61-62, 67, 90, 176, 179, 183, 201, 205, 215, 218
Galgal, 173
Geburah, 23, 45, 64, 99, 120, 131, 134, 178, 180-181, 186-187, 189, 215, 219, 221, 223, 226, 229, 232, 235-236, 239-240, 242 (see Gevurah)
Gedulah, 48-49, 64, 178, 180, 215, 253
Gematria, 187-189
Gevurah, 9, 48-49, 64, 90 (see Geburah)
Gnomes, 215, 218
Great Work, xxvi, xxvii, xxix, xxx, 10, 65, 121, 128, 136, 169, 186

H

Hcoma, 213, 217
Heilsweg, 108
Hermetic, xiii, xvii, xxix, xxxi, 54-55, 65, 82-83, 179-180
HGA, 190,
Higher Self, xxvi, xxviii, 10, 22, 42, 44, 48, 62-63, 65, 69, 78, 80, 82, 85, 91-93, 124-125, 128, 131, 134, 138, 167, 190
Higher Unconscious, 125, 131
Hod, 23, 45, 90, 131, 134, 180, 189, 221, 224, 227, 229, 232, 235-236, 242
Hypnosis, 107, 127, 129

I

Id, 26-27, 45, 106-108, 135

Ida, 162, 167
Individuation, 108-109, 113, 116, 118-119, 121

J

Jagrata, 39, 46

K

Kether, xxii, 45-46, 72, 74-75, 82, 86-90, 93, 131, 159, 178, 180-181, 189, 192, 210-211, 219, 223-228, 230-231, 233-234, 236, 241
Kundalini, 160-161, 167, 169, 174

L

LBRP, xxxi, 65-67, 82-83, 114-115, 175, 177-178, 183, 191, 194-195, 238, 247
Le-Olahm, Amen, 53, 176, 180
Libido, 3, 26, 29, 33, 37-39, 41, 57, 60, 107, 124
Logos, 31, 45, 177, 185
Lower Unconscious, 127, 134

M

Magic, xxii, xiv-xxiv, xxvi-xxxi, 1, 4-8, 10, 20-23, 25, 27, 33, 39-41, 43-44, 46, 49, 51, 55, 60, 65, 69-70, 76, 80, 85, 92-93, 95-98, 101, 103-111, 113-125, 127-131, 133-140, 142, 144, 146, 148, 150, 152, 154, 156, 158, 160, 162, 166, 170, 172, 174, 176, 178, 180, 183, 185-190, 192, 194, 196, 200, 202, 204-207, 210-212, 214, 216, 218, 222, 224, 226-228, 230, 232, 234, 236, 238, 240-242, 244

Malkuth, xxii, 36-37, 46-49, 53, 65, 67, 72, 74-75, 88-90, 98-99, 131, 135, 138, 159, 175, 178, 180-181, 191-192, 210-211, 215, 221, 224-225, 227-228, 230-236, 242
Mana Personality, 119
Manipura, 165, 170
Metaphysic, xx, 29, 48, 51, 54-55, 60-61, 70, 72, 139-141, 158, 185
Michael, 57, 61-62, 67, 90, 177, 179, 183, 202, 205, 214, 217
Middle Unconscious, 125, 134
Monad, 27, 29, 57, 183
Muladhara, 165, 169-170

N
Nadi, 162, 166
Nanta, 213, 217
Nephesh, 36, 39, 45, 72, 131, 134-135
Neshamah, 30-32, 36, 46, 131, 133-134, 136, 138
Netzach, 23, 45, 90, 120, 131, 134, 180, 221, 224, 226-227, 229, 232, 235-236
Neurosis, 14-15, 64, 69, 80, 114, 122-12
Notariqon, 66, 176, 192

O
Orgone, 123

P
Pentagram, xxi, xxiii, xxvii, 40-41, 47, 49, 51, 53, 55-67, 69, 76, 93, 98, 175-179, 181, 183, 185-197, 199-207, 212, 216

Pentagrammaton, 185
Pentalpha, 183
Persona, 30, 33, 108, 116, 118, 120, 128, 134
Phorlakh, 215, 218
Pingala, 162, 166
Prana, 138, 161-162
Pranayama, 96, 100, 161-162
Prithivi, 163, 165, 170
Projecting Sign, 93
Protecting Sign, 94
Psyche, 6, 8-10, 12, 14-15, 17-18, 25-26, 29-30, 32, 34-37, 39-40, 42-44, 46, 49-50, 65, 67, 69, 72, 83, 91, 105-109, 111-112, 114, 116-127, 129-131, 135-138, 155, 157-158, 160, 199
Psychiatry, xx
Psychoanalysis, xiii, xxx, 105, 108, 124, 127
Psychology, xiii, xiv, xix, xx, xxii, xxiii, 1, 3-6, 16, 19-21, 23, 25, 27, 30, 33, 35, 40-41, 49, 52, 98, 101, 103-105, 107-109, 111, 113, 115, 117, 119-125, 127, 129, 131, 133, 135-138
Psychopomp, 118, 130
Psychosis, 12, 174
Psychosomatic, 169
Psychosynthesis, 124, 128-129, 138
Psychotherapy, xiv, xix, xx, xxix, xxx, 4, 105-106, 123

Q

Qabalah, xv, xxiii, xxvii, xxxi, 9, 22, 30, 46, 65, 82, 92, 99, 109, 130, 179, 206, 243, 246-249
Quintessence, 51, 185-186

R

Raphael, 56, 61-62, 67, 90, 176, 179, 183, 201, 205, 213, 217
Repression, 11, 15, 19-20, 23, 34, 106-107, 123, 135, 137
Ruach, 33-34, 37, 72, 131, 133-136, 153, 215
Ruach Elohim, 153, 215

S

Sahasrara, 77, 167, 170
Salamanders, 214, 217
Sammasati, 13, 261
Self-realization, 120-122, 125, 127-129, 133, 135-136

Sephiroth, xxii, 23, 26, 36, 38-39, 42, 44-46, 48, 60, 64, 70-72, 82-83, 89-91, 95, 97, 99, 131, 133-134, 138, 159-160, 163, 180, 212, 222, 236, 240
Shaddai El Chai, 157, 210, 213, 221, 224
Shadow, xxvi, xxix, 34, 108, 111, 113-115, 117, 127, 135-138, 192
Siddhis, 169
Solve et Coagula, 127-128
Sphere of Sensation, 40, 42, 46, 57, 63, 76, 87, 89, 97, 222-223, 239

Subtle Body, 160-162, 167, 169, 241
Super-ego, 26, 106-108, 110, 138
Superconscious, 36, 124-125, 128-131, 133-134
Supernal, 32-33, 36-37, 45-46, 82, 131, 133, 181, 188
Sushumna, 162
Sushupti, 38, 46
Sutra, xxxii
Svadisthana, 165, 170
Swapna, 38, 46
Sylphs, xxi, 213, 217

T

Tabitom, 91
Talihad, 215, 218
Talisman, xx-xxiii, 83, 130, 183, 237
Tao, 29, 32-33
Tattva, 163-164, 170, 173 (see Tattwa)
Tejas, 163, 165, 170
Telesmatic, 60-62, 67
Tetragrammaton, 65-66, 83, 176, 179-180, 185, 191
Theurgist, 22, 181
Theurgy, 238, 257
Tiphareth, xxii, 9-10, 72, 74, 89-90, 131, 133-134, 138, 159, 178, 180, 190, 210-211, 221, 223-237, 239-242
Transconscious, 129-130, 138
Transpersonal, 105, 123-125, 129, 133, 135
Turya, 37, 46

U

Unconscious, xxvii, xxix, 3-4, 7, 11,
13, 15, 17-21, 23, 25-27, 29-37, 39,
41, 43, 49-50, 52, 55, 57, 60, 64, 69,
77, 86, 91-92, 105-106, 108, 110-
111, 113-114, 116, 118, 120-122,
124-125, 127-131, 133-135, 137,
165
Undines, 215, 218
Uniting Symbol, 122, 131
Uriel, 67, 177, 179, 183, 202, 205
(see Auriel)

V

Vayu, 163, 166, 170
Vegetotherapy, 123
Vibratory Formula, xxi, 40, 43, 72,
91-92, 95-97, 100
Visuddha, 166, 170

Y

Yah, 98, 124, 171, 179, 219, 223, 265
Yang, 30-31, 34, 36-37, 45, 49

Yechidah, 27, 29-30, 32-33, 36, 41,
44-46, 48-49, 51-52, 57, 72, 77, 82,
131
Yeheshuah, 185, 241
Yesod, 36, 45-46, 72, 74, 89-90, 131,
133-134, 159, 210, 221, 224-225,
227-230, 232-233, 235-236, 242
Yetzirah, 46, 65, 188, 190
YHVH, 56, 65-66, 72, 82, 90, 99, 157,
176, 185, 188-191, 210, 219, 221,
223-224, 239
YHVH Eloah ve-Daath, 210, 221,
223, 239
YHVH Elohim, 82, 99, 210, 219, 223
YHVH Tzabaoth, 90, 99, 157, 221,
224
Yin, 30-31, 34, 36-37, 45, 49
Yoga, xv, xvi, xxiii, 4-5, 22, 77-78,
88, 95-96, 100, 159-163, 165-167,
169, 171, 173-174

☽ LOOK FOR THE CRESCENT MOON

Llewellyn publishes hundreds of books on your favorite subjects! To get these exciting books, including the ones on the following pages, check your local bookstore or order them directly from Llewellyn.

ORDER BY PHONE

- Call toll-free within the U.S. and Canada, 1-800-THE MOON
- In Minnesota, call (612) 291-1970
- We accept VISA, MasterCard, and American Express

ORDER BY MAIL

- Send the full price of your order (MN residents add 7% sales tax) in U.S. funds, plus postage & handling to:

  Llewellyn Worldwide
  P.O. Box 64383, Dept. K140-6
  St. Paul, MN 55164–0383, U.S.A.

POSTAGE & HANDLING

(For the U.S., Canada, and Mexico)

- $4.00 for orders $15.00 and under
- $5.00 for orders over $15.00
- No charge for orders over $100.00

We ship UPS in the continental United States. We ship standard mail to P.O. boxes. Orders shipped to Alaska, Hawaii, The Virgin Islands, and Puerto Rico are sent first-class mail. Orders shipped to Canada and Mexico are sent surface mail.

International orders: Airmail—add freight equal to price of each book to the total price of order, plus $5.00 for each non-book item (audio tapes, etc.).

Surface mail—Add $1.00 per item.

Allow 4–6 weeks for delivery on all orders.
Postage and handling rates subject to change.

DISCOUNTS

We offer a 20% discount to group leaders or agents. You must order a minimum of 5 copies of the same book to get our special quantity price.

FREE CATALOG

Get a free copy of our color catalog, *New Worlds of Mind and Spirit*. Subscribe for just $10.00 in the United States and Canada ($30.00 overseas, airmail). Many bookstores carry *New Worlds*— ask for it!

Visit our web site at www.llewellyn.com for more information.

A Garden of Pomegranates

Israel Regardie

What is the Tree of Life? It's the ground plan of the Qabalistic system—a set of symbols used since ancient times to study the Universe. The Tree of Life is a geometrical arrangement of ten sephiroth, or spheres, each of which is associated with a different archetypal idea, and 22 paths which connect the spheres. This system of primal correspondences has been found the most efficient plan ever devised to classify and organize the characteristics of the self. Israel Regardie has written one of the best and most lucid introductions to the Qabalah.

A Garden of Pomegranates combines Regardie's own studies with his notes on the works of Aleister Crowley, A. E. Waite, Eliphas Levi and D. H. Lawrence. No longer is the wisdom of the Qabalah to be held secret! The needs of today place the burden of growth upon each and every person…each has to undertake the Path as his or her own responsibility, but every help is given in the most ancient and yet most modern teaching here known to humankind.

0–87542–690–5, 160 pgs., 5-¼ x 8, softcover　　　　　**$8.95**

The Golden Dawn

*The original account of the teachings,
rites & cermonies of the
Hermetic Order*

Israel Regardie

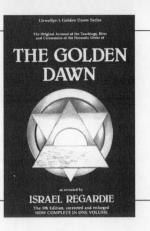

Complete in one volume with further revision, expansion, and additional notes by Regardie, Cris Monnastre, and others. Expanded with an index of more than 100 pages!

Originally published in four bulky volumes of some 1,200 pages, this 6th Revised and Enlarged Edition has been entirely reset in modern, less space-consuming type, in half the pages (while retaining the original pagination in marginal notation for reference) for greater ease and use.

Corrections of typographical errors perpetuated in the original and subsequent editions have been made, with further revision and additional text and notes by noted scholars and by actual practitioners of the Golden Dawn system of Magick, with an Introduction by the only student ever accepted for personal training by Regardie.

Also included are Initiation Ceremonies, important rituals for consecration and invocation, methods of meditation and magical working based on the Enochian Tablets, studies in the Tarot, and the system of Qabalistic Correspondences that unite the World's religions and magical traditions into a comprehensive and practical whole.

This volume is designed as a study and practice curriculum suited to both group and private practice. Meditation upon, and following with the Active Imagination, the Initiation Ceremonies are fully experiential without need of participation in group or lodge. A very complete reference encyclopedia of Western Magick.

0–87542–663–8, 840 pp., 6 x 9, illus., softcover **$29.95**

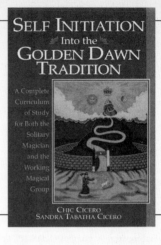